FROM YESTERDAY TO
TODAY

FROM YESTERDAY TO
TODAY

SIX DECADES OF AMERICA'S FAVORITE MORNING SHOW

By **STEPHEN BATTAGLIO**   *Foreword by* **MATT LAUER**   *Introduction by* **JIM BELL**

Running Press
PHILADELPHIA · LONDON

Books published by Running Press are available at special discounts for
bulk purchases in the United States by corporations, institutions, and
other organizations. For more information, please contact the Special
Markets Department at the Perseus Books Group, 2300 Chestnut Street,
Suite 200, Philadelphia, PA 19103, or call (800) 810-4145, ext. 5000,
or e-mail special.markets@perseusbooks.com.

ISBN 978-0-7624-4462-5
Library of Congress Control Number: 2011939379

E-book ISBN 978-0-7624-4548-6

9 8 7 6 5 4 3 2 1
Digit on the right indicates the number of this printing

Cover and interior design by Headcase Design
www.headcasedesign.com
Edited by Geoffrey Stone
Typography: Eames Century Modern, Forza, and Knockout

Running Press Book Publishers
2300 Chestnut Street
Philadelphia, PA 19103-4371

Visit us on the web!
www.runningpress.com

PHOTO CREDITS:

All photos courtesy of the NBC/Universal Photo
Bank unless otherwise specified.

Photo on page 209 courtesy of Katie Couric.

Photos on pages x, 180 (middle left), 180 (bottom
left and bottom right), 215 (top left), 215 (top
right), 232 (middle right and bottom middle), 241
(bottom two), and 268 courtesy of NBC News.

Photos on pages 236 (top right), 236 (middle
two), 236 (bottom right), 237 (top left), 237 (top
right), 237 (bottom right), 250 (top left) courtesy
of Debra L. Rothenberg/rothenbergphoto.com.

Page 126: AP Photo/Suzanne Vlamis; 127:
AP Photo/Charles Tasnadi; 139 (top left):
PA/PA Wire URN:9882483 (Press Association
via AP Images); 139 (top right): AP Photo, file;
139 (middle right): AP Photo; 139 (bottom right):
AP Photo/Handschuh; 177: AP Photo; 186 (top):
AP Photo/str-Alex Brandon; 206 (middle):
Peter Kramer/NBC/NBC NewsWire via AP
Images; 212 (top and bottom): AP Photo/Ed
Andrieski; 223: AP Photo/Bebeto Matthews;
226 (left): AP Photo/Marty Lederhandler; 226
(right): AP Photo/Chao Soi Cheong; 229:
AP Photo/Boudicon One; 233 (top left): AP
Photo/Henny Ray Abrams; 233 (bottom right):
AP Photo/Richard Drew; 239: AP Photo/Mark
Lennihan; 246: AP Photo/Richard Drew; 252:
AP Photo/Richard Drew; 256 (top): Peter
Kramer/NBC/NBC NewsWire via AP Images;
257 (top right): Peter Kramer/NBC/NBC
NewsWire via AP Images.

Photo on page 268 (and final front cover image)
by Andrew Eccles/NBC.

We hope we can give you enough to stay with you for a long time.

—Dave Garroway, January 15, 1952

FOREWORD

by MATT LAUER

I REMEMBER WATCHING BILL CLINTON BEING interviewed as he traveled to Washington, D.C., to be sworn in as this nation's 42nd president. When asked how he was feeling he replied, "I feel like the dog that's been chasing the pick-up truck and all of the sudden I caught it! Now what?"

I felt exactly the same way in 1996 when I got a phone call from the president of NBC telling me that he wanted me to become the next host of *Today*. Joy, excitement, shock, and fear all went through me at the same time. The dream of my professional life was coming true and a monumental challenge was about to begin.

> *"Well here we are. Good morning to you. The very first good morning of what I hope and expect to be a great many good mornings between you and me. Here it is . . . January 14th, 1952, when NBC begins a new program called Today, and if it doesn't sound too revolutionary, I really believe this begins a new kind of television."*

When Dave Garroway welcomed viewers to *Today* on that day in 1952, he ushered in a new era in broadcasting. And he changed the way Americans started their day.

The concept was simple yet dramatically different than anything that had appeared on the fledgling medium called television. It was a place where viewers could turn to each morning to satisfy their appetite for all things news and information. It was a destination for the curious to learn more about what had happened overnight and how the day ahead might shape up. And they would see and hear it all from the best storytellers in broadcasting.

I wasn't alive when *Today* debuted on that January morning, but five years later I would be born into what had already become a *Today* family. My parents raised me in a home where the likes of Garroway, Blair, Walters and Downs, Brokaw and Pauley, and Gumbel and Couric graced the screens.

Today become a part of my family's daily ritual. We sat mesmerized as the rich and powerful, the entertaining and the eccentric, the feared and the broken were questioned and held accountable. And yes, we were moved to tears by the suffering or simple kindness of total strangers.

And all before nine o'clock in the morning!

Today shaped the way I viewed my surroundings. It put the news into context, and it did something else. It ignited a desire in me to find a way to become part of the show's unfolding history.

Like my own path to *Today*, the path the show has taken over these past sixty years has not always followed a straight line. There have been detours and bumps along the road, including missteps and mistakes. But those were always followed by times of reflection and correction. In this book television journalist and historian Stephen Battaglio has not spared us or you an examination of those episodes. This is not a story of broadcasting perfection. But I think you'll agree that as *Today* reaches this milestone, it has managed to get more right than wrong. When we did fall, we got back up and in the game.

As you browse through these pages, I urge you to keep this in mind: In the past sixty years the world has changed in exciting, troubling, puzzling, and mind-blowing ways. We have all been witness to so much, perhaps even too much. There are very few things that remain the way they were when *Today* first went on the air. But despite all that change, the mission of the show has remained the same—to give you a window on the world, to bring you up to date and inform you, to prepare you for what the future may bring, and to offer a smile or two as a change of pace to what can be the stark realities of life.

We hope we have succeeded in delivering those promises.

Know too that we have had an absolute blast along the way. This job is a thrill ride that has opened doors for us all around the world. And we have gladly walked through them. Our bucket lists are left with very few unchecked items.

And one last thing. In the pages that follow you will see the faces and names of those of us who have been lucky enough to be the more visible employees of this formidable program. But make no mistake about it, we are not *Today*. We are just the high profile caretakers of this long-standing tradition. The handful of people like me, with classic good looks and thick luxurious heads of hair (sorry, the early hours have made me delirious), we

are the television equivalent of the tip of the iceberg, the part you can see that gets too much of your attention.

Today is the hundreds—or by this time thousands—of people who have worked tirelessly behind the scenes at ungodly hours to bring you the stories that move and enlighten you. And it is the innovators—the technicians who continue to push the envelope and make the impos-sible seem ridiculously routine. *Today* is everyone who has contributed their talent, energy, and passion to this broadcast over these past sixty years without asking for thanks or attention. They richly deserve both!

I hope you enjoy what we have gathered here and that you will join us each morning for the next sixty years . . . and beyond.

—*Matt Lauer*

INTRODUCTION

by JIM BELL

"Well here we are and a good morning to you. The very first good morning of what I hope and suspect will be a great many good mornings . . ."

—**Dave Garroway, January 14, 1952**

NEARLY TWENTY-TWO THOUSAND MORNINGS later, we can safely say that Mr. Garroway's hopes and suspicions have been confirmed. But the success of *Today* was hardly a sure thing. Before *Today* went on the air sixty years ago, morning TV was little more than test patterns. Literally, test patterns. Breakfast was a time reserved for radio. Most executives didn't believe that viewers could eat their breakfast, get dressed, and watch TV all at the same time. They didn't believe people could sometimes listen to TV rather than watch every frame.

But Pat Weaver, the NBC executive who created the *Today* show (as well as creating his daughter Sigourney) believed America was ready for, as he put it, "a revolt in their living rooms over eggs and bacon." The early reviews didn't entirely agree with him. A "morning news show" struck many as odd in 1952. The *New York Times* described it as "the latest plan for electronic bondage dreamed up by the National Broadcasting Company" and mentioned skeptics who said the show was "pretentious and in some cases pointless." Another critic told NBC to "roll over and go back to sleep."

The *Today* show, of course, prevailed over its harsher critics and today the broadcast that Pat Weaver and Dave Garroway started is not only a resounding and proven success, it's also essentially the same program it was sixty years ago. No degree of cultural change or technological tumult has altered Garroway's founding ideas that the show would "put you in touch more closely with the world we live in . . . in all fields of human endeavor" . . . so that the viewer would "know where you're going and what the world is like that you are going into."

From Yesterday to Today will bring you into our world. It represents the most ambitious and comprehensive effort to date at documenting the history of the broadcast. It should prove fascinating to viewers and non-viewers alike. Irrespective of one's morning TV habits, *Today*'s place in television history and American culture—as the closest thing we have to a national hearth—is secure. *Today* is where generations of Americans have begun their day, where the conversation begins, where viewpoints are stated, where news is made. It was also, of course, the first morning news show, and the first to have a woman and an African American as hosts. It invented television staples like the outdoor "plaza" studio and summer concerts, as well as signature annual events like "Where in the World is Matt Lauer?" and "*Today* Throws a Wedding."

For a book this ambitious, perhaps the biggest challenge has been deciding what to omit. Any compendium of *Today* would run the gamut of the last six decades' most significant events. Recently, on the tenth anniversary of 9/11, we re-watched how Matt, Katie, and another *Today* alum, Tom (no last names needed), took America through those initial hours that had no precedent. It was a reminder of how *Today*, perhaps more than any other broadcast, has been where history happens.

Today has fifteen presidential elections and inaugurations under its belt, spanning the administrations of Presidents Truman to Obama. There have been two royal weddings, countless trips to virtually every corner of the planet. There have been hurricanes, fires, floods, tsunamis, and earthquakes. And there have been, of course, the interviews. So many landmark and groundbreaking interviews. The *Today* show was where Hillary Clinton went when she decried that "vast right wing conspiracy." It was where Tom Cruise argued with Matt about "the history of psychiatry." It was where Katie grilled Bob Dole about whether cigarettes were addictive. And where the parents of the Columbine victims sat down with Katie for what became a national moment of grieving.

America has watched the *Today* show family grow and change as well. Jane Pauley and Katie had their babies. Katie tragically lost her husband to cancer and took the extraordinary step, as she honored his memory, of submitting to a colonoscopy on TV. We saw Matt get married and have three kids. And we saw Meredith Vieira make the tough decision, for family reasons, to step down from the anchor chair. The live good-bye to Meredith from the *Today* show staff has gone down as one of television's fondest and most heartfelt farewells.

People watch *Today* at the most vulnerable time of day. They're busy, sometimes they're stressed, and they don't have time to channel surf. Morning viewers make a choice and stick with it as they go about their morning rituals—making coffee, serving breakfast, packing lunchboxes, and looking for shoes. They choose *Today* because it informs and entertains them. And they choose it because it's family. A family of on-camera hosts who are genuine, curious, and authentic people. And a remarkable family, behind the camera, of production and engineering staff who decade after decade have pulled off television magic every morning.

Other television programs come and go. *Today* is now entering its seventh decade—remarkable longevity for a broadcast. And even more remarkable, it's just as vibrant, relevant, and exciting as it was when Dave Garroway and a chimpanzee named J. Fred Muggs were bidding the country good morning. We hope you enjoy the memories.

—*Jim Bell, Executive Producer*

DAVE GA

FLORENCE HENDERS

CHAPTER ONE

JACK LESCO

LEE MERIWETHER

CHA

J. FRED MUGGS

1952–1959

1952–1959

THE RCA EXHIBITION HALL ON THE STREET level of Rockefeller Center in Manhattan was lit up on the dark, damp, and unseasonably warm winter morning of January 14, 1952, as Dave Garroway looked into an NBC TV camera and introduced what he called "a new kind of television." It was being delivered, he said, from the "magnificent unparalleled means of communication, which NBC has assembled into a single room in New York." The network's publicity people had touted it as the "nerve center of the planet."

The camera scanned the twenty-two-by-sixty-foot studio filled with clocks set to various time zones, telephones, Teletype machines, reel-to-reel tape recorders, turntables, typewriters, and wall-to-wall world maps. The front pages of that day's newspapers from across the country were affixed to a board. Cigarette smoke wafted around the men in white shirts and ties and a few women in tailored skirts who created the image of a bustling newsroom. But some of them had to be wondering—is anybody out there?

(Opposite): A crowd in front of the RCA Exhibition Hall looks in on the first edition of Today. *(Top, from left): George Fenneman and Groucho Marx on* You Bet Your Life. *Milton Berle was "Mr. Television" on* Texaco Star Theater. *(Bottom): Bob Hope during his radio days for NBC.*

> ## The growth of television was already having an indelible effect on the leisure time activities Americans enjoyed.

When NBC's *Today* aired for the first time that day, there were 15.7 million television sets in the United States—up 5.2 million from the previous year. The growth of television was already having an indelible effect on the leisure time activities Americans enjoyed. They were reading fewer books and going to the movies less often. The flickering cathode rays in their living rooms brought them the vaudeville stunts of Milton Berle on *Texaco Star Theater* and the antics of Lucille Ball on *I Love Lucy*. They were emotionally absorbed by the works of a new generation of writing talent that in-cluded Paddy Chayefsky, Horton Foote, and Gore Vidal, who created original plays for live TV drama antholo-gies such as *The Philco Television Playhouse* and *Studio One*. Comedians such as Bob Hope, Jack Benny, and Groucho Marx had seen the massive ratings of their network radio programs tumble to a fraction of what they had been just three years before and began their transition into television.

NBC's parent company was the Radio Corporation of America, which developed and manufactured televi-sion sets. The network was driving sales by giving the public images of the kinds of events they were used to only reading about in newspapers or hearing on the ra-dio: the inauguration of President Harry S Truman, the Army-Navy football game and the World Series. In 1951, the "Shot Heard 'Round the World"—New York Giants outfielder Bobby Thomson's home run that stunned the Brooklyn Dodgers in the deciding game of the playoff for the National League pennant—was seen on NBC-TV.

As pervasive as television had become in a relative-ly short time, it had virtually no place in people's lives during the hectic early hours of the morning when they rushed to leave their homes for work, get the kids off to school, or prepare for a day of chores around the house

1953 — *First issue of Playboy magazine is published with a nude Marilyn Monroe on the cover.*

Garaway interviewing pedestrians in 1956

or the family farm. The living room was where TV was enjoyed, not the bathroom, the bedroom, or the kitchen, where people typically began their day. Some local stations offered morning programming—the brilliantly innovative comic Ernie Kovacs hosted a show on a local station in Philadelphia before becoming a network star. But it was considered almost decadent to watch TV early in the day— as if it was akin to having an alcoholic beverage before noon. None of the networks believed there was enough of an audience to program the hours before 11:30 a.m.

Enter Pat Weaver, the president of NBC Television. Weaver had taken over the network in 1949 after finding success as an executive in radio and advertising. He believed television could tap in to radio's morning audience just as it had in the evening hours. "I'd had 20 years in the business as a writer-producer of programming, and running the biggest of the radio agencies," he once recalled. "And in spite of what people said, I knew, and had known for many years, that there was a gigantic audience in the morning, with *The Breakfast Club*, and *Breakfast at Sardi's*, and at the CBS stations I worked at out on the West Coast. We had these immense hits in the morning. So I knew the audience was there."

After arriving at NBC, Weaver began to develop a program he called *Rise and Shine*. He described it as a "gang show" with a troupe of regular players that would greet viewers each morning with humorous routines, sketches, and songs. It was a formula that worked on morning radio. But Weaver's general tenant for television was that it needed to distinguish itself from radio. He sought a more distinctive format for his morning program and came up with the idea of what he called a "national newspaper of the air." The program would have cameras stationed wherever news was happening that a host could go to live. There would be fresh sports reports, weather forecasts, interviews with newsmakers, and reviews of the newest books, movies, and plays presented right in the studio that morning. Television news programs of the time were primitive—or "rotten" as Weaver described them. They were mostly composed of a staff announcer reading the latest headlines and wire reports, accompanied by still photos or newsreel footage. Weaver knew that emerging telecommunication technologies were going to transform television. While serving in Armed Forces Radio during World War II, he learned that magnetic recording tape could be used to record images as well as sound. Instead of having to send film to a lab, videotape was going to enable the immediate playback of moving pictures. Bulky cameras and other equipment were going to get lighter and more portable. Weaver was a member of the British Interplanetary Society where he heard its chairman, writer Arthur C. Clarke, predict that satellite communications would one day deliver pictures across oceans instantaneously. Weaver wanted a program that would take advantage of those developments as they arrived. On the advice of his wife, Weaver dropped the breezy name of *Rise and Shine*. He changed the name of the program he was developing to *Today*.

Pat Weaver knew how to package his business ideas with high-minded aspirations and the language of a scholar or philosopher.

Weaver had a strong business motivation for expanding NBC's reach into the morning hours. In the early 1950s, most prime-time TV shows were produced by sponsors or their ad agencies. Advertisers paid the networks for an entire time slot and largely controlled the programs they supplied, limiting the number of companies that could afford national network TV advertising. From the time he took on his leadership role at NBC, Weaver advocated a "magazine" approach where multiple sponsors could buy commercial time on the same program. The network had been successfully selling minute spots to several sponsors on *Your Show of Shows*, the wildly successful comedy and variety program with Sid Caesar. Weaver wanted NBC's morning show to be two daily hours that the network could control and sell to a wide range of advertisers who did not have the budget to produce or sponsor an entire program. It was a way to expand the TV advertising marketplace and bring more money into the network.

Weaver knew how to package his business ideas with high-minded aspirations and the language of a scholar or philosopher. To get affiliate stations on board, he presented a promotional film on a closed circuit telecast that outlined his vision for the show. He made it sound as if viewers would watch out of a sense of national obligation.

"A program like this is a magnificent use of the tool of television and its ultimate social responsibility," he intoned in the film. "John Smith, American, on this program will meet the people that he must know to be an informed citizen of a free society. He will hear the voices that count in the world. He will listen to the words that echo the story of history. He will see the places at peace, and the places at war. His horizon will be limited by neither time, nor place. John Smith will be there. He will know this is the real secret weapon of free men: to know, to understand, so that John Smith is ready for today, whatever it may bring."

NBC's affiliate stations were skeptical and somewhat resistant to Weaver's pitch. One reason was self-interest. Many TV stations belonged to larger companies that also operated morning newspapers. What would a

Garroway on the line with the U.S. Weather Bureau.

THE WINDOW

WHEN *TODAY* **SHOWED THE PEDESTRIANS** who peered daily into the window of the RCA Exhibition Hall, it gave America the opportunity to take a good look at itself.

Once or twice an hour while Dave Garroway played a record, the camera slowly panned across the glass and the screen filled with images of men in fedora hats, schoolboys in letter jackets, and women in kerchiefs and white gloves. The faces were white and black. Older people looked in amazement at the new technology that was transforming communication before their eyes. The very young often kept their eyes on J. Fred Muggs, who often stared right back at them. People smiled and waved and held up signs with their hometowns or the names of friends or relatives watching at home. One regular at the window was a man who delivered messages in sign language to his deaf mother in Atlanta (no one on the program ever knew what he was saying). It wasn't just common folks who pressed against the glass. Former President Harry S Truman made a habit of passing by the window when he took a morning constitutional during his stays in New York.

Perhaps the most haunting moment during the six and a half years *Today* aired in the RCA Exhibition Hall came on September 25, 1953. Frank Blair had read a news item on Gordon Dean, the retired chairman of the Atomic Energy Commission, who believed it "will only be a year before the Russians have the capacity to destroy us."

As Blair finished, the camera switched to Dave Garroway, shown taking a phone call at his desk. No voice was heard on the other end. "That's all right," Garroway said. "Let's do that right now. Let me tell the folks what's going on."

Garroway then informed viewers that an air raid drill had begun and sirens were blaring throughout New York. He explained that workers from the Office of Civil Defense would soon direct people to shelters (a bit of an obsession for the host, who built a well-stocked fallout shelter in the basement of his town house on the East Side of Manhattan). The pedestrians and cars cleared out. Viewers were soon watching a deserted West 49th Street.

"To slow down the big city to a dead stop in a couple of minutes is quite an art," Garroway calmly noted. "There is not a soul on the street. Not a vehicle in motion. It's very quiet outside. It's very quiet inside, too. The value of a civil defense thing like this is half I think in the drama of making you remember what the world might be like. I guess that's why they do it."

The sidewalk became an extension of the studio and gave *Today* instant access for person-on-the-street interviews. Some tried to take advantage of the daily television exposure the window provided. A local bakery had one of its trucks circle the block every morning for two hours in the hope of getting its name on screen. On one occasion, a man from a rival TV station came dressed in a gorilla costume and displayed a sign that proclaimed, "I'm J. Fred Muggs' long lost brother." When the camera came in for a close-up, he flipped the sign over and it read, "Tonight watch *King Kong* on Channel 9."

The era of the first street-level studio for *Today* ended in mid-1958, when the program moved to the more spacious Studio 3K inside the RCA Building at Rockefeller Center. It was a more modern facility, capable of more sophisticated lighting and elaborate staging. But a part of the show's authentic connection with the public was lost.

fresh, live TV news program with pictures do to their readership? The other issue was cost. Stations did not want to shell out money for programming the morning hours after *Today*. Only twenty-four stations committed to signing on to carry *Today* when it launched. When Garroway appeared on comedian Fred Allen's NBC show to promote the new program, the idea was mocked. "Let me ask you—if you're going on at seven o'clock in the morning, who is going to look at your show?" Allen asked. "Milkmen and roosters?"

When Weaver started considering a host for the program, he initially believed he needed "a buttoned up, hard-hitting guy, climbing up walls and taking us up-to-date all over the place." Instead he went for the soothing presence of Garroway, a known quantity at NBC who already demonstrated an ability to please viewers with his Chicago-based variety show *Garroway at Large*.

When Garroway heard about Weaver's idea, he immediately pushed for the hosting job (which Weaver, in his typically grandiose fashion, called "the communicator"). Garroway had been in the NBC page program in 1938. He studied at the network's school for announcers and fin-

ished twenty-third out of a class of twenty-four. But Garroway persevered, becoming a special events announcer for Pittsburgh radio station KDKA. While serving in the Navy during World War II, he had a regular disc jockey shift on a Honolulu station, where he developed a loose, relaxed style on the air. After the war he headed to NBC's Chicago radio station, WMAQ, where he became a local sensation with his popular evening jazz program *The 1160 Club*. As television emerged, Garroway became part of the medium's "Chicago School." Away from the show business hubs of Hollywood and New York, the Windy City's TV performers became known for their inventiveness and ability to create a feeling of intimacy with the viewer.

"I was built to do this show," Garroway said years later of his reaction when he first heard about *Today*. "All my training had been as a generalist, to specialize in nothing, and know something about everything. This show was made for me. And it was my show automatically, I felt. I deserved it." Garroway said he was so confident in the concept of *Today*, he signed a four-year lease on a large Park Avenue apartment after he moved to New York to take the hosting job.

IT WAS THE BEST PROMOTION *TODAY* COULD POSSIBLY HAVE.

Weaver's other bold move was to have *Today* broadcast at the RCA Exhibition Hall on West 49th Street in Manhattan, where the company showcased its television and radio models. The picture window facing the street allowed pedestrians to watch the program as it happened. The program's audio was carried over a loudspeaker. Weaver said it was the best promotion *Today* could possibly have. "People couldn't believe that anybody would be stupid enough to put a show when nobody would look," Weaver said. "That was the consensus of opinion. I knew they'd have to stop and look in when they'd hear it. As it got better known in New York word of mouth would zoom and it did."

Garroway was joined on *Today* by Jack Lescoulie, a personable actor and radio performer who served as announcer, sports reporter, and comic foil. Jim Fleming, one of NBC's veteran newscasters, was brought in to de-

liver the headlines several times an hour. But Garroway put his personal stamp on *Today* right from the start. He chose the show's theme music—"Sentimental Journey"—which had been a number one hit for bandleader Les Brown and His Band of Renown with lead singer Doris Day in 1945. The song seemed completely out of step with the futuristic mission of informing the world with state of the art communications technology ("Gonna take a sentimental journey"). But the selection resonated with the World War II veterans who had come home from Europe when it was a hit. They were the people heading out the door to work each morning and propelling the country forward through an era of rapid economic expansion.

Like the song, Garroway had an unhurried approach on the air. He moved gracefully around the complex *Today* set, always while speaking directly to the viewer at home.

He was commanding yet serene, relaxed and informal, unlike any other host of a news and information program at the time, yet always respectful. In the early years of the program, Garroway received the nationwide forecast over the phone from Jimmy Fidler at the National Weather Service in Washington, D.C. As Fidler described con-

ditions in different regions, Garroway effortlessly recorded them on a chalkboard map in the shape of the United States. What viewers didn't know is that production assistant Estelle Parsons (who spent five years on the show well before her acting career took off) had already put the information on the board in red chalk, which didn't show up on black-and-white TV screens.

Garroway was a comforting figure right down to his signature sign-off. Every morning he ended the two-hour broadcast by the raising palm of his right hand and stretching his thumb, so that it was almost at a right angle, as he said "Peace." Television writer Charlie Andrews said Garroway got the idea phrase from a charismatic black radio preacher who used it at the end of his broadcasts. "Dave thought it was the greatest sign-off in the world and adopted it," Andrews said in a 1998 interview with the Archive of Amerian Television. "He said it at the end of all his programs. He found it worked instead of any conversation. The other guy would say 'I think the Cubs should have won the game.' Dave would say 'Peace.'. . . He used 'peace' when he couldn't think

of anything else to say he would say that." Garroway delivered the "Peace" sign-off on *Today* with a combination of calmness and intensity. It felt like an acknowledgment that life in the new, faster-moving atomic age was more complex and uncertain.

> ## *Garroway was a comforting figure right down to his signature sign-off. . . . "Peace."*

Today had to grow into the technology that it promised. Technical malfunctions were the norm on the early shows. Segments were interrupted in mid-sentence by scheduled cutaways to local stations on the network. On the debut program, Garroway's phone conversations with NBC's foreign correspondents generated little in the way of news aside from a report of snow in Germany. When Garroway switched to live cameras in various domestic locations, there often wasn't much to see. The Washington camera was fixed on the parking lot at the Pentagon. "I'm getting tired of seeing cars," Garroway was heard saying off camera when the image came up a third time. When a reporter caught up with Admiral William Fechteler, the chief of naval operations, he was asked about the state of the navy. "Guess it's all right," he said. "It was there last night when I left it." Garroway managed to keep things moving with his fluid style. Still, the TV critics were dismissive. John Crosby of the *New York Herald Tribune* called the first show "an incredible two-hour comedy of errors, perpetrated as a new kind of television." He mocked the multitude of clocks on the set. "Who the hell wants to know what time it is in Tokyo?" he wrote. Janet Kern of the *Chicago Herald-American* said the program was "something without which TV can do very nicely."

But *Today* soon proved it had value simply by being on before everyone else. On the morning of February 6, 1952, King George of England suffered a coronary thrombosis and died in his sleep. Buckingham Palace

· DAVE ·
GARROWAY

DAVE GARROWAY WAS A TELEVISION ORIGINAL.

Unlike the biggest stars of the early years of the medium, Garroway had no experience on stage or in the movies. As a local radio personality, he didn't play a character or have a signature routine. Garroway became a star by just being himself.

David Cunningham Garroway was born in Schenectady, New York, in 1913. Two years after he graduated from Washington University, he headed east to work as a salesman. He was in New York, peddling a book about the most commonly mispronounced words, when he became intrigued by the radio business. At a party, he met a woman who supervised the page program at NBC. Garroway signed up and was soon escorting talent to the NBC studios at Rockefeller Center for $15.65 a week. After returning from military duty in World War II, he started a late night jazz program called *The 1160 Club*, which took its name from "11:60 P.M." a brassy fox trot number that was a hit in 1945 for Harry James & His Orchestra. *The 1160 Club* was a sensation with Chicago listeners, thanks to Garroway's laid-back on-air style and willingness to offer a dissertation on virtually any subject. He could comfortably use such words as "diaphanous" to describe a jazz trombone solo without sounding snobby or pretentious.

In 1949, coaxial cable enabled NBC to broadcast television from Chicago, and the network was looking for programs to emanate from the city. Garroway, who had become a local star from *The 1160 Club,* was signed to do a weekly half-hour network TV show called *Garroway at Large*. The original plan was to produce the show live on a stage in a Chicago theater, but Garroway was painfully shy and disliked performing in front of an audience, according to his writing partner Charlie Andrews. "He was an introvert," Andrews once said. "I'll never forget one time he said 'Charlie write me some funny stuff I can say at cocktail parties.'" To accommodate Garroway, his show was designed as a backstage look at a TV show while it was going on. As a troupe of performers presented songs, dance routines, and sketches, Garroway wandered through the proceedings, making wry but always friendly comments to the camera and microphone operators. It was a preview of the low-key but spellbinding style he used when presiding over *Today*.

"This rhythm that he had was absolutely unique," said Estelle Parsons. "It was just very slow. And it's like when you're in a movie, and you get an editor who adds those extra frames with a close-up, you have an impact. You can see Marlene Dietrich in movies where she got the extra frames, and where she didn't. When she doesn't get the extra frames she looks like any other beautiful woman. But when she gets those extra frames, she has an impact right into you. You know? And that was what he had. And it was absolutely unique."

Pat Weaver promised that *Today* would use state of the art communications technology to inform viewers in the morning. It was Garroway who put a human face on the program. His bow tie and large glasses gave him a professorial look befitting of a curious mind. His well-modulated, mellifluous voice and easygoing manner made him sound comfortable whether he was interviewing a nuclear physicist or a beauty queen. "On the air he can interview anybody about anything with his grace and sincerity," Paul Cunningham, a longtime *Today* staffer once said. "He always manages to make immediate contact and get the people talking easily." He had an innate ability to express the thoughts of the viewer at home. "I wonder what life is like in Frankenstein, Missouri," he said when he saw the small town came up on a list of local temperatures that slowly scrolled up the screen every half hour.

Garroway's on-camera skills made him a splendid pitchman, which is why advertisers eventually clamored to be on *Today*. He showed viewers his distorted reflection in a fun house mirror to demonstrate when they should go out and buy General Electric replacement tubes for their TV sets. When Saran Wrap was introduced in 1955, he placed a clear sheet over the camera lens. Stores quickly ran out of the product. Only Garroway could segue from pointing out Napoleon's tomb in Paris to a blurb for Rock of Ages, a maker of cemetery monuments.

"When you sell tombstones at breakfast time, you've got to be good," Jack Lescoulie noted at the time.

By the end of 1953—when *Today* had become a financial success—Garroway was earning a reported $300,000 a year. Even after he became a major star, he remained a loner. He preferred to spend time with the vintage sports cars he collected, which included an SS 100 Jaguar from 1938 that he had since his days in Chicago. He built the replacement parts with a metal lathe he had in his garage. Walking through Garroway's home, visitors would find microscopes, telescopes (he loved astronomy), a console from the first UNIVAC computer, and more than one hundred pairs of cufflinks, including one made of imitation eyeballs. Garroway's son remembered how his father had an actual Norden bombsight on display in his living room.

"He was fascinated by things," said Beryl Pfizer, who joined *Today* as a writer in 1959. "He had these pockets of incredible knowledge. People like that—something comes up and all of a sudden they are explaining something to you that is totally off your scope. He was good at that."

Years after she left the show, former "*Today* Girl" Helen O'Connell, was still in awe of how Garroway connected with the people he interviewed in the studio and the viewer at home. "He taught me how to listen and really hear what people were saying, and look at them and really see what was going on," she said. "And I still think that David Garroway has a knack of taking a story and telling it, and making it come so to life, and touch you deeply inside."

announced his death at 10:45 a.m. London time—5:45 a.m. in New York. The passing was too late for the early editions of the morning newspapers. Only one hour and fifteen minutes from airtime, the producers of *Today* scrapped their planned segments and devoted the entire program to reports on George's death. Garroway and the NBC News team reviewed the monarch's career and discussed how his twenty-five-year-old daughter Elizabeth would succeed him on the throne. They used only still photographs to tell the story. But they owned it. Not only was it a coup for *Today*, it demonstrated the clear advantage TV had in covering breaking news.

In its first six months on the air, *Today* was watched by an average of 1.4 million viewers, reaching 74 percent of the country on thirty-eight stations. The positive mail from viewers indicated that Garroway had made a connection with the audience. "Twenty of us on the faculty now meet every morning at the Faculty Club for breakfasts," wrote one university dean. "We watch the show in its entirety and we are well up on current events—much more so than when we read our local newspaper."

There was even the discovery that not everyone who watched the show was just getting up. "I am a nurse and I live alone and get home at eight o'clock in the morning," read one correspondence. "It's wonderful to have someone at breakfast with you."

So many letters poured in that NBC used them to attract sponsors who still weren't fully convinced that enough people were watching. Garroway, Weaver, and the network's ad sales department tried to make their point at a breakfast meeting for agency executives held in a New York hotel ballroom. After Weaver and Garroway made pitches for their support, several NBC pages entered with stacks of unopened mail. They dumped the letters onto the breakfast tables and passed out openers that were embossed with the *Today* logo that had the face of a clock inside the *o*.

The stunt generated some additional advertiser interest, but still not enough to make the program—produced for $60,000 a week—a financial success. At the start of 1953, there were rumblings throughout the TV industry that NBC was surveying its owned stations and affiliates about canceling the show. "*Today* May Become

(Left): Garroway with J. Fred Muggs. Right: Greeting beauty pageant contestants in 1954.
(Far right): Muggs returning from his world tour on August 14, 1954.

Yesterday Tomorrow," read the headline of a story in the show business newspaper *Billboard*. The producers scrambled to find an idea—or even a gimmick—that would get more people to watch. It arrived in the hirsute form of J. Fred Muggs.

Frank Blair, the longtime newscaster for *Today*, wrote in his 1979 memoir that producer Paul Cunningham and writer Len Safire were having a round of drinks at the New York celebrity saloon Toots Shor's when they came up with the concept of adding an ape to the cast. A newspaper cartoon that showed a gorilla newscaster handing his microphone over to a human newscaster inspired them. The caption read: "And now for the human side of the news!"

The seemingly bizarre suggestion turned into reality when LeRoy Waldron and Buddy Mennella—two former NBC pages turned New Jersey pet shop owners—showed up at the network's studios with an adorable baby chimpanzee for an appearance on another program. Safire brought Muggs and his trainers to *Today* producer Mort Werner who signed off on the idea of putting the chimp on.

Muggs was presented to the audience for the first time on February 3, 1953. He was greeted with an arrival outside of the RCA Exhibition Hall that parodied a Hollywood movie premiere. A black convertible sedan drove up to the door and a carpet was rolled out as an entourage escorted the ten-month-old pint-sized primate into the studio while photographer flashbulbs popped. Once inside, Muggs leapt up onto the desk on the *Today* set and into Garroway's arms. He then grabbed the host's tortoise shell glasses and put them into his mouth before Garroway could quickly snatch them back. From that moment forward, Muggs was a hit with viewers and the ratings for *Today* immediately soared. By the end of the month, he was signed to a thirteen-week contract.

Muggs's popularity and its effect on *Today* revealed it was children who were controlling the TV set in the morning. Even before the chimp arrived, about a third of the show's audience was made up of kids. Turning on *Today* so they could see the antics of Muggs likely aided in creating peace at many family breakfast tables across the country. Youngsters who showed up with their parents to stand in front of the window at the RCA Exhibition Hall were transfixed by Muggs, whether he was playing violin while wearing a white long-haired wig or dressed as a pilgrim on Thanksgiving. As a result, more grown-ups were tuning into *Today* as well.

Garroway was admittedly not an animal lover, but he was able to grin and bear daily life with Muggs if it meant success for *Today*. "Since he came on the show our rating has gone up two points," he said diplomatically when asked at the time how he felt about the new addition to the *Today* panel. "If he can help us that way, sure I want to keep him." Years later, Garroway said

FIRST
SHOW
1952

· JACK ·
LESCOULIE

LAST
SHOW
1966

THE FIRST VOICE EVER HEARD on Today belonged to Jack Lescoulie. He was the announcer who delivered the phrase "This is *Today*" on January 14, 1952. His bright friendly greeting opened the show for many years to come.

Lescoulie was a Sacramento, California, native who grew up in show business. At the age of seven, he did a soft-shoe dance act with his siblings and played vaudeville while growing up on the West Coast. His mother was a variety actress and his father was a technician who worked at the Hollywood studios. During his high school years, Lescoulie worked as a local radio announcer and sought a career as a stage actor. He liked to joke about how he made it to Broadway by providing the sound effect of an elephant in a play called *Achilles Had a Heel*. He returned to Los Angeles in the late 1930s and landed a job as host of an NBC radio show called *The Grouch Club*, in which listeners shared their beefs with the world.

When the U.S. entered World War II, Lescoulie headed overseas to serve as a combat reporter. He flew with the Air Force and recorded accounts of bombing missions over Italy. When he returned to New York, he found steady work as a radio personality, a game show host, and as an announcer for Jackie Gleason's TV programs. The affable Lescoulie became known for his all-American boy looks and big toothy smile. "Do you know why you were never a big hit in radio?" Gleason once said to him. "Because they couldn't broadcast teeth."

Dave Garroway remembered Lescoulie from *The Grouch Club* and suggested his name to Pat Weaver when he was putting together the talent lineup for *Today*. Along with his announcing duties, Lescoulie delivered sports updates and became known for his "Fearless Forecast" for college football games. He developed his on-air tone for *Today* after making a visit to the city room of a New York newspaper. "While there, I found a young man who used to come in and just kid everybody and no one seemed to resent it," he once said. "When I tried that on the set it worked beautifully, and did for many years."

Lescoulie was happy to provide comic relief on *Today*. He became someone Garroway could go to when an interview was going poorly or when a light moment was necessary. Garroway called him the Saver. "We worked out a great rapport," Lescoulie said. "(Dave) said to me, 'If you ever feel that I'm getting dull, or ever think that an interview isn't going right, just walk in, Jack.' Now, that kind of trust, you don't get very often."

Jack Lescoulie with actress Maureen Arthur

He was always game when the program required him to do sketches, play characters (most memorably in a *Caesar and Cleopatra* bit played with Jayne Mansfield in 1957), or even a pratfall into the Fontana di Trevi in Rome. But Lescoulie never forgot the news mission of *Today* and was adept at shifting from light-hearted material to a more serious tone when necessary. The role he created became a part of the fabric of *Today* and was filled in future decades by Joe Garagiola, Willard Scott, and Al Roker.

(Above, Left to Right): J. Fred Muggs, Dave Garroway, Lee Meriwether, Jack Lescoulie, and Frank Blair as portrayed by the top comic strip artists of the 1950s. (At right, top to bottom): Lescoulie with the weather at the 500 Club in

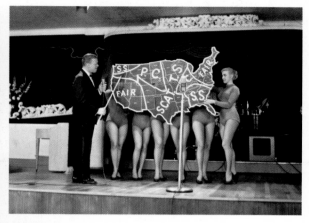

Atlantic City; Lescoulie with Dean Martin and Jerry Lewis on the Atlantic City Boardwalk; Lescoulie performing
Caesar and Cleopatra with Jayne Mansfield; Lescoulie giving his "Fearless Forecasts" on college football.

he was regularly chomped on by Muggs, resulting in nearly two dozen visits to the dispensary at NBC for tetanus shots.

Muggs grabbed the host's tortoise shell glasses and put them into his mouth. . . . From that moment forward, Muggs was a hit with viewers.

During the show, Muggs was kept on a restraint held by one of his trainers who stayed out of the range of the cameras. But he occasionally got loose in the studio. Jack Lescoulie said the staff often feared Muggs was tempting fate when he wandered into the spaghetti-like tangle of high voltage wire behind the set. "Every time he would run back there, why, we'd all hold our ears, expecting the flash and the crackle as the little monkey would be, uh, ruined," Lescoulie recalled.

Muggs's on-air antics clearly lightened up *Today*. The other cast members even started to address Garroway as "Uncle David," when Muggs, dressed in children's clothes and shoes, cavorted on the set. At times it was a tricky balancing act with the show's mission to report on breaking news. That became apparent during coverage of the coronation of Queen Elizabeth II. The event was a milestone for *Today*, which took to the air at 5:00 a.m. New York time to deliver the details live with the help of the latest advancement in telecommunications—a Mufax machine that transmitted pictures from London over short wave radio frequencies. The London bureau of NBC News took photographs off a television screen that showed the

BBC's coronation coverage. They were sent over and presented to *Today* viewers in as little as nine minutes after they were taken. As the still photos were shown, *Today* aired the BBC's radio feed. There was a lull in the audio during the communion ceremony at Westminster Abbey, leading Frank Blair to ask Garroway: "What do you have for us now Dave?"

Garroway used the moment as an opportunity to sit down with J. Fred Muggs, who was dressed for the occasion in a tartan kilt and hat. "Do they have coronations way in the deep jungle there?" Garroway asked. "Do you have a king and a queen, a government? Or do you just live and enjoy life?" Muggs grabbed a bowler derby that Garroway had been holding and started pawing and gnawing on it. "We just borrowed this Stetson for the day old boy, I wouldn't give it the usual Muggs treatment," Garroway warned. "It looks like we're going to be buying this hat, I can tell you without much doubt."

The British press was appalled when it learned of Muggs's routine during the NBC coverage. ("A TV Chimp Competed With The Queen," blared the headline in one Australian newspaper.) American TV critics were harsh as well. "Those responsible should be ashamed," Jack Gould wrote in the *New York Times*.

But it didn't matter. Americans loved Muggs and Garroway. *Today* became a habit in the morning for millions of TV viewers. As the program became more popular, viewers started making alterations in their homes so they could look out from their kitchens and into their living rooms to watch in the morning. Politicians and statesmen who wanted an electronic platform did not hesitate to appear on the program, even if it meant sharing time with the irascible primate.

In 1954, *Today* was the place to see Thurgood Marshall, then legal counsel for NAACP, discuss the United States Supreme Court ruling that declared racial segregation in public schools unconstitutional. Army generals and

(Opposite): Dave Garroway and J. Fred Muggs celebrate Today's *fifth anniversary.*
(Above): Mugg's successor, Kokomo Jr., breaking the news, 1957.

· J. FRED ·
MUGGS

J. **FRED MUGGS WILL GO DOWN** in broadcasting history as the ape that saved *Today*. Despite the huge amount of human effort going into the program during its first year, it was the arrival of Muggs that turned the show around after its rocky start. The chimpanzee born in West Africa was ten months old and thirteen pounds when he first joined the show in February 1953. Not only was he a ratings booster for the program, he was a licensing bonanza. Muggs' story was told in a children's Little Golden Book, and his likeness was used on puppets, dolls and other toys. At the peak of his popularity, America's favorite anthropoid was earning $1,275 a week at NBC.

Muggs was irresistible when he showed up on the set dressed in a pullover shirt and overalls, and Dave Garroway fed him with a baby bottle. He looked downright human when he slipped along on ice skates in the rink at Rockefeller Center or held a newspaper up to his face. An intelligent animal, it was said that Muggs knew when he was in the shot from the red lights atop of the television cameras. He tended to behave while on the air, but immediately acted up when the lights went dark. "The minute the camera went off, oh, things broke loose," Garroway once recalled. "And then we said, 'Well, what we'll do is, we'll turn the lights off on the camera so he can't tell which camera's on.' It took him all of two days to watch which camera was moving into him, and facing it. And that was all there was to that." Lee Meriwether remembered traveling on a plane with Muggs and seeing his eyes squint as sunlight poured through the window before takeoff. His hairy hand reached up and pulled down the shade.

In a few short years, the wildly popular Muggs quickly grew up, and his arms looked like those of a grown man. He became stronger and more difficult to control. He made a habit of attacking the desks of Jack Lescoulie and others in the *Today* studio. On one program, Garroway tried to mollify Muggs by giving him a roll top desk of his own. It was decorated with a sign identifying the chimp as Animal News Editor.

"I've never been happier about anything," Lescoulie said. "Now that he's got his own desk, he'll leave mine alone."

Not for long. After throttling his gift from Garroway, Muggs was led over to Lescoulie's desk and he proceeded to tear away at it. A grimacing Lescoulie struggled to keep it from toppling over until Muggs was pulled off.

Muggs charmed guests who appeared on *Today* up to a point. Frank Blair once recalled an incident with actress Kim Novak. "At one time Kim Novak had him on her lap because she

thought it would be cute," he said. "And he reached down and she squealed and she left the set."

Muggs's owners kept him on a harness as a means of restraint, but he still managed to get loose, especially when the show brought him on the road. One night during a trip in Beirut, he scampered by associate producer Mary Kelly when she answered a bellhop at her hotel room door. She had to chase after him down the hall wearing only a slip. "I never want to baby sit for a chimpanzee again," she told a reporter. Another time during a remote broadcast in Roanoke, Virginia, Muggs climbed to the top of a tree where he remained for hours as Garroway, Lescoulie, and Blair, all holding bananas, tried to lure him down.

But what ended Muggs's career on *Today* was his tendency to snack on human flesh. For the good of the show's ratings, Muggs's repeated chomps on Garroway's fingers and face were tolerated and even satirized in a *Mad* magazine comic depiction of *Today* called *The Dave Garrowunway Show*. After three and a half years, NBC decided to terminate its deal with Muggs. (The press release said the chimp was looking to "extend his personal horizons.") Muggs's owners filed a lawsuit against NBC, Garroway, and Lescoulie, claiming they damaged the animal's image and diminished his earning power. The suit, asking for $500,000, went on for years before a small settlement was reached.

In March 1957, a new chimp named Kokomo joined *Today*. His behavior was better. But he was no Muggs, who had been a true pop culture sensation. By 1958, *Today* became a people-only broadcast.

almost never the case. An obsessive hobbyist, he often stayed up late to work under the hood of one of his vintage sports cars, or stare at the night sky through one of his telescopes. To get through the day he always had a bottle nearby that contained a liquid mixture of Dexedrine and vitamins that he nicknamed "The Doctor." He made no secret of using the concoction, even offering it to colleagues and NBC executives. Hugh Downs recalled being with Garroway and an NBC producer in Nevada in 1955 during coverage of a nuclear test blast. Garroway pulled the bottle out of his pocket and was ready to pass it around. "We'd heard about it," said Downs. "And Garroway said, 'Do you want to take a sip?' I declined but the producer took what he said was about

"PEOPLE LIKED THE FACT THAT DAVE GARROWAY WAS UNPREDICTABLE."

U.S. senators appeared as they pondered the implications of France's surrender to the Viet Minh at Dien Bien Phu—a precursor to America's long and divisive military involvement in Southeast Asia. When the House of Representatives went from a Republican to a Democratic Party majority in 1954, *Today* went live to Kansas City to get a reaction from Harry S Truman. Publishers knew that when Garroway held their book covers up to the camera, it was a head start to the bestsellers list. Records that were played on the program soared up the *Billboard* charts.

Garroway was catapulted to a new level of stardom that America had never seen before. Unlike an actor in the theater or on the movie screen, TV put Garroway in millions of homes for ten hours a week. He did prime-time shows and radio programs for NBC as well. Over the years, the routine wore him down. "I felt sympathy for him in a strange way," said Beryl Pfizer. "I felt he was like a little boy who had come from Chicago and was overwhelmed by New York and Rockefeller Center. There was so much pressure on him."

While Garroway told interviewers he was in bed at 8:00 p.m. to make it in at 4:00 a.m. each morning, it was

a teaspoon, and didn't come down for three days. For years, Dave would do that in the daytime, and when it came time to go to bed, he'd take a handful of barbiturates with sleeping pills. He must have had the constitution of an ox."

According to Garroway's son David, his father suffered from depression since returning to Chicago after World War II. A physician Garroway met in a poker game introduced him to Dexedrine, and he became hooked. "He walked into the pharmacy and ordered two kilos of the stuff because he knew at some point it would not be readily available," Garroway Jr. said. "He kept it in a safe deposit box. He recovered from the drug use. But depression haunted him his whole life."

Over time, NBC executives became concerned about Garroway's condition. In the fall of 1958, he collapsed five minutes before the start of a broadcast and needed to be hospitalized. At the start of the 1959 season, they made his schedule easier by taping nearly all of *Today* in the late afternoon. Only Frank Blair's news reports were done live on the morning the program aired. "At that time, I said, they should have called it *Yesterday*," said Downs. "Because it was."

(Right): Garroway and Claudine Longet ride along the Champs-Elysées in 1959.

Going to videotape did allow *Today* to break its routine and leave the New York studio. In September 1959, the program traveled to Paris for a week of broadcasts, the first time an entire regular U.S. TV show emanated from a European country. Garroway traveled down the Champs-Élysées with Claudine Longet, who was Miss France at the time. When their horsedrawn carriage slowly moved away from the Arc de Triomphe, traffic slowed behind them and pedestrians gathered along the sidewalk. The images on screen were worthy of an Impressionist painting. Outside of the Eiffel Tower, Garroway greeted the dazzlingly sexy actress Brigitte Bardot. It was fitting to see the program near the Café de la Paix, known as a place where, if you sit long enough, you can see the whole world pass by. The same could be said about watching *Today*, just as Pat Weaver had envisioned.

–Beryl Pfizer

FIRST SHOW
1952

· FRANK ·
BLAIR

LAST SHOW
1975

NOT EVERY NEWSMAN was cut out for *Today*, which was more of an entertainment program in its early years. The program's first news editor, Jim Fleming, was a seasoned, knowledgeable journalist who had covered the Soviet Union for NBC. But he didn't care for the format and left after six months. His replacement, Merrill Mueller, hated the early hours and had an even shorter term of thirteen weeks. The producers then called on Frank Blair, a veteran radio announcer with thick wavy black hair who reported from NBC's Washington station. Blair was a protégé of legendary broadcaster Lowell Thomas and a consummate professional. As the father of six children in 1952, (he and wife Lillian would have two more), he was also well equipped for the chaotic atmosphere of *Today* while it was still finding its way. The South Carolina native had a commanding but warm bass voice that gave the right amount of gravitas to the news in the morning even if he had to follow Garroway's clowning with J. Fred Muggs. When *Today* went to Atlantic City for a remote broadcast that featured the final performance of Dean Martin and Jerry Lewis as a team, Blair read the news onstage in a tuxedo and looked totally comfortable doing it. His steady, unflappable nature helped make him a *Today* fixture for nearly twenty-three years.

C **HARLES VAN DOREN WAS** America's favorite egghead in the 1950s. The charming, handsome thirty-year-old Columbia University English literature professor riveted the nation over fourteen weeks in late 1956 and early 1957 as he piled up winnings of $128,000 on the NBC quiz show *Twenty-One*. The network created a new star and looked to *Today* to capitalize on it. With Dave Garroway's blessing, Van Doren was hired as a regular on the program for $50,000 a year. He was given a daily five-minute segment to report on cultural and literary events. On Fridays he read and discussed poetry. The home of J. Fred Muggs was now a platform for Van Doren's essays on non-Euclidean geometry and the works of English poet Sir John Suckling.

In the summer of 1958, reports began to surface that TV's quiz shows were rigged and contestants were being provided with information in advance. Van Doren testified before a grand jury investigation that he received no help during his run on *Twenty-One*. He later told the same thing to Garroway on *Today*. "I myself was never given any answers or told any questions beforehand, and as far as I know, none of the contestants received any coaching of this sort," he told the host and viewers.

It wasn't true. In October 1959, a House subcommittee inquired into the fixing of the quiz shows. Van Doren was subpoenaed and appeared at a hearing in Washington on November 2, 1959. In a statement, he confessed he was coached. He had lied to the grand jury, NBC, Garroway and the *Today* audience. "I have deceived my friends, and I had millions of them," Van Doren told the subcommittee. His contract with the network was terminated immediately.

Garroway had grown fond of Van Doren and admired how he used his popularity to spread knowledge and inspire intellectual curiosity in a way no one else had in the early years of television. He was crushed by the revelation his performance on *Twenty-One* was a fraud. But even more, he was hurt that a friend he worked closely with was gone. There were tears in his eyes when he discussed Van Doren's plight at the opening of the November 3, 1959, edition of *Today*.

"I'm sorry to break up this way," Garroway told the audience. "I know how much he loved to teach. I know his family. I know his charming wife. I watched his little girl grow up at his home, and through the pictures that Charles always carried with him. What do you want me to say? I can only say I'm heartsick."

TODAY GIRLS

FOR MOST OF THE PRE-FEMINIST 1950S, the women of *Today* were referred to as *Today* Girls. But it didn't start out that way.

Estelle Parsons was an aspiring singer from Marblehead, Massachusetts, when she arrived in New York City at the start of the 1950s. She was looking for a day job and learned from her roommate's sister, who was married to a vice president at NBC, that the network was looking for people to work on a new morning television program.

Parsons was hired to be on the staff of *Today* in September 1951, four months before it went on the air. When Dave Garroway went live on January 14, 1952, she was answering phones and handing off wire copy to newscaster Jim Fleming. As a production assistant, part of her job was to call the U.S. Weather Bureau in Washington and record the local temperatures for cities and towns across the country and write them down on a white board shown on the screen after the national forecast. Parsons also prepared book reviews for Garroway to present until one day he went over to ask that she deliver it on camera herself. Although paid a $75 a week salary, Parsons became the first female contributor regularly seen on the program, eventually having the title of woman's editor. She started going out of the studio for remotes. In 1952, she traveled to cover Estes Kefauver as he sought the Democratic presidential nomination. The assignment made her the first woman national political reporter on television.

Even though she had natural poise on the air and an easy rapport with Garroway, Parsons had no ambitions to be a television star. "I wasn't really interested at all in the job," she once said. "I wanted to sing in clubs." She was so capable that after she left her job at *Today*, she returned years later to fill in for Garroway when he went on vacation.

Parsons's skills as an actress, which later earned her an Academy Award, came in handy during the unexpected obstacles on the broadcast. Garroway once recalled the time Ava Gardner agreed to appear on *Today*. He sent Parsons to pick the actress up at her hotel and escort her to the studio. "When Estelle got to her room, she found the doors barricaded," he said, "Estelle knew she was in there but Ava refused to answer the bell, the phone or even to talk through the door. So Estelle returned to the studio and we put her on camera to impersonate Ava. She did a beautiful job."

Another early *Today* hire was associate producer Mary Kelly. She was a dark-haired, ebullient presence on the set, often seen at a desk next to Jack Lescoulie. She started out getting

Florence Henderson's first day as a Today *Girl in 1959.*

coffee for Garroway and others, and eventually worked her way up to writing scripts, wrangling guests, and on-camera interviewing. She was an essential member of the first *Today* team. As her airtime increased, she frequently received mail from young women who wanted advice on how to start a career in television.

Over time, the producers wanted a featured female presence on the program. But instead of using the self-assured women who helped get the show off the ground, they went for the "*Today* Girl." She was responsible for "tea-pouring segments," as they were called, dealing almost exclusively with fashion and family issues. She handled some celebrity interviews and the weather forecasts. The first was Lee Meriwether, a slender and wholesome looking brunette, who had been crowned Miss America for 1955. She was offered the job after appearing on the program as a guest. She lasted a year, as the *Today* Girl position over time proved to be a

(Top, left to right): Garroway with Estelle Parsons in 1954. Parsons at the temperature board in 1952. Blair,
Lee Meriweather and Lescoulie. (Above): Helen O'Connell and company celebrate the fifth anniversary of Today

Frank Blair, "Today Girl" Betsy Palmer, and Jack Lescoulie in 1958.

temporary one. But for most who served, it was an enjoyable one. Big band singer Helen O'Connell followed Meriwether and put in two years next to Garroway from 1956 to 1958. Years later, she was still getting letters from viewers. "People became very close to you," she said during a return visit to *Today* in 1972. "They identified with getting up in the morning and seeing you as a friend, across the breakfast table."

Betsy Palmer replaced O'Connell in 1958, but after a few months found it wasn't possible to juggle the morning hours with an acting career and her role as a panelist on the game show *I've Got A Secret* after a few months. Florence Henderson was in the midst of her successful career in theater and TV when she was recruited for *Today* in 1959. Right after she took the job, she became pregnant, a word, she said, that could not be used on the air at the time. Henderson—tired of disguising her condition by being strategically seated behind potted plants or furniture—said it anyway. "I remember getting a letter from a viewer that said how dare you sit up there in your hatching jacket," said Henderson. During Henderson's tenure, *Today* was taped in the late afternoon the day before it aired. But even when the program was not live, you had to expect the unexpected from Garroway. Henderson recalled the time he had a barrel of rhesus monkeys brought into the studio.

"Everyone uses that expression more fun than a barrel of monkeys and Dave said 'I'd like to see how much fun that is,'" Henderson said. "He brought in a barrel of monkeys and took the top off and they went berserk. I jumped up on the desk. They were little and they wound up in the grid where the lights are. They were pooping everywhere. I never knew how they got them down. I heard they had to shoot them. I don't know that for a fact, but a stage hand told me that."

A few of the *Today* Girls started out as writers for the program, including the last one hired by Garroway. Her name was Barbara Walters. In the 1960s, she would elevate the status of not just the *Today* Girl, but the American woman as well.

(Clockwise from top right): Claudine Longet, Bridgette Bardot, Van Doren, Lescoulie, and Garroway, the Arc de Triom...

way at a café, in front of the Eiffel Tower, taping on the streets of Paris, Van Doren with a local vendor in 1959

Frank Bla

BARBARA

CHAPTER TWO

Dave EDWI

Garroway John

Jack Lescouli

Hugh Downs

WALTERS

1960–1969

NEWMAN

Chancellor

JOE GARAGIOLA

1960 — *Ninety percent of all homes in the U.S. have a television set.*

Dave Garroway with Jackie Gleason and Jack Lescoulie.

1960–1969

IN JANUARY 1960, *Today* celebrated its eighth anniversary on the air with a program from Washington, D.C. Dave Garroway interviewed Senate Minority Leader Everett McKinley Dirksen in the Capitol and Supreme Court Justice William O. Douglas in his chamber. Jack Lescoulie took viewers on a tour of the Smithsonian Institution. Frank Blair did a dramatic reading of the Declaration of Independence. Florence Henderson sang "The House I Live In" from the steps of the Library of Congress. *Today* had become a more polished production and shed

some of the ramshackle spontaneity that made it an adventure to watch in its earlier years. Garroway appeared mellower than ever before on the air, while becoming more erratic behind the scenes. Yet when it mattered most, he always came through as a brilliantly skilled TV performer. The plans for the anniversary program included an exclusive interview with President Eisenhower. But it was never confirmed, and on the day of the taping, Eisenhower's press secretary informed producers that it wasn't going to happen. With a half hour of *Today* to fill,

Garroway's solution was simply to stand on the White House lawn and speak directly into the camera about past events that happened there. Using research that was gathered by his staff, he spoke into a tape recorder and the words were transcribed and put onto a teleprompter. On paper, the script seemed incoherent. When delivered in the calm, intimate style that Garroway had perfected, it conjured up vivid images of presidential history.

> **Today** *had become a more polished production. . . . Garroway appeared mellower than ever before on the air.*

Today got inside the White House the following year, when President John Kennedy gave an interview to Garroway to commemorate the 150th anniversary of Massachusetts General Hospital (he was on the board of overseers). It was the first time a sitting president appeared on a regularly scheduled TV program. Kennedy was relaxed, making his points about support for mental illness research and his own physical fitness program without notes or a teleprompter. He addressed Garroway as Dave, as if he were a friend who dropped by. It was a demonstration of Kennedy's comfort on camera and how he would use television to effectively disseminate his ideas to the public just as Franklin Roosevelt had done with radio in the 1930s. "As I was able to say to him 'anytime you want to use us, we're a tool at your disposal,'" an impressed Garroway said in the *Today* studio afterward. "Because he's the President of the United States. And if anyone can, he'll give us peace."

The Kennedy appearance turned out to be the last milestone of the Garroway era at *Today*. The host was always eccentric. But it was becoming more difficult for staff and management to navigate around his moods and whims. His continued use of Dexedrine to fight his depression and sleeping pills to come down from it was

Garroway with Lyndon Johnson (above) and with "Today Girl" Beryl Pfizer circa 1960 (below).

taking its toll. "He was using a lot of drugs at that time," said his son Dave Garroway Jr. Still, Garroway remained hugely popular with the audience and had nearly autocratic rule over what happened at *Today*. Beryl Pfizer recalled a revolving door of writers, producers, and *Today* girls during her tenure from 1960 to 1961.

1962 — *Tensions between the U.S. and Soviet Union escalate over installation of nuclear missiles in Cuba.*

"Garroway kept firing all these women," she said. "They came and went. When I was on the show, which was part of '60 and part of '61, there were four producers. So if he didn't fire the girl, he fired the producer." He tangled with NBC management more, but his clout was evident in the title of the program when it was changed to *The Dave Garroway Today Show*. It was the only time the network used a name other than *Today* in the morning.

Any turmoil on the set was overshadowed by tragedy at home. Garroway's second wife, Pamela Wilde, a former actress and ballet dancer whom he married in 1956, had problems with mental illness, alcohol, and controlled substances as well. On April 28, 1961, she died of a drug overdose in the family's Manhattan town house. Garroway's marriage had been under some strain at the time, according to his daughter Paris. When Pamela's death occurred, Garroway was out at the family's weekend home in Westhampton, Long Island, with his son David.

When Garroway returned to work after his wife's death, he no longer had the fight in him to get a new

They just wanted him to be a talking head and read the news and nothing more."

Garroway wished *Today* viewers "Peace" for the final time on June 16, 1961. His departure gave NBC News an opportunity to take over *Today*, which had been run by the network's program department. While NBC News was an integral part of *Today*, there was a bit of uneasiness with the show's freewheeling format and total independence within the company. In the early years of TV, radio was still the main platform for serious broadcast journalism. Many veteran reporters whose careers pre-dated TV tended to sneer at the show business aspects of the new medium.

"A lot of the old timers in those days resented it," said longtime NBC News correspondent Edwin Newman. "They didn't want to go to the trouble, especially in the days when you would go into a studio and have to be made up, and you might have to memorize a script in the days before the teleprompter. Or if you had the script in front of you, you somehow had to look into the camera and not appear to be looking down and read-

WHEN NBC NEWS GAINED CONTROL OF *TODAY* FOR THE FIRST TIME

contract (it was scheduled to expire that fall) and keep *Today* running his way. On May 26, 1961, he announced he was leaving the program to "make what contribution I can to peace" and devote himself to raising his children. But David said his father told him there was more to it.

"He told me he was forced out," he said. "He wasn't officially fired but they did everything they could to make him feel unwelcome, indicating to him that he should leave. He did resign officially, and the reason he left is that the show was going to an all-news format.

ing. There was some reluctance to recognize it as what the future was going to hold."

Newman was among the younger and more ambitious correspondents who understood the power of *Today* and were drawn to the program. "When the show came on in the early '50s, I was in London for NBC," he said. "*Today* made you known across the country. It gave you prestige; it gave you importance. People would see you. Friends and relatives would see you and write to you. In those days, even if you were on the staff you would get a fee when you went on particular shows. And the fee for

(Above): John Chancellor replaced Dave Garroway as host in 1961.

going on *Today*, as I recall, was larger than it was for any other program at the time."

When NBC News gained control of *Today* for the first time, executives found they inherited a beast that was not easy to tame. Veteran correspondent John Chancellor was named as the new host. The erudite newsman, who resembled film actor Ray Milland, had been covering Moscow. At that time—the height of the Cold War—it was the weightiest assignment at the network. Chancellor balked at the idea of being a breezy morning host, but was convinced to sign on after being told NBC News was running the show—and that his annual salary would jump from $20,000 to $100,000. "They do pay handsome overnight differential in salary," he once said. Newman was called in from his London assignment to join Chancellor on the show as newscaster. Both men were excellent broadcast journalists but had the kind of studious looks that were more suited to their brethren in print or radio.

When Chancellor took over, NBC returned to broadcasting the full show live at 7:00 a.m. after two years of taping the show the day before to accommodate Garroway. Jack Lescoulie chose to become host of a new children's game show instead of returning to the early morning grind. Since Newman was going to read the news, Frank Blair was designated to take Les-

mercials. The "can" referred to Alpo, the longtime dog food sponsor on *Today*.

Chancellor debuted on July 17, 1961, with Newman joining him the following week. It was a misfire right from the start. The program's greater emphasis on news upset the perfect alchemy of information and entertainment that eased viewers into the new day under Garroway's helm. Looking back, Chancellor realized the shift was too jarring after nine years of Garroway, who molded the program to his personality.

"I'm not sure I was able to fill those shoes. Dave was one of the most magnificent communicators I had ever known." —John Chancellor on Dave Garroway

---

"It was a very difficult act to follow," Chancellor said during a return visit to the show years later. "I'm not sure I was able to fill those shoes. Dave was one of the most magnificent communicators I had ever

EXECUTIVES FOUND THEY INHERITED A BEAST THAT WAS NOT EASY TO TAME.

coulie's role, handling weather and sports and providing some occasional comic relief. It was an ill-advised piece of casting. While Blair was a fun guy after a couple of drinks at Hurley's, the regular *Today* watering hole, his image as a broadcaster was generally steady and dignified. Any humor he brought to the program came through playing off of Lescoulie. But Blair was willing to handle most of the live commercials on the program—something that advertisers demanded and Chancellor resisted as a highly principled journalist. "He wouldn't hold the can" was the phrase used around NBC News to describe those who didn't want to do com-

known." One of the surviving tapes of *Today* from Chancellor's year as host is of him doing the show on location from the National Housewares Manufacturers Show at McCormick Place in Chicago. He could not muster wonderment over the latest kitchen and garden gadgets, something that would have come naturally to Garroway. "It was a great change for the program," said Barbara Walters, who wrote for Chancellor on *Today*. "And John, who was a delightful person, was considered too serious for *Today* at that time. And the audience just didn't respond to him." People inside NBC News said Chancellor missed being a correspon-

· EDWIN ·
NEWMAN

FIRST SHOW 1961

LAST SHOW 1974

EDWIN NEWMAN'S TIME as a *Today* panelist was brief. But he remained a distinguished member of NBC News for the two decades that followed. He frequently filled in on *Today* and was responsible for the only time a guest was thrown off the program. During a 1971 interview with Newman, comedian George Jessel, known at the time for being an outspoken supporter of the Vietnam War, referred to the *New York Times* and the *Washington Post* as *Pravda* and *Izvestia*, the official Soviet newspapers. Newman wouldn't put up with it and cut their chat short. "He in effect libeled the two leading newspapers in the country," Newman recalled. "I said, 'Well, that's enough. We won't want to hear anything more from you.'"

After *Today*, Newman frequently handled breaking news coverage during the day on NBC News. He was witty and acerbic, and looked more like an English literature professor than a TV broadcaster. His appearance was appropriate, however, as he was television's foremost grammarian. In 1974, he authored a book about language called *Strictly Speaking*. Executive producer Stuart Schulberg believed no one was more qualified to handle an interview about the book than Newman, so he used a split screen and had Newman interview himself. "For which he was paid," Chancellor once pointed out. "For plugging his own book on the air, he was paid. There's a *Today* show first."

· JOHN ·
CHANCELLOR

J

OHN CHANCELLOR WAS the pride of NBC News from the 1950s right until his retirement in 1993. While he looked and sounded scholarly on television, he didn't have a college diploma. Born on Chicago's North Side, he worked at various jobs— a tugboat deck hand, a hospital orderly, a dishwasher, and a busboy—before landing a job at the *Chicago Sun-Times*. He later joined NBC's WMAQ-TV as a summer replacement and developed a reputation for flirting with danger to get a story. He was once shot at while covering a shooting and had building debris fall on him during a fire that took the lives of four firefighters. His skills got him higher profile network assignments on the presidential campaign trail of Adlai Stevenson in 1956 and the battle over segregation in Little Rock schools in 1958. Chancellor was a high-profile foreign correspondent for the network when he got the call from NBC News to replace Dave Garroway in 1961. The job simply wasn't a good fit for someone who defined himself as a working journalist who enjoyed being out in the field reporting. One scribe noted at the time: "He has a ready wit, but he's inhibited on the air. That's a bad shortcoming." Chancellor also had little experience in doing live television, especially in the early morning hours. He said he once fell asleep on the air and flubbed Frank Blair's name. Chancellor's stint was mercifully short at *Today*, but the rest of his career at NBC News was highly esteemed. He was a key

figure in the network's political coverage. In 1970, he became co-anchor of the *NBC Nightly News*, a broadcast he was better suited for. After a dozen years in the anchor chair, he remained as a commentator, the last person to hold such a post on a network evening newscast. Chancellor always respected the endurance of *Today* and the connection it had with its viewers. "It's been very comforting for the American people to have the *Today* show," he said during a return appearance on the program in 1987. "NBC found some formula, some manner of civility, of comity, of ease that made people comfortable with this program in the morning."

· HUGH ·
DOWNS

H ugh Downs wrote a symphony, recorded an album of folk songs, made needlepoint squares, rode a motorcycle, loved astronomy, flew airplanes, and was an avid scuba diver. He was also one of the most popular hosts in the history of *Today*. "Hugh had the easiness that made people comfortable in the morning," said former NBC News president Dick Wald. "His wide range of interests gave him a little bit of knowledge about almost everything under the sun; and a general pleasant demeanor that made everybody feel comfortable. He was really the Everyman of that business."

Downs began his broadcasting career in 1939 as a radio announcer in Lima, Ohio, about 150 miles outside of his hometown of Akron. He worked his way to NBC's Chicago station WMAQ and became a staff announcer for the radio network by the age of twenty-two. While in Chicago, he became friendly with another WMAQ personality, Dave Garroway. The two men shared an interest in astronomy. "We used to talk about telescopes and stars and planets for hours," Downs wrote in his autobiography. Downs borrowed tools from Garroway's well-equipped garage in Chicago to build his own telescope.

Downs recalled the skepticism when his friend headed to New York to become host of NBC's new venture—a live two-hour morning program. "I'll never forget that people said to Pat Weaver, 'Nobody will tune in a television set at seven o'clock in the morning,'" Downs recalled. "And he said, 'Yeah, you're right. If you don't broadcast anything, they won't.'" But Downs had his own doubts when *Today* debuted in 1952. "The truth is I saw it, and I was impressed with the technology of the time and the people involved in it. But I said, I'm not sure this will last. It seemed a little gimmicky. But it did get the news out."

But after a first rocky year, *Today* was a hit. "I'm a hell of a prophet," said Downs, who did local inserts for the program out of Chicago. He eventually moved to New York where he became announcer, co-host, and sidekick on other NBC shows such as *Home* and *Tonight*. He later became the host of *Concentration*, a brainteasing game show that became NBC's top-rated daytime program. Downs did not tell jokes. His singing was passable. But he had an ability to talk extemporaneously on virtually any subject. His amiable style had given him a career. "I don't want to be anything but myself," he once told a journalist. "I have no talent. I am a personality, the best thing you can be on television. A personality is not talent so it can't be burnt out or overexposed. It has a fantastic kind of security."

Downs was not nearly as quirky or charismatic as Garroway. But he was the best option when John Chancellor failed to click on *Today* as Garroway's replacement.

When Downs joined the program, the trickiest part of the routine was not waking up in the morning, but getting dressed. He was totally color-blind. The condition required his wife, Ruth, to put his clothes out the night before. He also had numbers sewn into his wardrobe items so he could match them up himself when she wasn't around.

Downs's arrival in September 1962 steadied the *Today* ship. He was not a journalist, so he had no qualms about doing live commercials—the economic lifeblood of *Today*. Advertisers paid a premium for commercial time on *Today* when the hosts or panelists read the copy themselves. Some advertisers used cardboard cutouts of Downs for their in-store displays. While *Today* made an economic rebound with Downs at the helm, critical accolades came in as well. "*Today* is more than a good program," said a *TV Guide* editorial in early 1967. "It's a necessary one."

While Downs's gentle style was dismissed in some quarters as bland and superficial, he was never predictably mainstream in his views that he occasionally expressed on *Today*. "I came out for the legalization of marijuana, which created more of a stir than if I had said I'd just joined the Communist Party," he recalled. "It must have been the late 1960s or early '70s. And finally I quit using the word 'legalize,' because that's such a buzzword. It made people think that I wanted a nine-year-old to be able to go into a store and buy heroin, or nonsense like that. I believe in getting things under the law, since I believe in law. And when you outlaw something, you put it outside the law and hand it over to criminal elements." Downs's bosses at the network were not always happy when he used *Today* as a soapbox, especially on this issue. "Oh, they were very upset, and everything," he said. "But not quite enough to buy out my contract. Curiously, I had more support from the public than I would have expected."

dent. One producer quipped: "He had a bad case of trenchcoatitis."

Today producers tried to lighten up the proceedings by having Chancellor, Newman, and Blair perform in occasional comedy sketches. Chancellor wasn't comfortable mixing spontaneous light banter with the news and contrived merriment appalled him even more. "John was not happy with that," Newman recalled. "I had a bit more ham in me than John had in him. I enjoyed that kind of thing." (In 1984, Newman was the first TV news personality to serve as a guest host on NBC's *Saturday Night Live*.) While viewing remained high—twenty-seven million or one-third of all TV homes in America watched *Today* over the course of a month in 1961—panic set in at the network over a drop in ad revenue as sponsors missed Garroway. Newman was the first one to be thrown overboard. He was moved out of his role on the program after just six months.

There was one glimmer of hope for the future of *Today* during Chancellor's era. It came in the first on-air appearance of Barbara Walters, who was Garroway's last hire. On August 29, 1961, Frank Blair introduced her to viewers for the first time.

"We forced our staff writer Barbara Walters to go to Paris to cover the fashion openings," he said. "Today's the day that pictures of these clothes are released to the public, and we wanted to have them first. Barbara, would you tell me was this a very trying experience for you?"

"Oh Frank it was awful," Walters replied. "First of all, every day I had to go and look at fashion shows. And then I had to have lunch at Maxim's and drink champagne. And then I had to smell all the perfume at Dior's. I mean it was so trying that I took absolutely the very last plane that I could to get back here today."

Walters was coy and funny as she introduced her filmed report. When asked if she bought anything on her trip, she pulled out a bauble and placed it on a fingertip. It was a "nail ring" that cost six dollars wholesale. She put it on her index finger and stroked it against her cheek as the camera framed a tight shot of her face.

"I've looked at that tape," Walters said years later. "I think I was so thin. I think I was copying Audrey Hepburn. I think I was kind of cute. And I loved doing the fashion shows. I came back and reported on them myself. That was my breakthrough."

The Tonight Show *team of host Jack Paar, announcer Hugh Downs, and bandleader Jose Melis.*

Walters's career flourished after the next shake-up at *Today* came in September 1962. Chancellor was taken off the program. He was professionally unscathed by the experience as his star later rose at NBC News, where he eventually became the network's evening news anchor. NBC executives realized that *Today* needed a host who could handle the news, but who also had the ability to create the kind of comfort level that Garroway provided in the morning. They turned to Hugh Downs. Like Garroway, Downs's broadcasting career took off at WMAQ, NBC's Chicago radio station. Downs had become a durable, quick-on-his-feet broadcaster after effectively serving as a second banana for two of Pat Weaver's other NBC creations. He was Arlene Francis's co-host on *Home,* a popular daytime show that offered advice on cooking, fashion, and interior decorating. He later became the announcer and sidekick to Jack Paar on *Tonight.* Like Garroway, Downs had a natural curiosity and a penchant for collecting esoteric information in his head that could be dispensed at will. His ability to pull up facts during the wafer-thin conversations on *Tonight* gave him the reputation of being an intellectual.

In 1960, Downs was in the epicenter of the most notorious controversy during the emotional Paar's tumultuous five years on the late night show. During a monologue, Paar had told a humorous story that played on the initials W.C., an abbreviation for water closet, a British term for a room with a flush toilet. He was enraged when NBC's standards and practices department found the use of the term to be in bad taste and deleted it. The following night, Paar walked off of his program. "I'm leaving the *Tonight* show," he said as his voice choked up. "There has to be a better way to make a living than this." (He found there wasn't and returned the following week.) After watching in astonishment, Downs stepped in to host the rest of the program that night and filled in for Parr frequently enough to believe he had a shot at taking over as the permanent *Tonight* host. Instead the job went to Johnny Carson, and Downs was asked to host *Today.* NBC News executives were so desperate to get Downs in place, they were even willing to let him continue in his other job as emcee of a popular daytime game show *Concentration.* With Downs on board, Jack Lescoulie returned to the program and Blair went back to reading the news.

The images are: FIRST SHOW 1961, BARBARA WALTERS logo, LAST SHOW 1976.

"IT WAS A VERY DIFFERENT TIME,"** Barbara Walters recalled about her earliest days at *Today*. "It was before the women's movement. We had one female writer on the show and I mean only one. If she left they hired another female. But there were never two females."

When Barbara Walters was first hired at *Today* in 1961, it was on a freelance basis to write for Anita Colby, an actress and former model who was known as the Face after she appeared on the cover of *Time*. Colby regularly delivered fashion reports on *Today* sponsored by S&H Green Stamps. Walters's copy was never to come out of the mouths of Dave Garroway, Jack Lescoulie, Frank Blair, or any other man who appeared on the program. "I started out only being able to write for women," she said. "Can you imagine the breakthrough when I was allowed to write for men? I mean, this sounds as if I'm talking about the 1800s. I'm not."

The daughter of a Boston-based nightclub entrepreneur who operated the renowned Latin Quarter, Walters sought work in New York after her 1950 graduation from Sarah Lawrence College. Through her father's business, Walters knew many of the newspaper columnists in New York and the connections helped her land her first job in the publicity department of NBC's local station. She worked her way up into writing and producing positions at several local TV outlets and then spent five years writing fashion segments for a CBS morning show that tried to compete against *Today* with various hosts including Jack Paar, Dick Van Dyke, and Walter Cronkite. Walters didn't think she was attractive enough to be a TV performer herself. "It never occurred to me that I was going to be on," she said. "I didn't think I was beautiful, I wasn't a model, and I couldn't sing." But once Walters joined *Today*, she kept breaking barriers. Anita Colby was more of a looker than a talker, yet Walters's scripts for her were so strong they gained the attention of *Today* producer Shad Northshield. "Barbara can write anything," said Northshield. And she did. She was soon churning out copy for host John Chancellor and later crafted the introductory piece for his replacement Hugh Downs who was so impressed he became a major supporter of her work.

After her breakthrough appearance covering Paris fashions for *Today*, Walters was soon writing, producing, and directing the filming of her own pieces on a regular basis. "I spent a couple of days as a Playboy bunny," she said. "I did the day in the life of a nun. I traveled a lot for the program." One of her trips was a 1962 visit to India with First Lady Jacqueline Kennedy.

As Barbara Walters's star rose throughout the 1960s, she was described as brusque, pushy, hardworking, and unpretentious. With success, she transformed herself into one of

Barbara Walters, Billy Wilder, and Hugh Downs in 1966. Photo by Ron Ganley NBC/Newswire

the glamorous celebrities she often covered. She did fashion spreads in *Vogue* and *Cosmo-politan* and her apartment was featured in decorating magazines. "When I first went on the air, I looked boyish like Barbara Walters, Girl Reporter," she told *TV Guide* in 1967. "I looked a little tough. Now my eye makeup is different. I wear soft eyelashes, lighter lipstick. I have a softer look." Walters even made it into the lyrics of a pop song by the Neon Philharmonic called "Cowboy," which explained the range of her appeal. ("I woke up this morning and cried and cried . . . I turned on the *Today* show and wished it was yesterday . . . Barbara Walters, would you marry me? . . . Or maybe mother me?")

After *Today* made her a household name, Walters only took on more projects. She contributed segments to NBC Radio programs, wrote articles for *Ladies' Home Journal* and gave lectures at colleges and women's clubs. There was a reason for her tirelessness. Barbara Walters had spent her life being exposed to celebrities and deeply understood the public's fascination with them. She also knew that fame and fortune could be fleeting. As she became more prosperous in her career, she saw her father's business ventures falter. It only drove her to work harder. "I am always afraid it's going to be over tomorrow," she once said.

Dave Garroway, Hugh Downs, John Chancellor, Barbara Walters, and former T

(Clockwise from top right): At President Johnson inaugural in 1965, portrait from 1971, with Dave Garroway at 30th anniversary of Today, with Angela Lansbury in 1966, publicity shot coverage of the Investiture of Prince Charles in 1969 (large), with the short-lived NBC "N" logo in 1976, on the Today set in 1968, and publicity shot for 1972 convention coverage.

Today also tried to recapture the flavor of its early days by resuming its broadcasts from a street-level studio, this time in a Rockefeller Center storefront used by the Florida Development Commission to promote tourism. The set was not nearly as expansive or impressive as the RCA Exhibition Hall, where the show was staged in the 1950s. But it had a picture window that looked out onto West 49th Street. While it helped reconnect the show with the public, it was a less than ideal situation. During the day, the window was filled with paraphernalia associated with the Sunshine State—mannequins in flowered shirts, palm trees, thatched cabanas, and a tropical parrot in a cage. All of the items were stored and the birdcage was covered with a black cloth before *Today* set up. Barbara Walters recalled when the birdcage was left uncovered on a day Robert F. Kennedy was booked to appear on the program.

"The parrot said, 'What's your name?'

And he said, 'Robert Kennedy.'

And the parrot said, 'What's your name?'

decaying urban centers, and dramatic social upheaval throughout American society. It wasn't the on-air talent or NBC News management edicts that made *Today* more serious—it was the new crises that Americans faced every day. "It was a very turbulent time in this country, which made *Today* a much more important program," Walters said. "We used to say people tuned in to find out if the world was still there in the morning."

The maturation point for *Today*—and all of television news—came in the hours and days after the assassination of President John F. Kennedy in Dallas on November 22, 1963. The three networks broke into their programming to report on the unthinkable tragedy that afternoon and broadcast continuously to cover the aftermath. On November 23, *Today* aired on a Saturday for the first time. The program was woven into the fabric of the fifty-five hours of NBC News coverage.

"The shock of it in New York slowed everything down," a shaken Lescoulie told viewers that morning. "Trunk lines jammed in the telephone company. You

"THEY NEEDED REPORTERS SO BADLY THAT I WAS DRAFTED AS ON

And he said, 'Robert Kennedy.'

And the parrot said, 'What's your name?'

And he said, 'Goddammit, I told you, Robert Kennedy.' And he walked out after that into the studio, *furious*. Angry. He complained about the people backstage."

Even with the new cast, the program remained under the auspices of NBC News. As the 1960s progressed, the tensions that simmered under the seemingly carefree 1950s were coming to the surface: racial strife in the segregated South, growing military involvement in Southeast Asia, crime and civil unrest in the nation's

couldn't even get a call to your home. People wanting to tell everyone else, wanting to almost share this bad news with their reaction."

Frank Blair stood outside of St. Patrick's Cathedral on Fifth Avenue and reported that masses were being held every half hour until 10:00 a.m. when a solemn requiem mass was scheduled for the dead president. The camera he was on was set across the street inside Rockefeller Center as he appeared tiny on the TV screen with the massive church behind him. The camera panned across the street to Saks Fifth Avenue where

(Above): The second Today *window at the Florida Showcase on West 49th Street in Manhattan.*

all of the department store's picture windows were blacked out except for one that displayed a painting of the fallen thirty-fifth president of the United States. It was placed on a chair with and flanked by two urns of crimson roses.

The night before, Barbara Walters traveled all over New York City to gather the reactions to the president's death. She went up to Harlem, down to Greenwich Village, and into the arcades in the Times Square area. Her description of the bleak atmosphere that prevailed was simple, haunting, and riveting. She went into the Stork Club, the only nightclub she found open. "The people here tonight are like the people who are out Christmas Eve," the headwaiter had told her. "They have no home."

Walters then headed to Washington, where she covered the president lying in state. "They needed reporters so badly that I was drafted as one of them," she said. "And I was in the Rotunda for hours on end, commenting on the dignitaries, and the ordinary people who were coming to pay tribute. The whole nation was crying."

Walters's strong performance that weekend built a case for upping her status on *Today*. "For me, it was a most emotional assignment, but also one that proved I could—indeed, a woman could—play a more serious role," she said. Yet throughout the reinventions that *To-*

IF THEM . . . . THE WHOLE NATION WAS CRYING." — *Barbara Walters*

day went through in the early 1960s, the men running the show still held onto the notion of having a "*Today* Girl" who served mostly as an adornment on the program. (One journalist suggested *Today* producers believed that "too great a display of brains and competence in a woman would shrivel the mass audience.") After Beryl Pfizer left (and moved onto a successful career as a TV news producer), *Today* hired Robbin Bain, the 1959 winner of Miss Rheingold, a New York area beauty contest sponsored by a local brewery. TV and film actress Louise King, and former St. Louis weathercaster Pat Fontaine followed her.

BARBARA WALTERS
Interviews

TRUMAN CAPOTE

· · · · · · · · · · · · · · · · · · ·

BARBARA WALTERS ONCE wrote that she was shy about asking writer Truman Capote about his work when she met him at a party during the time when his book *In Cold Blood* was a literary sensation. But she soon learned that Capote loved talking on TV (perhaps more than writing), and he joined her for a lengthy *Today* chat in 1967. Once actor Philip Seymour Hoffman landed the lead role in the film *Capote,* he watched the interview dozens of times to pick up Capote's speech and mannerisms. It paid off, as Hoffman won a 2006 Academy Award for his performance.

DEAN RUSK

· · · · · · · · · · · · ·

BARBARA WALTERS GOT a lead on her first major political interview through a fan letter. During a summer in which she hosted *Today* while Hugh Downs was on vacation, a note came from Secretary of State Dean Rusk in which he expressed admiration for the job she was doing. "If NBC vice presidents ever begin to bother you, show them this letter and tell them to leave you alone," he wrote. Rusk was such a close Walters follower he once told her he preferred her hair long rather than short. Rusk never gave television interviews, but after he left his post in March 1969 he said yes to a persistent Walters. They talked for four hours in a suite at the Hay Adams Hotel in Washington, covering Vietnam policy and Rusk's work in the Kennedy and Johnson administrations. *Today* ran the interview in five segments over the course of a week. Once the interview was finished, Walters was taken aback at how both she and Rusk went outside the hotel by themselves to hail taxicabs. She had been used to seeing him over the years in limousines and with body guards.

PRINCE PHILIP

· · · · · · · · · · · · · · · · ·

BARBARA WALTERS'S CORDIAL professional relationship with President Nixon gave her entrée to other coveted interview subjects. In 1969, Walters met Nixon while she was filming an interview in the Rose Garden with his daughter Tricia. "He was happy with that interview," she said. "And if you could make it with one of his daughters, he then trusted you. So I did quite a few interviews with Nixon. Not only that, he arranged for me to get an interview with Prince Philip, who had turned me down. And Nixon talked to him, and Philip grudgingly did an interview with me because of Nixon."

The interview caused a minor international incident as Walters asked the prince if his wife Queen Elizabeth, II, had thought about abdicating and turning the throne over to Prince Charles. "Who can tell?" he insouciantly replied. "Anything might happen." Public outcry and rallies in support of the Queen forced Buckingham Palace to release a statement saying there were no such plans for her to stand down.

PRINCESS GRACE *of* MONACO

IN 1966, GRACE KELLY sat with Barbara Walters for her first interview as Princess Grace of Monaco. "It was difficult because it was like pulling teeth," Walters said. "It was the first time she had ever done one without a script and she was so nervous I had to put my arm around her to calm her."

The princess, who married Prince Rainier, III, in 1956, seemed sad and ambivalent even as she tried to respond to questions that required only basic facts. When asked how many rooms were in the royal palace she said, "I don't know really. I suppose there are over 200. I think I read that once."

Walters, as she often did, cleverly posited her last question to the princess as the one that "most Americans" wanted an answer to.

"Are you happy?" she asked.

"I've had many happy moments in my life," the princess said tentatively. "I have a certain peace of mind." Once the camera stopped rolling, she started to cry.

Hugh Downs championed the idea of making Walters a regular cast member when Fontaine left early in 1964. But executive producer Al Morgan (who never got along with Downs) went for another actress, Maureen O'Sullivan. She was well known to a generation of moviegoers who saw her play Jane to Johnny Weissmuller's Tarzan in the 1930s and '40s. After a brief respite from show business to raise her family (which included daughter Mia Farrow), she made a comeback on the Broadway stage in *Never Too Late* and was charming as a *Today* guest. In the age before television executives became obsessed with younger demographics, Morgan wanted the mature but still glamorous O'Sullivan because she would appeal to older viewers.

> *Barbara Walters's emergence on* Today *was heralded as a significant inroad for women in television news.*

It was immediately evident that O'Sullivan was not up to the task of performing on live television every morning. She botched cues and was a poor interviewer. Her inadequacy compelled the producers to pull her from the program during coverage of the Democratic National Convention in Atlantic City, where party members gathered to nominate President Lyndon Johnson for re-election. She was gone before her thirteen-week contract was up. She later admitted that she had a prescription drug problem that put her in a fog during most of her short tenure.

O'Sullivan's failure created an opportunity for Barbara Walters, who continued to work hard at turning out pieces for the program after being passed over. Hugh Downs pushed Al Morgan again to make her a regular cast member, and this time, he prevailed. "I always tried to promote Barbara because I figured that some of the glory would spill over on me," Downs said.

By the end of the year, Walters appeared at the desk next to Downs and Lescoulie three times a week. "The audience knew me and liked me," Walters said. "So they put me on for thirteen weeks. I stayed on for thirteen years." It wasn't only a victory for Barbara Walters. Once Walters became a regular, the title of "*Today* Girl" faded from the show's lexicon.

Al Morgan also hired newspaper film critic Judith Crist, who provided film and theater reviews, and Aline Saarinen, who reported mostly on culture and art. Aline was the widow of architect Eero Saarinen, who designed the exuberantly futuristic Trans World Airlines terminal at Kennedy Airport (then known as Idlewild) and the powerfully stark Manhattan glass tower known as Black

Walters' favorite times on Today *were alongside Garagiola and Downs.*

Rock, which served as headquarters for CBS. She was a natural on television when she appeared on *Today* to discuss her late husband's work during a remote broadcast at the opening of the TWA terminal. Coiffed by Jacqueline Kennedy's hairdresser, Mr. Kenneth, she exuded elegance and intelligence.

Walters shared panel duties with Crist and Saarinen but that changed over time as her stories and interviews impressed the program's producers and viewers. "Little by little, they began to use me more and more," she said. "So I learned a good lesson: just work as hard as you can; be as good as you can; don't complain; and become neces-

Downs with Marlon Brando in 1962, Walters with Garagiola in 1968, Robert F. Kennedy visits with Downs in 1964.

sary." In September 1966, Walters was named panelist and opened the program each day alongside Downs while Frank Blair did the news. But it was still Downs's show. "I was not a co-host," Walters said. "Women were not co-hosts then. I was the third member of the cast. I did most of the traveling. I did a good many of the more serious interviews. But, still, I was in my place."

During the early days of the feminist movement of the 1960s, Walters's emergence on *Today* was heralded as a significant inroad for women in television news. "The shift from the old *Today* Girl—who was usually a coffee-server and amiable lightweight—to Barbara Walters is the television industry's change of attitude in a microcosm," wrote Gloria Steinem in a 1965 *New York Times* piece with the headline "Nylons In the Newsroom." Saarinen also rose in the ranks at NBC News, where she eventually became a full-fledged correspondent covering earthquakes and space launches. She went on to become the first woman to be Paris bureau chief for NBC.

The women's liberation movement was largely ignored or dismissed by male TV journalists in the mid-1960s. Walters never positioned herself as a feminist, but used her perch to bring women's issues to a wider audience on *Today*. In 1967, she delivered a series of

reports on discrimination against women in the workplace. She also led a program-length discussion on the birth control pill, which included a group of longtime users who talked about the freedom and spontaneity it brought to their sex lives. Walters's adept and even-handed approach to the provocative topic earned praise in the show business paper *Variety*: "Without Walters's expert fielding this might have been a pretty bland pill of a show."

As Walters' career progressed, so did the technology that helped make *Today* more vital to viewers. The 1965 launch of the Early Bird space satellite facilitated the live transmission of transatlantic broadcasts. All of the networks raced to show off their ability to capitalize on the innovation and none did it better than *Today*. The May 5 program opened with Pope Paul VI speaking directly from the Apostolic Palace. Then it was on to London for Hugh Downs, who reported from outside Buckingham Palace for the changing of the Guard. In Paris, Barbara Walters interviewed actor Yves Montand and narrated a fashion show. Aline Saarinen reported from Rome and Jack Lescoulie from Holland, where he visited Madurodam, a miniature village and children's park. The broadcast demonstrated the new instantaneous

interview subjects in other fields so that his role could be expanded on the program. He became a panelist in December 1967.

For Walters, it began the happiest era of her time on *Today*. Garagiola referred to himself as "the six-pack guy" on the program who connected with Middle America. But like Downs, he was progressive in his attitude toward Walters's ability and how it was essential to the overall success of the program.

"You couldn't have a good Hugh Downs and a bad Barbara Walters and Joe Garagiola; and you couldn't have a good Barbara Walters and a bad Hugh Downs and Joe Garagiola; and you couldn't have a good Joe Garagiola and a bad Hugh Downs and Barbara Walters," he said. "It was either a good *Today* show, or a bad *Today*

global reach of television news and enabled *Today* to bring the world to viewers' breakfast tables in real time.

Starting in September 1965, the *Today* opening was proceeded by the animated peacock and the announcer who intoned that the show was airing "in living color on NBC." It required moving the set back inside of Rockefeller Center as the Florida Showcase storefront could not serve as a studio for color broadcasting.

The following year, Jack Lescoulie left the show for a final time and was eventually replaced by Joe Garagiola, the former Major League Baseball catcher who was part of the 1946 St. Louis Cardinals team that won the World Series. An amiable storyteller who became one of the first professional athletes to successfully make the transition into broadcasting (he did play-by-play work for the Cardinals, the New York Yankees and NBC's *Game of the Week*), Garagiola had been a contributor to *Today* since the early 1960s. He did sports reports, which included an iconic moment in the clubhouse of the 1966 World Champion Baltimore Orioles, when jubilant team members slathered Garagiola's face and baldhead with shaving cream as he tried to conduct postgame interviews. Garagiola was so likeable, executive producer Stuart Schulberg encouraged him to

Garagiola and Walters with Maharishi Mahesh Yogi in 1968

J **OE GARAGIOLA CALLS** *Today* his college education. "It made me get into areas that I ordinarily would not get into," he said.

During the 1920s and 1930s, Garagiola grew up in the Hill, a St. Louis neighborhood filled with Italian immigrants, many of whom worked in the city's clay mines. His boyhood pal was New York Yankees Hall of Fame catcher Yogi Berra. Garagiola's nine-year career as a second-string catcher in Major League Baseball was less illustrious. But he always said yes whenever his first team, the St. Louis Cardinals, asked him to attend a banquet, charity event, or Boy Scout dinner. He honed his skills as a storyteller at such appearances and eventually earned a spot in the Cardinals' broadcast booth after his playing career ended in 1954. By 1960, he was the author of a well-received book of anecdotes called *Baseball Is a Funny Game*. After appearing on *Today* to promote the book, the producers assigned Garagiola to cover the 1960 World Series with Jack Lescoulie. It was the year that Pittsburgh Pirates second baseman Bill Mazeroski won the seventh and deciding game against the New York Yankees with a walk-off home run, one of the most exciting moments in baseball history.

"It was in Forbes Field, and they gave us seats in the last row of the third deck, believe it or not, over the women's toilet," Garagiola recalled. "And every time somebody would flush, our seats would rattle. And when Mazeroski hit the home run, we could look over the whole city. And we saw it erupt. It was really funny to watch. I mean, it was eerie, because you could see confetti start to come out the window and kind of work its way down like a wave."

Garagiola reported from the losing Yankees' clubhouse, and began his long-standing membership in the *Today* family while taking on other assignments, including segments on NBC's *Monitor* radio program and baseball play-by-play work.

To expand his role on *Today*, Garagiola said he "had to prove that I could even interview guys outside of sports. I worked hard at it. I didn't want to look like an idiot." When Garagiola was assigned to interview an author on *Today*, he read the book cover to cover. He recalled once how he labored through a lengthy tome called *The Lawyers* by Martin Mayer. "That thing was so thick; I read every, every living word," he said. "And I had like a book report. I knew that thing backwards and forwards. And then they canceled him. And I said, 'Oh! You just can't do that, man! I put a week and a half into this thing. I'll go to his house and interview him, just for my own satisfaction.'" Garagiola once said his children were never more impressed then when he came home with books by Marianne Moore, a poet they read in school. "There never had been

Garagiola at the Macy's Thanksgiving Day Parade in 1970

any excitement when I brought home Mickey Mantle or Yogi Berra to dinner," he once told a journalist. "But all of a sudden I was a big hero because I was meeting Marianne Moore."

Garagiola's blue collar appeal worked best when he was sent into situations where viewers wouldn't expect to see him—like the time he was assigned to review the 1968 rock musical *Hair*. The Broadway show had caused a cultural commotion with its onstage nudity. Garagiola was able to connect it to his own experience: "I said that if I wanted to see naked bodies, I'd go into the Yankee clubhouse."

show. Anything you could do to help each other, you wanted to do it." Garagiola marveled at Walters's work ethic. "I don't want to hear anybody tell me anything bad about her, because I know how hard she worked, and I saw how hard she worked when we were on remotes. We would tape, and then we had to do it over and over, on cold, rainy days. And she never asked for anything. I mean, she was out there—just like the cameraman, just like anybody else, doing her part of the job. She's a thorough professional."

The trio of Downs, Walters, and Garagiola led *Today* for the rest of the 1960s. They were in harmony on-screen while the world they reported on became more discordant. Downs guided two full hours of *Today* coverage the morning after Martin Luther King Jr. was gunned down in Memphis on April 4, 1968. The nonviolent civil rights movement that King led was being overshadowed by the angry demands of the militant Black Panthers. Walters once listened to Kathleen Cleaver, wife of Eldridge Cleaver and Black Panther

DOWNS, WALTERS AND GARAGIOLA WERE IN HARMONY ON SCREE

Garagiola with John Saxon , E. G. Marshall and future Good Morning America *host David Hartman in 1969.*

spokeswoman, reel off the party's ten-point platform and program: ". . . Three: we want the end of the robbery by the white businessmen of the black community. . . . Point number six: we want all black men to be exempt from military service. . . . Point number eight: we want all black prisoners held in federal, state, city and county prisons and jail to be released because they have not had a fair trial."

Dissent over U.S. involvement in Vietnam had heightened on college campuses, and exploded onto the scene of the Democratic National Convention in Chicago, where *Today* aired for the week of August 26, 1968. The road to the nomination of Vice President Hubert Humphrey had been the most unpredictably shocking in American political history, from President Lyndon Johnson's surprise announcement that he would not seek a second term to the assassination of then New York Senator Robert F. Kennedy, whose entry into the race helped drive the incumbent president out.

The *Today* staff was housed at the Conrad Hilton Hotel across from Grant Park, where Chicago police and young antiVietnam War demonstrators were in bloody face-offs every night. The violence took its toll on the press as well. A *Today* production assistant was among the twenty-one journalists and photographers beaten by riot police with nightsticks that week. The hotel smelled of tear gas. Downs read a statement on-air denouncing the police action. One day he picked up the tab for a few thousand sandwiches that were given out to the young demonstrators.

That week, Joe Garagiola was on the street to film a segment on Chicago's underground theater scene when a young man approached him and said he was from his old St. Louis neighborhood, known as the Hill. The young man was an anti-war demonstrator who had been tear gassed the night before and was fearful over returning to Grant Park again.

HILE THE **WORLD THEY REPORTED ON** BECAME **MORE DISCORDANT.**

"Do you think they're going to gas us again tonight?" the young man asked Garagiola.

"I don't know," Garagiola replied. "They don't ever check with me. But if you're that scared, don't do it."

"I'm so scared," the young man said. "But I have to be here."

The memory stayed with Garagiola for years. "Here was a kid who grew up in the same environment as me," he said. "He was this scared kid who still believed in what he was doing, that he was going to do it in spite of being so afraid."

When *Today* completed its broadcasts from the convention location, film clips of the violence were shown under the closing credits with Frank Sinatra's recording of "My Kind of Town" playing over it. After a week of the terrifying images, even the dependably straight-ahead *Today* could not resist a little world weary irony.

Barbara Watlers and Hugh Downs

Frank Blair T O M

BARBARA WALTERS

CHAPTER THREE

Frank McGee

GENE SHALIT JIM

BROKAW

JOE GARAGIOLA

1970–1979

JANE PAULEY

HARTZ HUGH DOWNS

1970 — *Members of the Ohio National Guard kill four students at Kent State University during an anti-war protest on campus.*

Barbara Walters and Hugh Downs

1970-1979

AS THE 1970s BEGAN, America remained intensely divided over the war in Vietnam. Frank Blair's newscasts on *Today* reported on sit-ins and protests on college campuses as America's involvement in Southeast Asia widened. New social issues emerged as well. During the week of the first ever Earth Day on April 22, 1970, Hugh Downs devoted *Today* to the environmental crisis the country was facing as its air and water became more polluted. On the *Today* set that week were two renderings of Earth—one totally blacked out—and the words

"New World? No World." For one segment, *Today* invited representatives from major American auto companies to discuss the combustion engine's impact on the nation's air quality with consumer activist Ralph Nader. None of them accepted, so Downs conducted the interview with Nader next to some empty chairs for the no-shows.

It was also an era when *Today* provided viewers with a more global view. Said Barbara Walters, "We went to Paris. We went to Hawaii. We went to Puerto Rico. It was a time when the *Today* show could, and did, travel a lot. And we showed people the world." Downs, Walters, and Joe Garagiola spent a week in Munich, where they talked to leaders and opinion makers about the chances of reunifying Germany. They saw the sights in Romania, the first time the program had broadcast from a country behind the Iron Curtain. The final trip the trio made together was in the first week of October 1971. The Friday broadcast was a somber one from the Hiroshima Peace Memorial Park, where Downs listened to survivors give their grim recollection of August 6, 1945—the day a nuclear bomb leveled the city at 8:15 a.m. Downs held up the rusted remains of a clock that had been melted by the blast, the hands stopped at the eight and three positions.

For the cast, the trip was also personally poignant, as it was Downs's final day as host of the program after nine years. "As much as I had enjoyed hosting *Today*, the hours made it feel like a debilitating disease from which it might take years to recover," Downs wrote in his autobiography. Walters was genuinely sad when she embraced Downs and told him good-bye. She had good reason to lament his departure. She had blossomed into a true equal in their on-air partnership. They complemented each other's skills when they handled interviews together. Downs was genial and conversational in his inquiries. Walters was sharper and more direct in her questions. The fact that they appeared to truly like each other made Walters more acceptable as a woman broadcaster in an assertive role.

As he did in the 1960s, Downs championed the idea of Barbara Walters as a *Today* host. "When I left *Today*, I recommended to NBC that they hand over the program to Barbara," Downs said. "I think the public was ready for it. But the industry wasn't quite ready for it yet."

Watching Downs was like having an affable, interesting guest at the breakfast table.

According to the memoir of Reuven Frank, the NBC News president at the time, the idea didn't get any consideration. Frank was determined to put what he considered a serious journalist back in the host role. Downs succeeded John Chancellor on *Today* because

Hugh Downs at Lion Country Safari, 1971.

the news division had stumbled in making the choice back in 1961. Frank wanted to prove that NBC News was capable of developing a *Today* host from its ranks who could keep the program commercially successful. He designated Frank McGee, a distinguished correspondent for the network throughout the 1950s and '60s. "He seemed to me perfect by aspect and experience," Frank wrote in 1991. "His controlled, interesting baritone, his measured speech and lyrical way with a phrase, his lifetime in news, his capacity for long hours, and his pleasant face, attractive without being too handsome, added up to my idea of the perfect host." The appointment of McGee was a solution to another problem at NBC News. In 1970, Chet Huntley had left the network's highly successful evening newscast *The Huntley-Brinkley Report*. The program was renamed *NBC Nightly News* and had

1971 — *All in the Family premieres on CBS.*

a troika of anchors with McGee, David Brinkley, and John Chancellor. Some combination of two of the three appeared on the program each night, including weekends. It was a confusing format that had viewers switching in droves to CBS and Walter Cronkite. Reuven Frank's real priority was to fix the evening news, his division's prestige-building broadcast. "He saw *Today* as a burden," said one friend.

People turned on Today *in the morning to find out if the world was still there.*

Going from Downs to McGee was a significant shift for *Today*. Watching Downs was like having an affable, interesting guest at the breakfast table. McGee's manner was often described as ministerial or worse. "Everybody thinks I'm an undertaker," McGee once told his pal Jim

Hartz. But Reuven Frank got his way. He used a hefty salary increase to get McGee to overcome his qualms about taking the job, which he thought would hurt his reputation as a newsman. He was wrong. On many mornings, McGee was the first voice to report on times that appeared to be even more precarious than the 1960s. On October 26, 1973, *Today* opened with an image of a flag flying over the White House in the predawn light. "This is the White House in Washington on a morning when a major confrontation between the United States and the Soviet Union appears to have been averted. The United Nations is sending a peacekeeping military force to the Mideast, lessening fears that Russian troops would intervene unilaterally in the Arab-Israeli war," McGee said. "Nevertheless, American military forces around the world remain on alert." The notion that people turned on *Today* in the morning to find out if the world was still there had never been more accurate.

Today, like the rest of network TV news at the time, was not always on the leading edge of the social changes going on in America. When Barbara Walters suggested stories on the feminist movement during its nascent days,

Walters leads a feminist roundtable at the 1972 Democratic National Convention in Miami with Bella Abzug, Liz Carpenter, Gloria Steinem, and Betty Friedan.

Barbara Walters and Frank McGee covering the 1972 Democratic National Convention (DNC) in Miami, Florida.

a note would come back from her bosses that said, "Not enough interest." When gay rights activists were taking to the streets demanding better treatment in the early 1970s, they were given scant attention by network news—until one surprising moment on *Today*.

On the same October 26 broadcast, Frank Blair was reading the news in the 7:00 a.m. hour, when a young man—with shoulder-length hair and dressed like a college student—stormed onto the set. "Gay people are sick and tired of the bigotry at NBC," he shouted before the audio was cut and the picture blacked out. It was Mark Segal, the head of a Philadelphia-based group of activists called the Gay Raiders. Its members had been disrupting live broadcasts of various programs to bring attention to how gay people were ridiculed and stereotyped on television programs and ignored by TV news. They posed as students from Temple University's radio, television, and film program to secure passage into the studio in advance. Segal was on the set as an observer before he rushed into the camera's shot. After Segal was hauled off by guards, Walters followed him out into the studio hallway to speak with him. "Wait a minute. I want to find out what this is all about," said Walters, even though she was supposed to be on the air. She listened to Segal explain his cause and later told viewers what happened: "He was protesting against an NBC program *Sanford and Son,* which is aired on Friday nights. He said the program was unfair to homosexuals or as he put it 'unfair to gay people,'" she said in a sympathetic tone. Segal was sent on his way without even a call to police. (The *Today* disruption—or "zapping" as the group called it—was just a warm-up to interrupting the *CBS Evening News with Walter Cronkite* two months later. Segal said that incident resulted in more coverage of gay issues by the network.)

● ● ●

BARBARA WALTERS
Interviews

MAMIE EISENHOWER

. . . .

AS BARBARA WALTERS scored more newsmaker interviews in the 1960s, she developed a reputation for getting famous people to offer up revelations about themselves. "I had a line in which I would say, 'What are the greatest misconceptions about you?' And very often, they would bring these things up. That's what happened with Mamie. I didn't say, 'Do you drink?' I said, 'What's the greatest misconception?' And she said, 'People think that I'm a drinker. But I'm not. I have an inner ear imbalance.'"

When Walters landed an interview with legendary opera soprano Maria Callas, she was told Callas would not discuss former paramour Aristotle Onassis. The Greek shipping magnate had dumped Callas and married former First Lady Jacqueline Kennedy. Walters agreed but gave Callas an opening.

"I said, 'What's the biggest misconception about you?' Callas said, 'That people think I'm jealous of Jackie Kennedy.' And it all came out. She had never intended to talk about him, but she spoke rather longingly about him."

MARTHA MITCHELL

. . . .

DURING THE WATERGATE ERA, there was no one more quotable than Martha Mitchell. The rambunctious, attention-loving wife of John Mitchell, Nixon's attorney general and manager of the president's re-election campaign in 1972, freely offered journalists barbs about the corrupt activities that eventually took down the Nixon presidency. "If her facts were shaky, her opinions were not," said Barbara Walters. "For the press she was marvelous . . . she knew a headline when she made one." In a *Today* appearance in 1974 after her husband had separated from her, Mitchell was so incoherent that Walters's asked if she was an alcoholic. But Walters knew Mitchell made great, unpredictable television. During their first interview, Mitchell pulled a copy of Walters's book *How To Talk with Practically Anybody about Practically Anything* out of her voluminous handbag and proceeded to rave about it. Even a pro like Walters appreciated that move. "It was a shrewd and, I must say, successful way to divert a reporter from her line of questioning," she said.

Martha Mitchell repeatedly told Walters she was going to write a tell-all book on Watergate (and was hoping to promote it on *Today*). It never happened. When Mitchell died in 1976, Walters said, "My opinion is that she had told all and that she knew very little more."

HENRY KISSINGER

• • • • • • • • • • • • • • • • • • • •

BARBARA WALTERS'S STRONG connections in the Nixon White House gave her an inside track on interviews with Secretary of State Henry Kissinger. Their meetings on *Today* were substantive, often challenging Kissinger to rationalize America's role in a guerrilla war in Southeast Asia. But viewers could count on Walters to probe powerful figures in areas left untouched by traditional Beltway journalists. Walters once recalled how Kissinger reacted when she asked about his status as one of Washington's most socially active bachelors. "I love it," he told her. "Now when I bore people they think it's their fault."

RICHARD NIXON

· · · · · · · · · · · · · · ·

BARBARA WALTERS WAS on vacation from *Today* in early March 1971 when a call came from the White House. The fifty-ninth birthday of President Nixon's wife, Pat, was coming up and he wanted to pay tribute to her by having conversations with a group of female journalists. Walters was the only television reporter chosen. The president liked Walters and aided her in booking important guests. But he had never given her or any other lone TV reporter a lengthy interview since he took office. Walters immediately went to Washington with a film crew and talked to Nixon in the Blue Room of the White House for nearly ninety minutes. There were ground rules— the discussion was to be about the president's wife, his family life, and the role of the First Lady. *Today* also had to agree to run the interview in its entirety. Walters was able to get the president to talk about a wide array of issues, including equality for women. Nixon said the women who covered the White House (including UPI reporter Helen Thomas) were as good as the men. He said he saw no barriers to a woman being on a presidential ticket. In discussing his wife, Nixon revealed her ambivalence toward political life and that he could understand if she became weary with his stubbornness. "If I were a woman living with a man who happens to be president of the United States I would say it would be a lot easier to be someone who is not quite dug in," he said a bit clumsily. When the interview aired on the March 15, 1971, edition of *Today*—taking up most of the two hour program—it was as close as American TV viewers had ever gotten to seeing a personal side of Nixon who was always extremely reserved in public. Walters knew how to flatter Nixon. She was perhaps the only reporter to ever describe him as sexy.

(Above): Barbara Walters with Ray Bolger on The Tonight Show *in 1976.*
(Right): Walters interviewing Israeli Prime Minister Golda Meier.

While Downs was an essential ingredient to the success of *Today* during his nine-year run, it was Barbara Walters who had emerged as the star of the program. She wanted recognition of the fact with the title of co-host when McGee came on board. McGee would not go for it. "He was not at ease with professionally equal women," Reuven Frank wrote. That was an understatement. "The idea that he had to work with a woman appalled him," Barbara Walters said. McGee went to NBC chairman Julian Goodman and demanded certain conditions for working with Walters. In any *Today* interview they conducted together, he would ask the first three questions. "He was a very difficult and complicated man," Walters said. "And he was the one who said, 'She can't come in until the fourth question.'" The demand was particularly humiliating for Walters. She had already ably handled her own *Today* interviews with President Nixon, Henry Kissinger, Egyptian President Anwar Sadat, and Israeli Prime Minister Golda Meir.

Barbara Walters had emerged as the star of the program.

The rule only motivated Walters to go out and land more newsmaker interviews and assignments away from the studio. When President Nixon announced he was making what would be a historic visit to China in 1972, Walters jumped at the opportunity to cover it for *Today*. "Going to China was like going to Mars," Walters said. "This was the time of the Cultural Revolution and I was the only female television reporter. It was very heady stuff for me." NBC News bosses had chosen Walters to join *NBC Nightly News* anchor John Chancellor on the trip (which was fine with McGee, whose reaction, when

told Walters would be gone for a week, was, "China's not far enough").

"I went to the Great Wall of China with Richard Nixon," she said. "He introduced me to Chou en Lai, who was one of the major figures in China at the time. He said, 'This is Barbara Walters. We're just breaking her in.' What a way to get broken in." Walters was nervous and unsure of herself in China as the other networks had sent their heavyweight (and male) anchors and correspondents to cover it. She returned to learn that she had done more stories than anybody else on the trip.

When the Watergate scandal consumed the Nixon White House, Walters spent much of her time in Washington, giving her plenty of opportunities to get around the three question edict. On-air, McGee and Walters always appeared cordial. Behind the scenes, their hostility toward each other was not as well concealed. McGee made condescending comments about her in the press.

There was a larger issue brewing under the inequitable situation. NBC News management wasn't sure of what to make of Walters, who had become a high-profile journalist comfortable with both hard, serious news and softer, entertaining features. She even filled in as a guest host for Johnny Carson on *The Tonight Show*, and did a dance number on the program.

"It wasn't that Barbara had to become the co-host, so much as it was that the corporation couldn't get its mind around the fact that Barbara was a powerful figure in the equation," said Dick Wald, who succeeded Frank as NBC News president and inherited the uncomfortable arrangement. "It isn't that they didn't see that she was a star. Yeah, they sort of understood that. But what they didn't understand was that she was essentially the future, and the era of the male host, and everybody subordinate, had passed. They thought that dynamic was what made *Today* popular. Changing that dynamic made everybody extremely nervous."

· FRANK ·
McGEE

F **RANK McGEE'S DEFINING MOMENT** as an NBC News correspondent came in September 1957 on *Today*. He conducted a live interview with Arkansas Governor Orval Faubus in which he repeatedly asked why nine black children were not allowed to enter Little Rock's all-white Central High School after the local school board voted to comply with the Supreme Court ruling on desegregation. The students were kept out by Arkansas National Guard troops under the control of Faubus, who claimed the public's safety was at risk.

"If the Negro students were obeying the law, those who would prevent them from entering the school would be violating the law," McGee told the governor.

"No they're obeying the law and keeping peace and order in the community," said Faubus.

McGee, ordered by his boss to do the interview, once recalled how he thought it was a terrible idea. "I think I was afraid to do it," he said in 1972. "But I did it. . . . [Faubus] said the same thing over and over and over and I kept him at it for fifteen minutes."

A dismayed Garroway played the interview twice and then asked the audience—in a way that only he could—"On this cool September morning, 1957, it is a fair question to ask yourself I believe: Is this the United States of America? Is this our home? Is this the country that we knew?" The students were admitted to the school later that month.

It had been McGee's gutsy reporting on the civil rights movement on NBC's Montgomery, Alabama, affiliate that punched his ticket to the network. He did the first television interview with the Reverend Martin Luther King Jr., then a minister at the Dexter Avenue Baptist Church. He gave early national attention to the story of Montgomery seamstress Rosa Parks after she refused to move to give up her seat to a white passenger on a city bus. As news director, McGee regularly had the station do stories on the inequitable treatments of black citizens.

McGee became a familiar face to viewers with his network coverage of the space program. When John Glenn orbited the Earth in February 1962, McGee was on the air for eleven consecutive hours to report on the mission. "You did everything perfectly," Julian Goodman, then an NBC News executive, said afterward. "We've just got to find a better way for me to go to the bathroom," McGee replied. Glenn's flight established McGee as NBC's Rocket Man, with an ability to explain complex NASA missions with clarity. "I never knew anything about the space program," David Brinkley once said. "How those things flew around the Earth—I don't understand it. Frank McGee would walk up to the blackboard with a piece of chalk like a professor of physics and would explain it to me. I always knew if I could understand it, the American people

Frank McGee moderating the Great Debate between Nixon and Kennedy in 1960.

(Clockwise from top left): McGee as a Washington correspondent in 1959, Frank McGee with Richard Nixon and John F. Kennedy for the second 1960 presidential debate, McGee anchoring NBC's Kennedy assassination coverage in 1963.

could." McGee presented the coverage without being a cheerleader for NASA. At times he was critical of the agency for wasteful spending.

The space program sent McGee's TV career into orbit after his very down-to-earth beginnings. He grew up in Oklahoma, where his father worked in the oil fields during the Dust Bowl era of the 1930s. "Those were the type of conditions that either break you or make you very tough and Frank was a very tough man," said Jim Hartz, his friend and fellow Oklahoman. After five years in the army, McGee studied fiction writing at the University of Oklahoma, and then went into local television news. He joined NBC News in Washington in 1956 as an assignment editor and worked his way up to being a correspondent out of New York, where he was often featured on *The Huntley-Brinkley Report*. He moderated the second of the 1960 presidential debates between John F. Kennedy and Richard Nixon. He also was anchor of *The 11th Hour Report*, the late newscast for WNBC, as it was the days when NBC News correspondents typically had assignments at both the network and one of the owned and operated local stations. McGee was also anchor of the network's weekend newscast called *The Frank McGee Sunday Report*.

McGee was generally evenhanded on the air, but did not fear taking a stand. His experience in Montgomery made him an outspoken supporter of the civil rights movement. While Walter Cronkite's criticism of the Vietnam War in 1968 was seen as a turning point on public opinion toward the conflict, it was McGee who was likely the first journalist on network television to pointedly oppose the country's involvement. At the end of an NBC program called *Vietnam December 1965*, McGee stated emphatically that if the British and the French were able to withdraw from Southeast Asia honorably, so should the United States. The network received mail that complained about his views, but he continued to speak out against the war. He did an award-winning documentary, *Same Mud, Same Blood,* which examined the lives of black soldiers as they fought side by side with whites in Vietnam. To cover the story, he lived nearly a month in the field with a platoon of the 101st Airborne Division.

Jim Hartz described McGee as "kind of a bantam rooster." He was wiry, intense, blunt, and often abrasive. "He was a tough guy to get along with," said Hartz. "He was an absolute perfectionist. He was a brilliant writer and a strong editor. I never had problems because we were good pals. But he chewed people up and down in the newsroom." McGee even ridiculed the *Today* writers on the air. He did not possess the kind of mild temperament that made *Today* go down easy for viewers in the morning and wasn't about to change when he reluctantly agreed to succeed Hugh Downs as host in 1971. "I am cursed with the character I have," he told *Look* magazine. "I cannot create a new one. Nor would I try." Yet the typically buttoned-up McGee told Hartz privately that he hoped viewers would see a lighter side of him on the program (they rarely did). McGee's two-and-a-half-year run on *Today* has mostly been remembered for his unwillingness to tolerate Barbara Walters. But *Today* remained potent—journalistically and financially—while he was at the center of it.

Walters had also become a more sympathetic figure to the audience, thanks to an attempt by CBS to try to compete with *Today* with *Washington Post* style writer Sally Quinn, who was ten years younger. Despite having no television experience, Quinn was made the co-anchor of the *CBS Morning News* with veteran newscaster Hughes Rudd in the fall of 1973. Although Walters and Quinn were friendly—Quinn had written a flattering profile of Walters the year before—the press billed the morning matchup as a newswoman catfight. "The problem is Sally is beautiful, slick, and glamorous," Aaron Latham wrote in *New York*. "The women in the television audience may not be able to identify with her the way they seem to with Barbara Walters. Moreover, a wife in curlers may not want to invite a stunning woman like Sally into her home at breakfast time. It can hurt to be a blonde." CBS didn't help Quinn's cause by portraying her as a sexpot in its on-air promotional spots. The

cause. "*Ms.* magazine wanted me to sign a paper saying I had an abortion," Walters told the *New York Times* in 1972. "I didn't sign it because I hadn't had an abortion, but I wouldn't have signed it anyway." Quinn crashed and burned after six months on CBS and went back to the *Washington Post*. But it did not change the fact that Walters was a second-class citizen at *Today* with McGee at the helm. The situation took an unexpected turn in the early spring of 1974. By that time, it was apparent to NBC management that McGee was ill, but no one was sure how serious it was. He had kept his failing health a secret from his colleagues. On the set, he sat in a chair that was designed to relieve severe back pain. He grimaced when he got up to leave the set, often needing assistance from a stagehand. "I was his best friend," said Jim Hartz, who was working as an anchor at NBC's New York station at the time. "I knew something was wrong with him, but I didn't know

McGEE'S PRESENCE HAD TURNED *TODAY* INTO A SHOWCASE FOR NBC NEWS

network showed her making an offhand remark that "a senator will tell you more over a martini at midnight than he will over a microphone at noon."

Walters once recalled the public's reaction after the start of Quinn's ill-fated run on CBS: "I remember we were doing our show outdoors from Rockefeller Center and people would come up to me and say, 'It's okay, you've still got your job.' People began to look at me as a human being, as someone who also could bleed." Before that moment, the trailblazing Walters couldn't win. Men in her profession resented her and leaders of the feminist movement—who gained a higher profile in the early 1970s largely through exposure on television talk shows—had been criticizing her for not being more supportive of their

what. The rumors were starting to get pretty bad. He was having episodes of having to be helped from the studio and so on. He had bone cancer."

Hartz was asked by NBC News brass to take McGee to lunch and question him about his condition. They went to Pearl's, a popular Chinese restaurant near Rockefeller Center. As they sipped martinis, Hartz raised the issue. "There are a whole lot of rumors floating about you that you've either got to put down, because they're going to be destructive, or figure out some way to live with this." Hartz said to McGee. "Are you sick?"

McGee put up his right hand and looked Hartz right in the eye. "I swear to you, there's nothing wrong with me," he said.

(Above): Frank McGee, 1973

At that moment, Hartz had no reason not to believe him. "I was thinking back on it after it happened," Hartz said. "He looked great."

But he wasn't. Not long after that lunch, Hartz received a late night phone call at home from McGee's daughter, Sharon. "Jim, get over here," she said. "Dad is dead."

"He'd gotten a roaring case of pneumonia that was facilitated by the chemotherapy that he was on," Hartz recalled. "It took him suddenly."

On the morning of April 18, 1974, *Today* opened with the news that its host, Frank McGee, had died. Most of the morning was devoted to recollections of McGee. Clips were shown of his career as a correspondent courageously covering the Vietnam War and the civil rights movement in the South. Barbara Walters led the program as professionally as she did any other morning. There was not a hint that there had been any conflict with McGee. "Our own Frank McGee will not be with us this morning or any other morning," Walters said with an empty black chair to her left.

Soon afterward a search began for a new host. But NBC management was also informed by Walters's agent, Lee Stevens, that his client was contractually entitled

been on the hard news side," said Hartz. "Hugh Downs was a brilliant guy but he was not a news guy, so the program had a different flavor." McGee's replacement—Walters's co-host—was going to keep the program in the news realm. But there was no obvious successor. "It was very traumatic for the company and the program and all of his friends," said Hartz. "Nobody had really been groomed for the job."

Dick Wald had his eye on Tom Brokaw, then a young and aggressive White House correspondent who had become a fixture for viewers through his coverage of Watergate. But Brokaw was unwilling to walk away from his role as the network's lead reporter on the greatest political scandal in American history. "It was the story of my life," he recalled. "I didn't want to leave the White House." He was also adamant about not wanting to hold up a can of Alpo dog food or any other product as the talent who worked on *Today* were contractually obligated to do. "I'm a reporter not a huckster," he told a newspaper columnist at the time. "And I find doing commercials repulsive."

After weeks of tryouts with several NBC correspondents, Wald turned to Hartz, who had substituted frequently for Frank Blair at the news desk. Like Brokaw, he had risen in local TV news during the time NBC stations

... BROKAW WAS GOING TO KEEP THE PROGRAM IN THE NEWS REALM.

to a promotion. The three-year deal Walters had signed with NBC in September 1973 stipulated that in the event McGee left the program voluntarily or involuntarily, she would be named co-host. NBC executives probably didn't think it would be enacted. *Today* ratings were strong—averaging nearly six million viewers each morning—and McGee was only fifty-one years old. They did not know the full extent of his health issues.

By the end of April 1974, Walters got the co-host title she had sought after twelve years on the program. "It took that long," she said. "I didn't wave any flags. I didn't burn my bra. But if there's something I'm very proud of, it's that occasion."

Frank McGee's presence had turned *Today* into a showcase for NBC News. "All of Frank's experience had

Tom Brokaw as a White House correspondent.

· GENE ·
SHALIT

E **VEN IN THE HIRSUTE DECADE** of the 1970s, some *Today* viewers didn't know what to make of Gene Shalit.

Early in Shalit's tenure on the program, NBC chairman Julian Goodman received a piece of viewer mail that said, "When are you going to get that bushy haired fairy off the air before he starts luring little girls into his car?" Goodman passed it on to Shalit with a note to "please answer." Shalit replied: "It doesn't say Gene Shalit and it doesn't say movie critic—why did you send me the card?"

But Shalit knew his look was unusual and was proud of that. "In a sense, I was a pioneer—chopping down trees, proving that you didn't have to look like a Princeton graduate," he once told *Parade*. When a reporter once asked him if NBC ever tried to make him change his trademark look he said: "Look—those people who complain about mustaches, would they prevent Albert Einstein from being an NBC science reporter because he had bushy hair? Would they stop Albert Schweitzer from being medical editor of NBC because of his mustache?"

Shalit's appearance became iconic. It was satirized by comedians and animators (he became Gene Scallop on *SpongeBob SquarePants*) all through his career. "If imitation is the highest form of flattery, Gene was flattered over and over again," said Jane Pauley.

Shalit was a public relations expert and a magazine writer before he became an unlikely television star after NBC started using him as a movie critic on its TV stations and *Today* in 1969. His "Critic's Corner" became a regular feature on the program and Shalit himself became the regular third wheel after 1973. While best known for his pun-happy reviews ("*Smokey and the Bandit* is an affable, mindless ninety minutes of non-stop driving—drive, drive, drive—what the audience needs is just one break"), Shalit started on *Today* as a culture critic, introducing millions of viewers to jazz and literature. "He was passionate about books," wrote Reuven Frank, the NBC News president who adored Shalit and put him on television. "There were years when Gene Shalit sold more books than any other American."

After Frank moved on, NBC News management had Shalit focus on film because "what people did was go to the movies," according to Dick Wald. Shalit was a clever writer who considered himself a serious movie critic, just not a solemn one. His humor at the *Today* desk even loosened up Frank McGee. But no one laughed as hard as Shalit did himself, especially on a memorable morning in 1979 when he interviewed Broadway legend Carol Channing, who recounted a London dinner party with Lady Astor and Sir Benjamin Harrison. Channing told them she was heading to Istanbul, and Sir Benjamin said, "When you go to Istanbul, you must taste the cherries. They're

as big as golf balls." Channing imitated Sir Benjamin's overbite and barely decipherable Mayfair accent and then told how she finally asked Lady Astor to interpret. "How do you know what he said?" Channing asked. Lady Astor replied: "Oh that's what they always say when you're on the way to Istanbul." Shalit was laughing so hard, he almost looked as if he was weeping.

"He could not complete the interview," said Tom Brokaw. "He put his face down on the desk and (the camera) just stayed on us. And I was off to the side, laughing every bit as hard as he was."

As Shalit put it: "I laughed my Lady Astor off."

Shalit created a relaxed atmosphere for the many famous actors he interviewed on *Today*. He even got Richard Burton to put his rich, sonorous voice to use by reading names out of a telephone book.

had expanded their news broadcasts in the 1960s. Hartz had a velvety smooth voice and a hint of a southwestern drawl from his Oklahoma upbringing. While he was a solid journalist, his even-tempered personality would provide a soothing presence—and he tolerated having to do commercials. "I'm opposed to it, but it's one of the things that grew up with the show," he said at the time. The *Variety* story on the new *Today* co-host was head-lined: "Tap Hartz To Scale Alpos."

Hartz considered McGee his mentor at NBC, but did not share his disdain for Barbara Walters. Hartz didn't care if she asked the first question when they jointly interviewed a guest. He admired her tenacity. "She and I were the first co-hosts," Hartz said. "Barbara was the first woman in television (news) to attain a high degree of visibility. A lot of folks wrote things that they knew were not true about her and the people who picked some of the crazy stuff up didn't know her or never worked with her. She was one of the most dogged reporters I have ever worked with. She worked the phones like nobody you had ever seen in your life. If she wanted somebody on the program she would call four, five, six, ten times a day. I think a lot of people just gave it up and said 'OK, here I come.' Working with her was a real treat. I enjoyed it."

Life on the set was better for Walters, too. "There were no interviews that I was denied," she said. "I probably did, after Frank McGee left, all of the major political interviews. And there were women now in all aspects of television. There were women who were foreign correspondents. There were women behind the cameras. There still were not enough women executives. But it was a time when women were coming into their own. So, in that sense, it was a good time. The women's movement had borne fruition."

Hartz and Walters were so compatible they even had a flirty catchphrase they used with each other. "The two of us had interviewed this woman who had written a book about how to hang onto your husband," he recalled.

"I remember one thing was you were supposed to meet your husband at the front door wrapped in Saran Wrap. You were also supposed to call him up at the office and say 'I crave your body.' The phrase became kind of a cute little secret code between Barbara and me." Once Walters was traveling with President Gerald Ford on his 1975 state visit to China and could not hear New York shortly before she was to go on the air live for *Today*.

"I can hear her fine, but she can't hear me," Hartz recalled. "And there's a big flap over the technical problems. Somewhere along the line, Barbara sort of lost her feeling for how many people were listening. And all of a sudden, her microphone opens up and she can hear me. And I said, 'Good morning, Barbara.' We're not on the air, but you know, it's going by satellite around the world about six times. And she very softly said, 'Jim, I crave your body.' And that sort of meant everything is okay."

Once Walters and Hartz were in place, Wald called for another significant change in the *Today* cast. Frank Blair had been with the show since the beginning as Washington editor and had read the news for nearly twenty-three years. He was the last link to the era of Dave Garroway and J. Fred Muggs. Wald believed that Blair "was slipping" and it was time for him to hang it up. Blair didn't agree with the assessment of his work, but he didn't fight the decision. By 1974, he had developed a serious drinking problem.

Shalit makes friends with a Muppet.

In his autobiography, Blair revealed that he had gotten into the habit of bellying up to the bar at Hurley's not long after his final newscast. The word around the *Today* set was that the tavern even opened early on occasion so Blair could get a drink during the program. On the way home, Blair said he made stops at the English Grill or the Barberry Room at the Berkshire Hotel before arriving at his apartment on East 56th Street. There were cocktails at lunches with *Today* advertisers a couple of times a week. He was a regular at Toots Shor's. Blair knew he had a problem and occasionally stopped at St. Patrick's Cathedral to pray for help. Blair said he left *Today* because he believed a change of scenery and routine might aid him in recovering from his addiction. He bid farewell to viewers and his *Today* colleagues on March 14, 1975. He said he quit drinking a few weeks later and spent the rest of his years living with his wife, Lillian, in Hilton Head, South Carolina. Lew Wood, a smooth, nattily dressed anchor for the local news on WNBC, was brought in to replace Blair.

Flanking Hartz and Walters was Gene Shalit, who first joined the program in 1969 as a movie critic and became a panelist after Joe Garagiola departed in 1973. His Brillo-pad hair and oversized walrus mustache made him a highly identifiable foil capable of taking on subjects with a lighter touch. "He was a change of pace, a different look," Wald said. "He was somebody who was out of the normal realm of what television was giving you. He had strengths of performance and of intelligence that were palpable."

While the new *Today* team was taking shape, the Watergate scandal had been consuming the Nixon presidency. "We went to Washington and practically camped out there," Walters said. Hartz and

The *Today* team in 1974. (Clockwise): Jim Hartz, Lew Wood, Gene Shalit, and Barbara Walters.

Walters recalled being on the air when Nixon left the White House for the last time on August 9, 1974. "He was in the helicopter, on the way to San Clemente," Hartz said. "It was a powerful moment. I mean, none of us had ever seen that before, a president who resigned in disgrace. He made a little speech before he went and got on the helicopter. You know, 'Don't get mad at your enemies—it'll only hurt yourself.' And then striding out and boarding the helicopter, and then the kind of awkward salute."

Said Walters, "It was a very poignant time for me because I had seen Pat Nixon come into her own in China, when she went with the president. It was the first time that people saw Pat Nixon—'Plastic Pat,' they used to call her—as a human being. I had interviewed both Julie and Trisha Nixon. I had reported on their weddings, and now Richard Nixon was leaving in disgrace."

The following year, *Today* tried to help the nation heal from what had been a dark period of the country's history with an ambitious celebration of the nation's upcoming bicentennial anniversary. Every Friday, starting in the summer of 1975, the program traveled to a different state in the union, covering all fifty and the District of Columbia until the final stop in New York Harbor for an all-day celebration on July 4, 1976. "The Tall Ships were there," said Hartz. "It was a grand glorious day." Hartz did the bulk of the roadwork for the bicentennial shows. "I traveled a quarter of a million miles and never got out of the country," he said. "Looking back on it, it was sort of like seeing a snapshot of America, all at once, on its 200th birthday. And it was really fascinating. I mean, if you'd told me when I was a little boy growing up in Oklahoma that I'd be in every state of the union, especially in one year, and get to meet nearly every governor, and senator, and important person, and ordinary people, all over that period, I would have said, 'What a dreamer you must be.'"

Before *Today* reached the end of its transcontinental journey, it was rocked by an announcement that forever altered the network TV news landscape. Barbara Walters had been offered $5 million for a five-year contract at ABC News. The network wanted to make her a co-anchor of the *ABC Evening News* with Harry Reasoner. It was a chance to be the first woman to hold the title of anchor on a network evening newscast. The deal also included four one-hour prime-time specials each year for ABC's entertainment division. It was a shrewd strategic move. After years of being an also-ran third place network, ABC was having its first real run of success in prime time with such hit shows as *Happy Days, Laverne & Shirley, The Bionic Woman,*

Fred Pierce hired Barbara was not so much to bring her to their news division, but to take her out of *Today*, so that he would be able to move *Good Morning America* into the winning position," said Wald. "He wasn't shy about saying he got two bites out of that apple."

While much attention was given to the large salary that ABC dangled in front of Walters, it actually wasn't tremendously more than what she was earning at NBC at the time (between *Today* and her earnings from her syndicated daytime talk show called *Not for Women Only*, she was already in the high six figures annually). Walters wanted to stay at the network that had been her professional home for fifteen years. But she also had a desire for more input at *Today* so her role would not be dictated by the whims of a new producer or another chauvinist co-host. "I couldn't bear the thought of another Frank McGee," Walters wrote in her memoir. Such requests were dismissed during her negotiations with NBC management.

> *Barbara Walters was way ahead of the rest of the industry in understanding that TV journalists, even serious ones, were TV personalities as well.*

"I TRAVELED A QUARTER OF A MILLION MILE

Starsky and Hutch, and *The Six Million Dollar Man*. The network now had its sights on improving its performance on the evening news and in the morning. It had started a news morning program called *AM America* in 1975, a *Today* clone soon replaced by *Good Morning America*. The prime-time ratings improvement of ABC—and the departure of Walters—meant *Today* could have its first serious competitor in the morning. "The reason that (ABC President)

There were numerous factors that led to Walters' departure from NBC. As a divorced single mother, she thought the evening news job would give her more time with her adopted daughter, Jackie. "I struggled over that decision," she said. "I had to weigh a program that I loved, that was successful, that would go on long after I left, with a new challenge and a new opportunity, and a chance to sleep late."

Corporate upheaval at NBC's parent company, RCA, had distracted executives from focusing on keeping her. There was also continued ambivalence at the network over the unique role that Walters carved out in television news. In retrospect, Wald said she was way ahead of the rest of the industry in understanding that TV journalists, even serious ones, were TV personalities as well—something that viewers and executives now take for granted. "You have to look at Barbara as a person who did something nobody else had been able to do, which was essentially to straddle completely the world of entertainment," he said. "Either she saw the future, or she intuited the future. There was never any doubt in my mind that she had a better grasp of where these programs had to go, or were going, than anybody else. She thought that she could marry serious news with entertainment values. And she was right. But the people who ran the company thought that she could not become, and never thought of a way to make her become, a serious newsperson, in addition to the entertainment things they knew she could do. She would have stayed, had somebody had the wit to say, 'Hey, look. *Meet the Press* could use a really high-powered moderator who could bring in the big guns of the world' or, 'There is a magazine program in which Barbara Walters could be a major figure.' Nobody had that wit. It was all a question of: 'What do we do on *Today?*'—and not thinking of her as an asset to be used in other parts of the empire." After a miserable start on the *ABC Evening News*, where many of the promises made to her were not kept, Walters became an even more iconic TV star on ABC. For more than three decades, she regularly delivered high-profile interviews on prime-time specials that often delivered staggering ratings, hosted a hit news magazine in *20/20*, and developed her own successful daytime talk show, *The View*.

ND **NEVER GOT OUT** OF **THE COUNTRY."** — *Jim Hartz*

•   •   •

· JIM ·

HARTZ

FIRST
SHOW
1974

LAST
SHOW
1977

J **IM HARTZ WAS** the calm after the storm on *Today*.

In nearly every story written about *Today* in the early 1970s, journalists couldn't resist sneaking in a mention of the ongoing antagonism between Barbara Walters and Frank McGee. The chatter was based in fact, especially in the months before McGee's death when the respected newsman (in pain from his illness) had gone from being scrappy to downright cantankerous and erratic. The difficult time was eased by the arrival of Hartz, a well-liked anchor with a more placid demeanor, who had led a two-hour early evening newscast on NBC's New York station.

The son of a fundamentalist minister, Hartz was a few credits away from a premed degree at the University of Tulsa when he left school to pursue a career in television. One of his friends was another young TV journalist named Tom Brokaw. "Tom and I knew each other prior to either one of us being hired at NBC," Hartz recalled. "He had some relatives in Tulsa, where I was working, my hometown. He used to come in once in awhile, and we'd have a couple of beers and would discuss how he could get out of South Dakota, and I could get out of Oklahoma." The plans of both men were realized when NBC expanded its local newscasts on its owned and operated stations. Brokaw ended up in Los Angeles, while Hartz, just twenty-four years old, landed in New York, where he shared anchor duties with McGee on WNBC. He was the youngest on-air talent at NBC News.

His low-key style made him distinct from the rest of the New York's TV newscasters. He was also known for his decency toward everyone he worked with. "Hartz came here as a nice guy and he's still a nice guy," an NBC cameraman told *People* in 1974 after the *Today* assignment was announced.

Hartz had a passion for aeronautics—his brother was an air force pilot—and it led to a network assignment covering the space program. He covered every NASA mission from 1966 to 1976.

While Hartz enjoyed his time on *Today*, he admitted he disliked the early morning hours and the workdays that often lasted well into the evening. "I was burnt out fairly early," he said. "Maybe we traveled more than usual. It is a grind sometimes. The hours are horrible. I left parties at my own house to go to bed. It may be the hardest job I ever did in the amount of hours you put in and the knowledge you are expected to have." After two years at the *Today* desk, he became a roaming host for the program, working outside of the studio. He left NBC, but remained a TV fixture as the host of the PBS shows *Over Easy* and *Innovation*. As of 2011, he was living in the Washington, D.C., area and serving as chairman of the Will Rogers Memorial Commission.

When Walters agreed to defect to ABC, her contract with NBC had another four months to run. She later described it as "staying in the same apartment with an ex-husband." Management decided to end her groundbreaking run on the program on June 4, 1976.

Walters's final appearance on *Today* was actually on tape. She had done the bicentennial visit to Massachusetts, her home state. Her final live appearance was the day before on June 3. There was a minimum of fanfare. She talked about a lunch that was given to her by the ad agency for Alpo. ("Wasn't it odd that when you

First Lady Betty Ford with Tom Brokaw.

walked in the restaurant that all the plates were on the floor?" cracked Shalit.) Walters sold a lot of dog food for the company. She was always charming and good-humored whenever a dog had to be restrained during the live commercials she did for the brand. ("Sometimes a dog practically dragged me across the set to get to its food," Walters recalled years later. "I don't think they starved them, but I've never seen hungrier dogs.") The agency showed its appreciation with a double magnum of champagne, chilled in an ice bucket that looked like a red fire hydrant, and presented her with a bejeweled pin in the shape of a Scottish terrier. Walters did feel compelled to address her ABC deal, which was largely derided by the press and news industry veterans as an unhealthy merger of show business money and TV jour-

nalism. (Walter Cronkite told *Newsweek* he experienced a sickening sensation when he heard about Walters's move.) She never complained, but did point out to *Today* viewers that a double standard was being imposed on her in regard to her salary.

"I will be the first female anchor person on the evening news and that's both a challenge and a responsibility," she said. "It saddens me that much more has been made about the money than about the precedent of my new assignment. However this money was offered to me and it is the American way not to turn down a raise. Indeed I doubt that any of my fellow newsmen ever turned down raises. As a matter of fact, I'll bet they'll all ask for more." (She was right, as Dan Rather became a $1 million-a-year anchor for CBS when he took over for Cronkite in 1981.)

The next day, the taped show aired with a final and more emotional farewell from Walters. She thanked Hugh Downs and Joe Garagiola, whose support allowed her to prosper on the program. She mentioned how Garagiola teased her over how she felt she was always auditioning.

"I'm not auditioning anymore Joe," Walters said.

After thanking Gene Shalit (whom she called "a confidante"), Walters proceeded to name assistants, secretaries, hair stylists, makeup artists, prop handlers, wardrobe mistresses, floor managers—names that were largely unknown to the audience. It was a gracious and generous acknowledgment of everyone behind the scenes who contributed to her success.

During Walters's entire tenure at ABC, she always recognized the importance of *Today* to her career. "*Today* made me what I am today," Walters said years later. "It can take all the credit and all the blame."

With the loss of its signature talent, Wald believed *Today* had to be rebuilt. He pushed again to bring in Tom Brokaw to replace Hartz, who he believed was too laidback on the air. Brokaw once again raised his objection to doing live commercials. Believing Brokaw was the best choice, Wald convinced his bosses to change the policy and assured Brokaw he would not be a pitchman. Brokaw signed on. "I remember specifically Dick Wald saying, 'Look, you don't have any choice this time,'" Brokaw recalled. "He said 'We'll get rid of the commercials. You've got to start doing this in the fall of 1976.' He was nice about it. But they were saying 'this is really what we want you to do.'"

There was no apparent successor for Walters. In the months that followed, various women filled in during what had become a series of on-air auditions. NBC News correspondents Cassie Mackin, Linda Ellerbee, and Betty Rollin and Los Angeles news anchor Kelly Lange were among those considered. The strongest candidate was Betty Furness, a commercial spokeswoman who became an effective government consumer affairs advocate and one of TV's first consumer reporters (a role she eventually had on *Today*). But Furness had been around long enough to have actually dated Dave Garroway back in the mid-1950s. The *Today* audience was large but aging and Dick Wald believed he needed younger talent. Just how young was a surprise to the entire TV industry. "I was twenty-five years old, and I succeeded Barbara Walters on *Today*," said Jane Pauley, still with a bit of disbelief thirty-five years later. "Four years out of college. I was one year from the big news, *Weekend Edition*, in Indianapolis. One year. To be twenty-five doesn't seem too extraordinary now. It did then. It was extraordinary because not only was I female, but anchormen and the few women around such as Barbara Walters were people with credentials. Maturity was something that was valued. They had seasoning. I had freshness. And it just didn't make sense to me."

Pauley was young, but up-and-coming. After her stint in Indianapolis, she became the first woman to anchor a major newscast in Chicago at WMAQ. She hung in despite having detractors in the local press, known for being extremely tough on its newscasters. "One critic said that I had the I.Q. of a cantaloupe and I hadn't crossed the Indiana-Illinois state line yet," she recalled. "I literally hadn't started working."

But Pauley scored high with viewers during the days she filled in for a few mornings on *Today* after Walters

left. Compared to the other women who tried out, Pauley had won every category in audience research but one. "And that was experience," she said.

Jane Pauley had the "red light reflex," according to Paul Friedman, who became executive producer of *Today* that year. "I mean, that red light went on and her personality came alive," he said. "She was just great on television. She was pretty without being threatening. She was bright. She was charming." Brokaw, who had seen her on the air and met her briefly in Chicago, liked her too. "I was always struck by her poise," he said. "For a young woman, she was very self-confident. She seemed to be a natural."

Time magazine described her as a corn-fed Catherine Deneuve. Other writers thought she was similar to Walters in appearance and her speech intonation—comparison that both women dismissed. But critics had little else to analyze, which was one of the reasons why Dick Wald wanted her. "*Today* needed to bring in more and different viewers," he said. "I thought the way to do that was to get a blank slate, somebody who was not defined by other things. I was looking for somebody who was in the age group I wanted to attract and didn't have a track record."

When Tom Brokaw and Jane Pauley were assigned to lead *Today*, it was the start of a new era of morning television. "We have two innocents thrown into this row boat and set adrift onto the seas of the *Today* show at a time when ABC is gearing up," Brokaw said. "Jane and I kind of found our way together." ABC's entertainment division produced *Good Morning America*, giving it the latitude to be a far more relaxed presentation. There was no hand-wringing about news values at ABC, since it did not have much of a news tradition at the time. TV actor David Hartman served as the lead host of *GMA*, a move that *Today* never tried even in its breeziest early days. *GMA* also expanded on the concept of the morning TV family with a virtual neighbor-

Above: Brokaw was NBC's star White House reporter before he joined Today.

· TOM ·
BROKAW

T **OM BROKAW REMEMBERS** his very first time on *Today*. He was a tourist visiting New York with his wife, Meredith. They stopped by the Florida Showcase storefront window on West 49th Street that *Today* used for a studio in the mid-1960s. "I came here from Omaha for the World's Fair," he recalled. "Two bigger rubes never crossed the streets of Manhattan that summer. We went down and held up a little sign that said 'Watch *Today* in Omaha with Tom Brokaw on Channel 3.' I thought that was going to be my one network shot."

The South Dakota native could not have been more wrong. He made it to NBC News in 1966 and eventually distinguished himself as the network's White House correspondent when the presidency of Richard Nixon collapsed under the weight of the Watergate scandal in 1974. When Brokaw agreed to come to New York to be host of *Today* in 1976, it was not what he had in mind for his career. "I was a traditional reporter," he said. "I never thought I'd end up doing a show like *Today* and some of my friends didn't think it was the best idea in the world. But I wanted to bring my news sensibility to it."

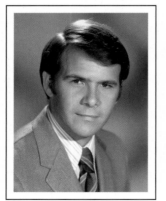

Brokaw was always crisp and commanding on *Today,* especially after he learned how to shift gears from questioning potent political leaders to chatting with beauty pageant queens. "I learned not to have such a terribly hard edge," he said. "But I suppose it came with some confidence that you could get something from authors and entertainers and cultural figures that would be useful and interesting to the audience without treating them like they were suspects in the Watergate case."

Over time, he used the program to pursue stories that satisfied his own intellectual curiosity. "One of the things I took some pride in was that authors would come on and always be quite surprised that I'd read, if not the entire book, most of the book. And I was always interested in how they learned to write. And we did some things that you can never do now. Joan Didion is a famous author who lived on the West Coast. And John Cheever of course is a famous author who lived on the East Coast. And they reflected their geography and their culture. And so I did a story about the two of them, and we ran it on successive days. It was about how the West Coast and California had influenced Joan's writing. And it was about the East Coast and Westchester County, and how it had influenced John Cheever's writing. That would never happen today, but I loved doing that story."

Brokaw traveled extensively for the program. One Friday morning he hosted *Today* from a bunker in the Strategic Air Command headquarters. He flew out of a blizzard in Omaha that afternoon and into Miami. There, he changed airplanes and headed for Panama, where he broadcast live from the Panama Canal. In 1980, he covered the presidential primaries and reported from the floor of the nominating conventions, and then hosted *Today* in the morning. (During the Republican National Convention that chose Ronald Reagan, Brokaw revealed on *Today* that former President Gerald Ford was discussing a plan to be Reagan's running mate and serve in a "co-presidency.") Brokaw's tirelessness as a live broadcaster earned him the nickname of Duncan the Wonder Horse.

"Tom would finish interviewing one person and be told who he'd be talking to next with no preparation," Jane Pauley said. "He's the best ad-libber in the business, and he ad-libs in prose. If he'd run out of steam, I'd put another log on the fire."

Brokaw was so solid and reliable; there was no sign of panic on the *Today* set when he once overslept and showed up late for the program. "We had been having some work done in our apartment and apparently we had a short," he recalled. "I had an electric alarm, which I never relied on again. I woke up at about ten minutes to seven and got there at about five after seven or something. And no one called! And they said 'Well you know you've come from all over the world and made it here on time. We just thought you were going to walk in at the last minute.'" Despite the incident, Brokaw never complained about the early hours. "I liked the idea of getting up and the most important thing that you were going to do, you did first," he said. "At seven o'clock you came on and the whole country was there. It was like taking your oral exams, as I used to say, on national television. You had to know what you were talking about."

The most difficult experience of Brokaw's time on *Today* came on November 18, 1978. He had to tell the country that two of NBC's own—Los Angeles-based correspondent Don Harris and his cameraman Bob Brown, were killed in Guyana, where cult leader Jim Jones had led his followers in a mass suicide. They had gone to cover a trip to Jonestown by Congressman Leo Ryan, who also was gunned down. "The Jonestown Massacre was one of the worst days of my life," Brokaw said. "Our crew was down there doing an assignment for us. It never occurred to me that it was going to have this kind of an ending to it. And when the word began to filter back that there had been a massacre, and that our crew had been ambushed at the airport, it was devastating to me. Don Harris was somebody I'd known well from California. Bob Brown was one of our very best cameramen. Congressman Ryan, I had known from my California days. And it came in waves: more bad news, more bad news. And it was so bizarre that it was just hard to process, frankly. I think I was in a funk for four or five days after that. I mean I had a hard time functioning. I remember talking to Don right before he went down there. There was a producer by the name of Bob Flick who survived, who got away from the airplane. And Steve Sung, the soundman, who got wounded: I knew them all well. And they were going off to do this story for us. It was their idea, but even so, it was a nightmare. I'm not sure it was as emotional for the country as it was for the rest of us. The country had a hard time understanding it. Jim Jones was a weird cult figure, who had been quite successful in San Francisco before he'd taken this turn onto the dark side."

Pauley remembered it as the most horrific story during her time on *Today*, in part for how it affected Brokaw. "The pop, pop, pop, the camera lying on its side," she recalled. "Tom knew how it was to be on a tarmac like that. He could put himself in the shoes of the correspondent. I rarely saw Tom lose it. He's a very emotional man. As a journalist we count on him to be strong. That was a very challenging and emotional moment for him for a lot of reasons."

Brokaw interviewing Jane and Henry Fonda, 1979.

Skitch Henderson was at the keyboards when Ethel Merman, Abe Burrows a

Barbara Walters paid tribute to composer Cole Porter on Today in 1965.

J **ANE PAULEY, THEN TWENTY-FOUR YEARS OLD,** had been doing the Saturday newscast on WMAQ in Chicago for nine months when her boss came into her office and said: "Do you want to go to New York and go on *Today* for a few days?" It was in the short period after Barbara Walters left the program and Betty Furness was doing most of the fill-in work. "I came to New York," Pauley recalled. "I got a phone call from my sister at the hotel, who told me she read in her Pittsburgh newspaper that I was auditioning to replace Barbara Walters. That was the first I knew of it. I assure you, it hadn't occurred to me that, at my age and with barely four years' experience in the business, I was going to take Barbara Walters's seat on *Today*. I slept forty-five minutes that night, if that. I did the audition with Lloyd Dobyns, whose sense of humor just meshed with mine. He was so wry. He wasn't going to take this seriously. It was exactly what I needed. So the audition went very well. And I'm told that there was a network convention, and that the network executives, having taken their spouses, their wives, apparently picked me of the half a dozen or so women who were the final contenders for this job."

Pauley returned to fill in for another week and by October 1976 she joined *Today* as a panelist next to host Tom Brokaw. It was a bit intimidating for a young woman just a few years out of Indiana University to try and replace a broadcasting icon. "I would say Tom Brokaw was really replacing Barbara Walters, though, from a gender point of view, the spotlight did fall on me," she said.

The good news for Pauley in those early years was that most of the press and industry attention was focused on Walters and her $1 million contract at ABC ("Which Is She—Journalist Or Cher?" asked *TV Guide*). Walters's on-air rapport with *ABC Evening News* co-anchor Harry Reasoner was so bad it likely made her pine for her days with Frank McGee. "There was attention on the fact that the chemistry between her and Harry was not working," said Pauley. "I think that really gave me the cover of months, or possibly even years."

In Brokaw, who was finding his way as well in the job after developing an image as a sturdy hard news reporter, she found a comrade and supportive friend who helped her through the journey. "Tom Brokaw was really a big brother to all of that," Pauley said. "He helped me find my apartment, which had a terrace and a southern exposure and a rent which, at that time, you know, people would have killed for. He and Meredith gave me a place to go on Thanksgiving, my first Thanksgiving when I didn't go home. He really looked after me. He introduced me to Garry, so I guess you could say he found me a husband."

"MAYBE YOU'RE WONDERING HOW I GOT HERE—I AM TOO."

— Jane Pauley on her first day at Today.

Brokaw had met *Doonesbury* cartoonist Garry Trudeau during President Gerald Ford's state visit to China in 1975. Barbara Walters, still with *Today*, was also on the trip. Brokaw and Trudeau hit it off. They played Frisbee together on the Great Wall and became good friends. But it was after Pauley joined *Today* that Trudeau began hanging around at Brokaw's office at NBC. "My wife, Meredith, said to me, 'Dummy, he wants to meet Jane,'" Brokaw recalled. "So we had a little dinner, and I don't think they ever left each other's side after that evening."

"We had a lot in common," Pauley recalled. "We talked at dinner about how we both recently stepped up from Morton's frozen chicken pot pies to Stouffers frozen dinners, which was an upgrade."

Pauley and Trudeau were married in 1980. She later said she doesn't know who her husband would be if it had not been for Brokaw. "Tom Brokaw and Barbara Walters and a cartoonist named Garry Trudeau are among the press corps in China. Barbara leaves. Garry meets Tom. I replace Barbara," she said. "What's it all mean?"

hood of characters—the renegade long-haired journalist (Geraldo Rivera), the show business yenta (Rona Barrett), the handsome mayor (John Lindsay), the woman's career counselor (*Cosmopolitan* editor Helen Gurley Brown), and the angry gadfly (muckraking Washington columnist Jack Anderson). The *GMA* set looked like a suburban living room with comfy furniture. The producers admitted they were trying to copy the more free-wheeling atmosphere *Today* had when Dave Garroway was host back in the 1950s. Back at the real *Today*, the on-air team sat behind a formal news anchor desk with its strange clock that only had a minute hand. (The reason behind the missing hour hand is that the two hours of *Today* did not run in sequence in the west and Midwestern parts of the country. In Chicago, for instance, the program opened with the second hour live, followed by

the first hour on tape. As a result, the host or newscaster always said "eight minutes after the hour" never 7:08.) NBC News was always concerned how much substantial content *Today* needed to have. Now the faster-paced *GMA* had made it look plodding and staid in comparison.

> *When Tom Brokaw and Jane Pauley were assigned to lead Today, it was the start of a new era of morning television.*

"JANE PAULEY WAS VERY SELF-CONFIDENT

Brokaw said he and Pauley were "like two kids who got the leads in the class play."

HE SEEMED TO BE A NATURAL." — *Tom Brokaw*

The press started to notice that *GMA* was making inroads with its less formal feel. "Times are changing and so are viewers' preferences," wrote *Us* magazine in 1977. "Some just might prefer Rona Barrett's Hollywood gossip to an interview with a Washington official. It's a formula even stodgy old *Today* is watching carefully." *Today* responded by shortening the length of interviews and features, which had typically run eight minutes or longer, and taking Brokaw and Pauley out from behind the desk and onto a brightly colored set. It cut back on the number of book authors who appeared. A backdrop of the Manhattan skyline was later put up on the set to give the feeling of a picture window. Even as *GMA* was building an audience, NBC's research said *Today* matched up well in every area except one. Viewers loved David Hartman. "They thought that David asked the questions they wanted to see asked," said Paul Friedman. "He was down to earth and friendly, kind of one of the guys. Warm. But mostly he was kind of the viewers' representative. He asked questions out of curiosity and desired to learn the kind of things that they, if they had the chance, would ask. That was the single biggest finding in the research—his popularity."

Hartman's just-folks personality was likely a sharp contrast to Brokaw, who, while boyishly handsome, still had the intensity of a hard-charging correspondent covering the Nixon White House. "I remember I did an interview with Miss America and I think I asked questions as if she had stolen the tiara or it was somehow a corrupted process of some kind," Brokaw recalled.

In their first two years together on *Today*, Brokaw and Pauley staved off the upstart *GMA* in the ratings. Many of the ABC program's viewers were new to the morning television habit. But it became more of a struggle as ABC added more hit shows and its dominance grew in prime time while NBC's lineup was in a prolonged slump. ABC was able to use its hot streak to trade up to stronger affiliated stations in some cities. As a result, in May 1979 *Good Morning America* had done what no other morning program had done before in the twenty-seven-year history of *Today*. It topped *Today* by a slim margin to become number one in the ratings. Said Brokaw, "We were not prepared for the kind of competition they put up against us."

TOM BROKAW
Interviews

ROBERT REDFORD

· · · · · · · · · · · · · · · · · · · ·

TOM BROKAW TALKED with actor Robert Redford outside of the United Nations on "Sun Day"—a nationwide event on May 1, 1978, aimed at promoting solar energy. "Bob somehow persuaded the Mormon Tabernacle Choir to open *Today* live with an old hymn about sunshine," Brokaw recalled. "We tried a lot of different things."

JIMMY CARTER

· · · · · · · · · · · · · · · · · ·

AFTER VIETNAM AND WATERGATE, President Jimmy Carter
"came along as somebody fresh and new from the South," said Brokaw, shown
here in December 1977 during a White House press conference with Carter
and Barbara Walters of ABC. "He wasn't part of the establishment that seemed
to have made such a wreck of things. Vietnam had ended, and there were the
consequences of all that. So Carter came along and he seemed to be a fresh
face and a fresh voice. It turns out that he was not as prepared for the job as
he needed to have been, given the challenges that were there before him."

BRYANT

DEBORAH NORVILLE

CHAPTER FOUR

GENE SHALIT

JOHN PALMER   TOM

GUMBEL

· WILLARD SCOTT ·

1980-1989

JANE PAULEY

BROKAW

Today *began the new decade with Gene Shalit, Jane Pauley, Tom Brokaw, and Willard Scott.*

1980–1989

AS THE 1970s DREW TO A CLOSE, fifty-two Americans were being held hostage in Iran after radical Islamist students seized the Unites States embassy in Tehran. Gasoline prices were rising and motorists had to line up to fill up. Interest rates were sky-high and so was inflation. "Jimmy Carter never used the word malaise, but that was the feeling," Tom Brokaw recalled. "That America had malaise for the first time in the post-war years. . . . The country wanted something to be done, but it didn't know what. We were dealing with the Ayatollah Khomeini. And he was the subject of late night jokes, but he was this utterly sinister and powerful figure who was determined to hurt the United States."

Brokaw said the hostage crisis forced Americans to focus on the political complexities of the Middle East. "We only knew it as a gas station," he said. "That's where we went to get our oil. I was often invited to interview the shah of Iran. He appeared on *Today* several times. [The United States] had made a big investment in him. It turned out not to be a very wise thing to do because he had abused his people, in his own elegant way, for a long time, by not sharing the oil wealth. It mostly went to his friends."

> ### *Today* was on firm ground as well. The program continued to revolve around Brokaw's solid journalistic presence.

For months, Brokaw had the first word each morning on the ongoing hostage crisis for *Today* viewers. It ended on January 20, 1981, the same day as the inauguration of Ronald Reagan as the fortieth president of the United States. Brokaw, Jane Pauley, and weathercaster Willard Scott, in Washington for the inauguration, were still in awe of one of the most stirring days that television had ever witnessed—a new president coming into office while the hostages were being freed. "Some of the most emotional pictures you'll ever see," Brokaw said on the morning of January 21 as video showed medevac planes landing at an air force base in West Germany "They are now officially described by the air force not as hostages or as President Reagan called them prisoners of war—they are returnees."

"Cecil B. DeMille and Walt Disney in their finest hour could not have produced a greater script," said Scott.

Today was on firm ground as well. The program continued to revolve around Brokaw's solid journalistic presence while loosening up the proceedings to combat the lighter and brighter *Good Morning America*. It was working with the addition of Willard Scott, who joined the program from NBC's Washington station WRC. At six foot three and 240 pounds, Scott was as big as he was buoyant. He always had a wide smile and a fresh colorful

(Top): Ronald and Nancy Reagan; (middle): Tom Brokaw covering the 1981 inauguration; (bottom): Pauley interviewing Reagan's daughter, Patti Davis in 1981.

"Steve Friedman was very good, because he was a contemporary young guy," said Brokaw. "And he knew how to organize the show."

flower in his lapel. The weather forecast he delivered was secondary. His purpose was to give viewers' spirits a lift when they got up in the morning. "If you're really a weather fan, come to New York today. Don't bother to go to Miami," he said on his first day in April 1980. "New York is the fun sun capital of the world! I saw a groundhog with a Pucci bag open walking down Fifth Avenue smiling with sunglasses—fifty-two degrees!"

Today had never had a personality as ebullient or irreverent as Scott, and it was an adjustment for the sedate sensibilities of some viewers. "I was such an oddity that there was a lot of mail that was against me," Scott recalled. "I was too fat. I was corny. I wasn't dignified. I wasn't this. I wasn't that."

But Brokaw was supportive. He knew Scott from his days in Washington and was clearly amused by his

act. He also appreciated not having to be the source of mirth on the program. "Tom was a big fan," Scott said. "That's one of the things that saved me. And within six months, everything turned around. I mean, it's just unreal."

NBC News had also turned over the executive producer reins to Steve Friedman, a brash thirty-one-year-old Chicago native who had overseen the program's West Coast coverage in the late 1970s. He had developed a knack for turning out innovative, offbeat segments. When the Arab oil embargo was lifted, he put together a music video showing Americans filling up at gas stations and visiting car showrooms while the Peaches and Herb hit "Reunited" played underneath. Friedman came to New York with a mandate from NBC management to freshen up *Today*.

(Left): with Tom Brokaw circa 1980. (Right): Willard Scott as pop star Boy George in 1985.

"I was supposed to get them out of the poetry reading business," was how Friedman described it. He wasn't joking. Actress Julie Harris once appeared on *Today* to recreate her stage role as Emily Dickinson, typical of the high-minded fare favored in the 1970s.

"Steve was very good, because he was a contemporary young guy," said Brokaw. "And he knew how to organize the show. They used to do whatever they wanted to do on kind of a random basis. Well, we got more segmented and we were more responsive to what was going on across the country. We got the ship righted, as it were."

Friedman's vision of what *Today* needed to be was fully realized on the program that covered the death of John Lennon. On the night of December 8, 1980, Lennon

was shot to death by an obsessed fan named Mark David Chapman outside of the Dakota, the apartment building on West Seventy-Second Street in Manhattan, where the former Beatle lived with his wife, Yoko Ono. In the hours after the stunning news broke, grieving fans gathered and formed an all-night vigil at the site of the murder. Flowers were placed in the black iron gate outside the building. Fans sang along to Beatles music that blared from portable radios on a sidewalk aglow with lighted candles.

Steve Friedman called Brokaw that night. He told him he wanted to tear up the planned lineup for the next morning's program and devote most of *Today* to the Lennon story. Brokaw was skeptical at first. The impact of the loss of Lennon simply did not immediately resonate with him. He wasn't alone. Even in 1980, rock music was viewed as a cultural force that catered to youth and still did not earn much respect from adults. Network news rarely paid attention to it. When Elvis Presley died the afternoon of August 16, 1977, *NBC Nightly News* led with the story, but the *CBS Evening News with Walter Cronkite* opened its broadcast that night with a report on the Panama Canal treaty.

Lennon was the voice of the generation that came of age in the 1960s. He provided the rebellious attitude

ON *TODAY*, JOHN LENNON RECEIVE

and musical grit for the world's most popular rock 'n' roll band of all time. Friedman believed the shock of his sudden loss was on the scale of the assassination of President Kennedy. He was right, as millions of young adults gathered all around the world to mourn Lennon's death over the week that followed. On *Today*, Lennon received the kind of coverage that had been reserved for a head of state. "Steve Friedman was of that generation more than I was, and he understood the global ramifications of this," said Brokaw. "I knew it was a very big deal. But I was a political animal. And I didn't know that it would take off the way that it did."

On the morning of December 9, the entire first half-hour of *Today* was devoted to Lennon's death and career. Throughout the program there were reports with reactions from London and live remotes from the Dakota, where fans were still gathered that morning. A panel was assembled in the studio that included Dave Marsh, a record critic for *Rolling Stone*; Laurie Kaye, a young radio reporter who interviewed Lennon only the day before as he was still promoting his *Double Fantasy* album; and Barbara Graustark, a music writer from *Newsweek*. None of them really knew Lennon very well. Friedman insisted that the program include Richard Lester, the director of the Beatles' two feature films, *A Hard Day's Night* and *Help*, who had a deep and authoritative understanding of Lennon as a man and as an artist. But Lester was in Oslo. "I said 'Okay, let's get him on anyway,'" Friedman said. "And somebody figured out a way that they could hit a satellite from a television studio in Norway and do it live." Lester was the most compelling and insightful interview subject that morning. "[Lennon] represented a sense of optimism, certainly in England, that everything was possible," Lester said. "It turned out to be a false dream that John had, but if there was any one person in that I've ever met in my life that gave people that hope and that opportunity, John had it." Mil-

or experts instantaneously. Broadcast satellites had been in operation since 1965, but usage was limited by high costs and the need to order transmission time in advance. As more satellites were launched and the expense came down, TV news coverage was revolutionized and so was *Today*.

"Satellites were making it possible for us to go live in ways that we had not before," said Brokaw. "And that was good news and bad news. The good news is that you

HE KIND OF COVERAGE THAT HAD BEEN RESERVED FOR A HEAD OF STATE.

lions of Americans learned of what happened to Lennon through *Today*, which presented the story with immediacy and depth. "It was an instant news special about one of the most important cultural figures of the twentieth century," said Brokaw. "That's what live television, and especially what morning television, should do. When you wake up in the morning and something has happened overnight, and it's big, and it's historic, then producers have to have the courage to say, 'Blow everything out. We're going with this story.'"

It also demonstrated how satellite transmissions could bring viewers the best possible journalists, guests,

could get on the air from there; the bad news was that you had to fly all night to get there to get on the air."

But on-the-scene reporting played to Brokaw's strength on *Today*. After a gunman's bullets struck and severely wounded Pope John Paul II as he entered St. Peter's Square on May 13, 1981, Brokaw stayed on the air until four o'clock in the afternoon that day. "And then I went out and got a plane to Rome," he said. "And the next day—it was like midday in Rome by then, because of the time difference—I came on with, 'Good morning, live from St. Peter's Basilica in Rome,' from Vatican Square."

THE DEATH OF JOHN LENNON

DECEMBER 8, 1980

JANE PAULEY WAS already a veteran of *Today* when she turned thirty years old in 1980. As a baby boomer growing up in Indiana, her mornings in the 1950s were spent watching *Captain Kangaroo* or Dave Garroway on *Today* (once admitting to being transfixed by the clocks on the set). As a teenager in the 1960s, she grew up to the hits of John, Paul, George, and Ringo. "My life was set to music," she said. "It was Beatles music. Every event of my life is attached to some song." It meant the death of John Lennon was more than just another tragic news story reported on the program.

"For many of us it marked a final coming of age," said Pauley. "That event kind of brought us up. It was time for youth to retire."

Pauley was asleep the night of December 8, 1980, when Lennon's murder was first reported. Her husband Garry Trudeau did not awaken her. Instead, he went into his record album collection in their Manhattan apartment and pulled out several selections by the Beatles, including *Sgt. Pepper's Lonely Hearts Club Band,* and Lennon's solo work, *Imagine.*

"When I woke up he told me what happened and handed me the albums," she recalled.

Pauley showed the iconic covers during the program, but was almost too anguished to articulate her feelings. It was not just the shocking, violent way that Lennon's life ended. It was the sense that her youth was yanked away from her in one sudden moment. "I came from

a generation that pretty much had a lot more invested in youth than probably any other generation," she later said. "And that morning it was over." The realization hit Pauley in the closing minutes of *Today*, as a montage of photographs of the Beatles and Lennon filled the screen while "Imagine" played in its entirety. "Tom Brokaw and I are done," Pauley recalled. "I just put my head down on the desk and sobbed."

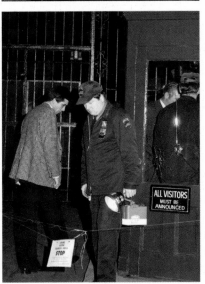

AT&T divested its Bell System companies, ending — 1984
its monopoly over local telephone service.

Brokaw was on *Today* the morning of October 6, 1981, when a voice from the control room told him there was a report that Egyptian president Anwar Sadat had been assassinated. "We were waiting to try to get some confirmation," said Brokaw. "And then the first footage came in. It was actually ABC, as it turns out. It was just flying through the air, and we put it on. And ABC quickly said this should be made available to everyone. It was the scene at the site of the assassination." Brokaw, joined by *NBC Nightly News* anchor John Chancellor, stayed on the air for several hours to report the story. He then took an overnight flight to Egypt that afternoon and spent the next several days handling live coverage for *Today*. Friedman called it an "active style," showing viewers images as they came in rather than editing and digesting them first. "When a picture came in from Cairo, we saw it at the same time the audience saw it," Friedman said.

class background, I don't get very excited about birthright. But when I got there and saw the excitement of the British people, and the whole sense that this was not just a British royal wedding, that this is the British Empire as family, and everybody, in effect, was invited to the wedding; when I saw that, I knew that this was going to be a big deal. And it grew every day. We were outside. It was midday. Jane looked fabulous, obviously. We had the Queen's Guard, the band, play the *Today* theme, and march through our set. We were wired at St. Paul's Cathedral. Kiri Te Kanawa, who is one of the great opera singers in the world, was going to sing and I had interviewed her the day before. And then she came and was on the set with me afterward. So it was really a memorable time."

All three networks covered the royal wedding ceremony that morning, but most viewers—44 percent of them—were tuned in to *Today*. "The biggest audience we ever had," said Pauley.

ALL THREE NETWORKS COVERED THE ROYAL WEDDIN

Today showed it could cover celebratory moments in history with the same vitality when it headed to London for the wedding of the Prince of Wales and Lady Diana Spencer. *Today* presented royal weddings before, but Friedman believed *Today* had to be embedded into the atmosphere of the event. "This was going to be the big story, and I wanted to own it and the only way to own it was not to send the program for a day, but send them for a week," he said.

Brokaw initially had his doubts, but became a convert once he arrived on the scene. "I had not been, until that point, either a fan or a student of the Royal Family," he said. "I guess because I come from a working

While Brokaw thrived—and ratings climbed—with the emphasis on live breaking stories, Friedman believed *Today* had to offer something more. He wanted viewers to see spontaneous moments that they could talk about during the rest of the day. "He was always producing against type," said Brokaw. "So if, for example, if Cher came on and she was in an outrageous outfit, he'd make sure I interviewed her." Brokaw was generally a good sport about it. But one *Today* segment in particular helped him decide that it was time to move on.

"You're going to interview Charlene Tilton," Friedman told him. Tilton was the compact, buxom blond cast member of *Dallas*, the hottest prime-time show on television.

"I had no idea who she was," Brokaw recalled. "I didn't watch *Dallas*. And it turns out she was effectively a T-shirt pinup girl that they had hired out of a drugstore somewhere. She had nothing to say. I promise you, she had nothing to say. I do remember she gave me a two-handed handshake, and it was very, very sincere." Brokaw's body stiffened as he conducted the interview from the edge of his chair, his arms crossed tightly. At the end of the program, he got up and walked into the control room and said to Friedman, "That's it. I'm out of here."

Brokaw believed the long curve of his career was serious journalism, and if he stayed too long on *Today*, he would be diverted from it. His next contract with the network made him anchor of the *NBC Nightly News*, where he remained for the next twenty-three years. It meant *Today* had to go through another transition in the host chair with no consensus within the company on a successor. Fred Silverman, who had come over from red-hot ABC to run NBC, wanted Phil Donahue, who had been appearing on *Today* as a contributor. His taped segments delivered topics that were similar to what he covered on his daytime talk show. Some were timely (tax reform, discrimination, violence against women in films, child custody for working mothers)

REMONY. . . BUT MOST VIEWERS WERE TUNED INTO *TODAY.*

while others were titillating (sex therapy, vibrators, extramarital affairs, women who murdered their husbands). The news division favored Chris Wallace, the son of *60 Minutes* legend Mike Wallace and the network's Washington correspondent. Steve Friedman pushed for an unorthodox choice in Bryant Gumbel, who had become the signature star of NBC Sports. Friedman admired Gumbel's ability since he first saw him covering sports in Los Angeles in the early 1970s. Gumbel was an extraordinary live broadcaster—quick, facile, and diligent. As the primary host for NBC Sports, he had a razor sharp memory and a keen ability to get across a lot of information quickly without a script.

PRINCE CHARLES AND LADY DIANA

JULY 29, 1981

SOON AFTER TOM BROKAW arrived in London to cover the royal wedding for *Today*, he went out to dinner with Tina Brown, a young British editor for *Tatler* magazine. Brown was hired to be a part of the program's coverage, along with actor Peter Ustinov. She was not experienced in television but she could bring an insider's view on the Prince of Wales, the thirty-two-year-old heir to the British throne, and his bride, Lady Diana Spencer, then a shy nineteen-year-old teenager. "I said to Tina, 'You know, this will be a huge audience. But don't worry about it. Just be yourself.' And that made her very nervous," Brokaw said. "And then the first thing I said, as she sat by my side on the air was 'All right. Here comes the new princess. Oh, my God. Look at her feet. Her shoes are as big as gunboats.' After I said that, Tina said she knew she could say almost anything." (Brown went on to reveal that one of Diana's nicknames was "Hey Big Spencer.")

But there was one issue where they showed restraint during the seven hours of coverage. Brokaw remembered hearing the rumors about Prince Charles during the week *Today* spent in London. "There was a buzz underground," he recalled. "I had dinner a couple of times with people who were close to the Court, women who knew the relationship. And they all said the same thing: 'This is an arranged marriage. He has another.' It was Camilla (Parker-Bowles). 'He has another girlfriend that the Queen will not approve of him marrying.'" Looking back, Jane Pauley recalled how Diana shot a sidelong glance at Camilla as she came down the enormous aisle at St. Paul's Cathedral during the ceremony on July 29, 1981.

It was not what the worldwide audience of 750 million was tuning in for. They wanted a respite from assassination attempts and civil unrest and that now came to them faster than ever on television. They wanted a fairy tale, and the royal family gave one for the media to serve up. "I think we gave them a pass," Pauley said. "You know, 'Oh it was a wedding, and the dress and she was lovely.'"

Brokaw learned how big an appetite the public had for the story when he returned to the States and met up with a group of his mountain-climbing friends at Grand Teton in Wyoming. "All of their wives and girlfriends had rented motels in the middle of the night to watch the wedding," he recalled. "And I thought, well, that really is a commentary on what the country is looking for. They're looking for a little joy in their lives, a little uplift."

"PEOPLE WAITING IN THE CHURCH DIDN'T HAVE THE SEATS THAT WE HAD" —*Jane Pauley*

The Oprah Winfrey Show premieres. — **1984**

Once during a sports update, he learned that New York Yankees owner George Steinbrenner had fired his seventh manager, Gene Michael. When he reported the story live, he proceeded to fire off the names of the previous six. He also had a penchant for confronting sports figures with tough questions instead of fawning softballs. Friedman brought Gumbel onto *Today* in the fall of 1980 for a regular interview segment called "Sportsman of the Week." One of the athletes featured was a five-year-old golfing phenomenon named Tiger Woods.

Bryant Gumbel in the studio on NBC's NFL '80.

Gumbel had no journalism experience outside of sports, but Friedman believed he was the perfect choice to host *Today* as it evolved toward more live breaking coverage. "I felt the procedure was play-by-play news," Friedman recalled. "I wanted somebody who could do that. And nobody could do it better than Bryant. Television was changing. It was no longer pre-written, pre-digested tape. It was live as it's happening. And you need somebody who can do it without studying for it, being able to call it up like he did football. And I had no concerns that he couldn't. You know, interviewing presidents is no different than interviewing football coaches—you

just ask different questions. It's about listening and being prepared. And he always was."

Executives at both NBC News and NBC Sports resisted the idea. News purists did not believe a sportscaster should get the job. NBC Sports did not want to lose its star. ("Why do you want to give up seventy-two million viewers for five million?" Gumbel was asked by his boss, referring to the massive audience that watched him on the National Football League pre-game show *NFL '81*.) "There was also the wondering, if you will, whether a black sportscaster—and I don't know which one hurt him more, being black or being a sportscaster—could sit next to Jane Pauley in the morning in 1982," Friedman said.

Gumbel was an extraordinary live broadcaster—quick, facile, and diligent.

Once NBC president Bob Mulholland got behind the idea, the job belonged to Gumbel—if he wanted it. He was aware of the news division's reservations. "I was a thirty-two-year-old kid who really had his dream job already," Gumbel recalled. "Why would I leave that to jump into something where most people, as I begin, really don't even want me there?"

As Gumbel considered the offer, he met with Joe Garagiola—the only other sportscaster to have had a significant role on *Today*—when they were both in Cleveland for the 1981 Major League Baseball All-Star Game. Garagiola remembered their conversation.

"You've got to do it," he told Gumbel. "You're one of the brightest guys I've ever been around. You're more than curveball, touchdown, or slam dunk. You've got to do it."

"Well, what do you mean 'You've *got* to do it?'" Gumbel asked.

Garagiola was blunt with Gumbel about the significance of being the first African-American host on a TV

Gumbel, Pauley, and Scott traveled the world for Today *in the mid 1980s.*

· BRYANT ·
GUMBEL

MORE THAN ANYONE ELSE who anchored *Today,* Bryant Gumbel let you know where he stood. Viewers who watched him over his fifteen-year run on the program learned that he loved a good cigar, collected teddy bears, hated cheese, was terrified of snakes, separated his M&M candies by color before he ate them, and was obsessed with golf. (Once on *Today* Gumbel mentioned how he would choose a good round on the links over sex.) He could tell you the exact number of years, months, and days he had been married.

Gumbel admitted that his translucent personality was not ideally suited for the objectivity often required on his job. "I've never been good at putting on a reporter face, to be honest," he said. "It's my curse and my blessing in life. I doubt that you'd find many people who watched me, whether they loved me or hated me, who would say 'I never had any idea what he was thinking.'" Off camera, he would just tell you even if you were a journalist. On interviewing Mick Jagger's longtime girlfriend Jerry Hall: "It's like talking to a window." UN Ambassador Jeane Kirkpatrick: "Five minutes with her is an eternity."

He knew his blunt honesty could be polarizing in a business where you needed to be liked in order to succeed. "I think what happens is if you don't like me I'm arrogant," he once told Barbara Walters. "If you like me, I'm self-confident."

But no one could ever argue with Gumbel's skills as an interviewer. His unrelenting preparedness enabled him to be relaxed, smooth, and always in control. He could ask a pointed question without seeming prosecutorial ("Are you the power behind the throne?" he suavely asked First Lady Nancy Reagan in 1984). He did not give up easily when he didn't get an answer. "He always had that great question: 'Why?'" said Al Roker. "That great follow up."

Gumbel brought the proper intensity when talking with state or defense department officials because he was mindful that their decisions could result in putting troops on the ground. The lighter segments came easily to him. "It didn't take long for me to study for a cooking spot or a fashion spot," he said. "Doing ten minutes with Casper Weinberger and James Baker, that was a different deal."

Gumbel was a stickler for preparedness and life could be unpleasant for colleagues who did not share his commitment. "He didn't suffer fools lightly," said John Palmer. "If somebody wasn't prepared or he felt people were bullshitting him, he would let them know of his displeasure."

"The one thing he never tolerated was stupidity," Steve Friedman noted.

In August 1985, *Today* celebrated its comeback season with a live prime-time edition on Rockefeller Plaza. The producers planned a segment with David Letterman that would also air on his NBC late night show. Instead, Letterman grabbed a bullhorn and attempted to disrupt *Today* by shouting from the window of an office in the RCA Building while Jane Pauley was conducting an interview with the stars of *Miami Vice. Today* viewers could not hear Letterman's proclamation, "I am Larry Grossman, the president of NBC News, and I'm not wearing any pants. " But Letterman was taped on his end, and the bit became a legendary clip on his program. Gumbel called the stunt sophomoric and didn't speak to Letterman for years. "Bryant did not expect it to be a juvenile prank," Friedman said.

Gumbel was born in New Orleans in 1948. Richard D. Gumbel was a lawyer who moved his family to Chicago. He became a probate judge under Mayor Richard Daley's Democratic machine but was known for his independence on the bench. Gumbel idolized his trailblazing father,

who put himself through law school while holding down two jobs to support his family. It likely drove him toward being a perfectionist in his own life. "The only reason I have what I do now is because of what he did back then," Gumbel once said of his father, who died in 1972—before he could see his son on TV. "I don't think there's a day that goes by that I don't think about my dad. I think anything I do that's good, I attribute directly to his influence."

Richard Gumbel demanded that Bryant and his siblings "listen carefully and speak properly," and that advice paid off.

After graduating from Bates College in 1970, Gumbel headed to New York and became a corrugated box salesman. He learned he wasn't great at sales, but was good at sports writing and landed a job with *Black Sports* magazine. He was soon sought after for broadcasting positions. Once Gumbel got on the air at KNBC in Los Angeles, producers were awed at his seamless ability as a live broadcaster. That reaction continued as he headed to *Today* in 1982 through the unlikely route of NBC Sports.

While Gumbel's emergence as the first true African-American superstar of TV news could not be denied, he never wanted it to define him. "I think Bryant wanted the work to speak for itself," said Roker. "He didn't want to be 'Oh that black host of *Today*.'"

Nor did Gumbel dwell on the high-wire aspect of doing two hours of live TV each day. Often, it was life at fast-forward that did not always offer time for reflection. "The good part of the program is exactly the worst part about it," he said. "If you screwed up there was another chance the next day to make it well. The bad part was, when you said goodbye, you were twenty-two hours removed from saying hello. In a student sense—with a deadline facing them, or test facing them, or a paper due—the show was always right there. You know, no matter what you did, it was right there." But he was always ready when it was.

(Left): Bryant Gumbel with Johnny Carson. (Top right): with Chris Wallace and Jane Pauley in 1982; (center): with Pauley in 1987, (bottom) with Katie Couric.

1985 — *Actor Rock Hudson is the first high profile death related to the AIDS virus.*

program that stood as an American institution after nearly thirty years on the air. "Well, Bryant, you're almost like Jackie Robinson," he told him. "Take a look at television. You'll be behind one of the most prestigious desks in television. You just have to do it. You owe it to yourself, and you owe it to what we're all about in this country."

Gumbel never gave much thought about breaking any color barriers on *Today*. "That's flattering for Joe to say that," he said in a 2002 interview. "I never looked at it that way, to be honest. I guess most TV jobs that I

It took nine months (and a new boss at NBC News, the returning Reuven Frank) to figure out that three hosts was one too many. Wallace was reassigned to the White House and John Palmer, a veteran correspondent with a seasoned, authoritative presence, joined the program as newscaster in New York. The team of Gumbel and Pauley became the center of the program. Meanwhile, *Today* had lost its leadership position in the ratings, with *Good Morning America* taking a firm hold on first place. Even CBS became a player in the

WHEN *TODAY* DOES ITS JOB IT CAN'T BE BEAT.

have held, by virtue of timing, I've always kind of been the first. I was the first black host of a network sports program. So that wasn't something that occurred to me at the time." Gumbel remembered being more concerned about the resistance he received from NBC News. "There was a certain degree of snobbery," he recalled. "It was like, 'How on Earth can you take a jock and put him in a position as host of the *Today* program? How is that possible? When you have all these other wonderful people who are applying for the job, with wonderful news credentials? How on Earth could you do this?' And that's the way a lot of people felt. I mean there was talk of people refusing to do reports for us; other people who would refuse to talk to me on the air. It was pretty ugly."

Friedman attempted to placate NBC News by making Chris Wallace a co-host as well. He read the news and handled interviews with all Washington-based guests. It was unwieldy from the start. On Gumbel's first day on the air, January 4, 1982, he did not have much to do aside from going to Willard Scott for the weather.

morning with a newscast that was co-anchored by an attractive former Nixon White House aide named Diane Sawyer. *Today* was still the top brand name in morning television, but viewers were more fickle than ever. "When *Today* does its job it can't be beat," said Friedman. "When it wavers from its job, that's when others get a chance."

For Frank, who had spent the previous few years making documentaries, the TV news business had changed. During his first go-around as NBC News president, he faced the wrath of affiliate stations that shared the Nixon White House's view that subversive forces existed within the network. In the early 1980s, the leading complaint was that Jane Pauley's dark blond hair was too long and made her look like a toy doll. But Frank was convinced by Friedman to believe in the Gumbel-Pauley pairing and gave them time to grow.

Over time, Pauley developed a strong connection with Gumbel that differed from her days with Tom Brokaw. When Pauley first arrived on *Today* in 1976, she was

Steve Friedman (center) led Today *back to the top in the mid 1980s.*

inexperienced and willing to let Brokaw run the program. "He really looked after me," she recalled. "That's the good side. The bad side is, to sit next to Tom Brokaw is to feel completely intimidated." With Gumbel, closer to her in age and experience, she felt more comfortable bantering and pushing back when they disagreed.

Their differences made them interesting together and to each other. Pauley was an aspiring homecoming queen from Indianapolis, where her father was a salesman and her mother a church organist. She had confidence and natural ability on camera, but a self-deprecating sense of humor and an instinct to not make waves. Gumbel was a smooth Chicagoan who could be glib and unapologetically opinionated. Pauley enjoyed the fact that Gumbel "didn't have an edit button" as she liked to say. "I think Bryant and I had a fabulous working relationship," she said "We just complemented each other.

The kind of spicy quality to his personality really enhanced what might have been a little bland about my own. He forced me to be a little edgier than I would have been inclined to be on television. And I think I kind of cut the heat sometimes in his personality."

Pauley also overcame her unhappiness that Gumbel had been named host on the program while she was still co-host, even though she had seniority. She strongly believed that they should have equal billing. "I was very serious about it, and argued strenuously that I had earned it, that the times demanded it. And they heard me, and turned me down. I lost, but I felt that I made my case, made a good argument. But on the other hand, Gumbel was the first African-American cast member . . . never mind host. So it was really hard to argue on the basis of the prevailing feminism that I had to be given that honor."

THE SOVIETS CHOSE TO ANSWER THROUGH GUMBE

Bryant Gumbel with Richard Nixon in 1988

In 1983, Pauley became pregnant with twins. It was seen as a turning point for the new team. Unlike a previous era on *Today* when an expectant Florence Henderson had to hide her condition for months, the program could now reflect the generation of women in the workplace who were getting pregnant, admitting it, and were proud of it. On *Good Morning America*, motherhood and family life had helped define its co-host Joan Lunden, who openly discussed her pregnancies and child rearing. Pauley was not as upfront about her condition, but it was apparent to *Today* viewers. "I never talked about it in public," she said. "Except when you're sitting next to Willard Scott who, every day, has little twinsie teddy bears, or little tiny twinsie T-shirts." After Pauley confirmed that she was having twins, Scott noted once that *Today* had "twice as many babies coming as any other morning show!"

Gumbel with Sir Paul McCartney

AKING HIM APPEAR AS A BROKER OF DIPLOMACY.

Pauley got visibly larger to the point it became a topic of conversation among guests. "Bill Cosby was on the show one day and I was wearing a purple dress, and he called me a big, purple ball," she recalled. "And the cast broke up." She eventually went along with it. "I look like I'm going to be a float in the parade tomorrow," she told viewers on the day before Thanksgiving.

Once Pauley went on a three-month maternity leave, the ratings dipped, but not for long. "I think the ratings on my return were 25 percent greater than before I'd left or something like that," she said. It was further proof of the emotional connection that viewers had with their morning hosts. *Today* viewers had watched Jane Pauley grow up.

"I was in my thirties and no longer too young," she said. "I'm one of the few people on Earth who just couldn't wait to turn thirty, because I'd been too young for too long. I wasn't any longer. I was suddenly a mature person who had had six or seven years' experience on an important network television show."

Over the years that followed, viewers saw Pauley, who had a third child in 1986, as a role model for the women who were raising families while navigating through their careers. "I really tried not to talk about the twins too much; never was photographed with my children, no magazine covers; didn't talk about them on the air," she said. "And nonetheless, I think I definitely was strongly identified as a working mother, or so I'm told—that people would kind of gauge how deep the bags were under my eyes, you know, whether 'Jane was up that night with the kids.' I did meet a lot of women—once again, the baby boom factor—who had pregnancies about the same time I did who felt like they went through it with me. And a lot of them were among the first generation of women to have babies, and then after a couple of months, or six months, go right back to work. So I think I did represent something."

The ratings bounce that occurred after Pauley's return from her maternity leave continued through 1984. Gumbel proved his skills as a news interviewer every day. In some ways his background in sports became an asset. Richard Nixon, a serious football fan, wanted to appear on *Today* so he could meet Gumbel, who was later invited to the disgraced former president's home for dinner. (He accepted, even though he once called Nixon "the embodiment of evil.") An avid golfer, Gumbel occasionally hit the links with Gerald Ford. ("There's a part of me that never wants to forgive him for pardoning Richard Nixon.") But what silenced critics for good was the week in September 1984 when Gumbel headed to the Soviet Union as part of an NBC News contingent. He reported live from Moscow every day, a first for a morning program. "That turned it around dramatically," he said.

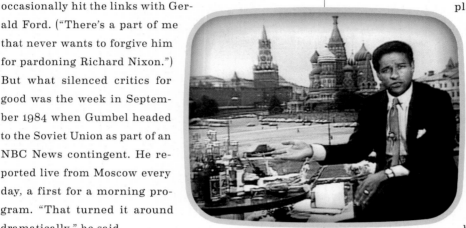

On the first day of the trip, he interviewed Georgi M. Korniyenko, the first deputy foreign minister, and Marshal Sergei F. Akhromeyev, the new Soviet chief of staff. Gumbel got the usual stonewalling from Soviet officials when he asked about the health of Soviet leader Konstantin U. Chernenko. But he moved the needle when

he went to Bates and studied Russian history," John Palmer said. "He was perfectly equipped." Gumbel won an Edward R. Murrow Award from the Overseas Press Club for his work that week.

As the new *Today* cast found its way, the program remained what Gumbel called "an American meeting place," that could examine frothy fads (Cabbage Patch Kids), new social classes (Yuppies), and technological breakthroughs (Silicon Valley). It sounded warnings on new dreaded threats, such as crack addiction and AIDS. Celebrities who came on *Today* pushed their ideas as well as their movies and books ("I know I don't die," said actress and reincarnation believer Shirley MacLaine). While Gumbel brought a more sophisticated approach to the anchor desk, the program stayed in touch with the heartland through reports from correspondents Mike Leonard, Boyd Matson, and Bob Dotson.

• • •

"THIS WAS A SHOW WHERE WE SAID TO YOU, 'WE WAN

he asked Korniyenko if a meeting between President Reagan and Foreign Minister Andrei A. Gromyko would be more valuable. "The meetings of statesmen are always useful," said Korniyenko, indicating that the Soviets were willing to resume talks on nuclear disarmament. Later that day, the White House announced that Gromyko and Reagan were to meet later that month. The administration had already asked for the meeting, but the Soviets chose to answer through Gumbel, making him appear as a broker of diplomacy. It was a stature-building moment. He also landed an interview with the new head of the Soviet army. "People didn't realize that

As Bryant Gumbel convinced NBC News and viewers that he was more than a sports guy, the press often mused about how he represented his race. In the early 1980s, there were only a few other African Americans with high-profile broadcast network news jobs—Ed Bradley on *60 Minutes*; Max Robinson, who was part of a trio of anchors on *ABC World News Tonight*; Charlayne Hunter-Gault, the primary substitute on *The MacNeil/Lehrer Report*; and Bernard Shaw, the principal anchor on then nascent cable news channel CNN. But the viewers' relationship with a *Today* host was more intimate and that put Gumbel's look and on-air style under great-

Bryant Gumbel spent a week reporting from the Soviet Union in 1984.

Mikhail Gorbachev implements his policies of greater openness and economic reconstruction in the Soviet Union.

er scrutiny, some of it condescending. "He is a handsome man with subtle features," wrote David Blum in *New York*. "He speaks with a voice so clear and modulated that it betrays no hint of racial origin. He dresses in outfits that most Americans, black or white, could never dream of affording." *The Crisis*, the official publication of the NAACP, said although the hiring of Gumbel was a breakthrough, he was not part of the struggle for racial equality: "Gumbel seems to represent that new generation of blacks—better schooled, vitamin-enriched, pleasant, like the boy next door, but self assured, strongly goal-oriented, a bit of an over-achiever, and possessing the distinct ability and inclination to speak mainstream (meaning white) language and underneath, a hardnosed bottom liner."

Gumbel always minimized the importance of his color, but those who worked with him said it cannot be discounted in the evolution of America's attitude toward race in the 1980s and beyond. "Bryant likes to say that it was a bigger deal that he came from sports than that he was African American in getting that job," said Jeff Zucker, who joined *Today* as a producer near the end of the decade. "It was a big deal that he was from sports, but it was a bigger deal that he was African American. It was an incredibly bold move by NBC's

sional parents and their college-bound children. (Gumbel grew up in the integrated Hyde Park neighborhood of Chicago where "everyone was professional and there was a high priority on education," he once said.) *The Cosby Show* was an immediate hit and went on to become one of the most successful situation comedies in the history of television. It also sparked a ratings turnaround for NBC's prime-time lineup, which had been in a slump for nearly ten years.

> *Bryant was the right guy, and the right choice. . . . He broke the barrier, both for that program and for society.*

By March 1985, *Today* topped *Good Morning America* in the ratings for the first time in three years. Shortly after *Today* broke the streak, the program went to Rome for Holy Week. Tim Russert, then a special assistant to the president of NBC News, supervised the coverage and arranged

UR FAMILY TO WATCH OUR FAMILY." — *Steve Friedman*

management at the time. But the fact was, Bryant was the right guy, and the right choice, because he was so incredibly talented. And at the end of the day it was talent that won out. But it really broke the barrier, both for that program and for society—the fact you were waking up with Bryant every morning. This had never been seen on television."

A case can be made that Gumbel's ascension on *Today* paved the way for another TV show that depicted the lives of African Americans in a way viewers had not seen before. In the fall of 1984, NBC debuted *The Cosby Show*, starring Bill Cosby as the head of the Huxtables, an upwardly mobile Brooklyn family of prosperous profes-

for Pope John Paul II to meet with the *Today* cast. High-ranking politicians, royalty, and world-famous celebrities regularly passed through *Today*, and Gumbel and Pauley did not feel any special sense of anticipation on this trip. But that changed when they were shuttled from the Sistine Chapel into the Pope's private chapel. "Happy Easter, Your Holiness," said Gumbel as he put both hands on the Pope's. It was a big moment for a former alter boy from Chicago. Pauley brought a picture of her children for the Pope to bless. As the Pope left the room, Gumbel and Pauley kept their eyes on him. They were oblivious to the camera as Gumbel put out his hand and gave a quick brotherly rub to Pauley's back as if to say, "It's OK."

(left): Jane Pauley and Bryant Gumbel meet Pope John Paul II;
(right) Willard Scott, Jane Pauley, and Bryant Gumbel on the SS Norway *1986*

"I wasn't even aware of it," he told *Playboy* in 1986. "It just happened." But the moment solidified them as a team in the eyes of *Today* viewers. The morning family—originated by *Today* in the 1950s and adapted by *Good Morning America* in the 1970s—had fully coalesced with the current cast. "This was a show where we said to you, 'We want your family to watch our family,'" said Friedman. "And you had the brother and the sister, in Bryant and Jane; you had the crazy uncles, in Willard and Gene Shalit; you had the stern taskmaster school teacher type in John Palmer."

On *Today*, the family that traveled together stayed together. The program regularly went on the road in the late '60s and '70s, but had gotten away from it. In the new era of morning TV ratings battles, remote telecasts from American cities (outside of the jaded hubs of New York, Chicago, and Los Angeles) and exotic overseas lo-

cales became a powerful weapon for *Today*. (As one *People* magazine headline put it: "It's War as Jane Pauley and Bryant Gumbel Take *Today* on the Road.")

"They came in rapid succession, and all of them enjoyable," Gumbel said of the trips. "But I've always believed that television, in general, and, when I was there, *Today*, in particular, should be about introducing people to and showing them things that they would otherwise not see or hear. It should be something that transports you to someplace you don't have the opportunity to see, or tells you something you haven't had the opportunity to learn. And so that's what I would like to think those shows accomplished."

Gumbel went to Ho Chi Minh City to help NBC News examine Vietnam ten years after the fall of Saigon. The *Today* cast took a whistle-stop tour on a specially equipped Amtrak train, stopping in Houston, Memphis,

A terrorist bomb explodes on a Pan Am 747 over —— 1988 •
Lockerbie Scotland, killing 259 passengers.

Cincinnati, and the birthplaces of Gumbel (New Orleans) and Pauley (Indianapolis). In 1986, it was on to Rio de Janeiro and Buenos Aires, a week of shows from the SS Norway, and three days in London to cover the wedding of Prince Andrew to Sarah Ferguson. In 1987, *Today* headed to Australia and China. "Just another day at the office," Pauley said one morning as she and Gumbel opened the program with a stunning view of the Great Wall of China behind them. In 1988, they boarded the Orient Express for a weeklong transcontinental tour of Europe. "Before I got into television I had never been west of the Mississippi," Gumbel said. "Before I went away to college I had never been on a plane. Going overseas—you've got to be kidding."

Every trip was a visual feast for the viewers and a culinary one for Gumbel, an adventurous gourmand. His fearless sampling of unusual local dishes became a regular highlight of the broadcasts. Said Gumbel, "I'll try anything," including duck feet, winkles, jellyfish, moth larva, and snake blood. The travels of *Today* always delivered a ratings spike during "sweeps" months, which local affiliate stations used to set their advertising rates. Needless to say, they were happy when the *Today* crew rolled into town by rail or by sea.

Today had become so successful that NBC expanded the program to the weekends in the fall of 1987. The first co-anchors for *Sunday Today* were Boyd Matson and Maria Shriver, who had joined the network as a newsmagazine correspondent. "It was becoming a seven day a week world—how could you be on just five days a week?" said Steve Friedman, who launched the program before he left NBC. The new edition became a farm team for new talent. It gave the first national exposure to an engaging New York weathercaster named Al Roker. When the Summer Olympics aired on NBC in 1988 for the first time since 1964, Bryant Gumbel was the prime-time host of the festivities from Seoul, South Korea. It was the first

time since the days of Dave Garroway that a *Today* personality was given such a vast broadcasting platform beyond the morning hours.

The *Today* juggernaut seemed to be rolling along until February 1989. when a front page story of the New York City edition of *Newsday* became the talk of the TV industry. Gumbel had written a confidential memo to *Today* executive producer Marty Ryan five months earlier that assessed the program's strengths and weaknesses. It had been leaked to a *Newsday* television reporter. The story described it as a "four page single spaced" critique of the program that Ryan had requested. Over time, the document was simply referred to as "the Memo." Every aspect of the program was analyzed with the exception of Gumbel's co-host Jane Pauley. But it was most harsh when it dealt with Willard Scott, who Gumbel said "holds the show hostage to his assorted whims, wishes, birthdays and bad taste" by ignoring time constraints and cues.

"He was really truthful," said John Palmer, whose newscasts were also criticized in the document. "It wasn't a vindictive thing. If Bryant is anything he's an honest guy. It was a damaging thing that it went out. Bryant talked to all of us. We knew it was for the good of the so-called family to keep a stiff upper lip and try to accept all this and move on with it because it was our careers and was something we wanted to do and liked to do. We honestly had been a close family. When you get up at four in the morning and go to work five days a week, there is a certain camaraderie that comes with suffering as a group. We all have the same sleep problems. We were all dealing with family issues complicated by the hours we kept. So we were friends and we would talk about these concerns."

Scott said he never held a grudge with Gumbel over the matter. "He liked me," Scott said. "It was never personal. He had feelings about the show and he had feelings about me. I had to agree with him. I am corny. But Guy

ON JANUARY 14, 1982, *Today* turned thirty years old. The milestone was celebrated with an on-air gathering of every major surviving personality associated with the program, including the original *Today* "communicator" Dave Garroway.

At the time, Bryant Gumbel had been host of *Today* for only two weeks. He did not grow up watching the program and came into the job without being awed by its storied history. But on that morning—which felt like a family reunion—Gumbel began to understand the legacy and the power of the platform he now presided over. "*The* adventure—it changes you from one man into another," Garroway told him during the program. "And you will feel differently about the world."

Gumbel and Garroway immediately hit it off. "Dave, unlike a lot of people at NBC News when I joined, was willing to talk to me, and didn't have an ax to grind," Gumbel recalled. "He and I had a couple of very good conversations. And one of them I had quoted often is when he told me: 'Do the program for five years. If you do it for any more than five years, you'll wind up talking to a moose.'"

Garroway was featured prominently on the anniversary program and his spirits seemed good. He had been to a rehabilitation facility where he succeeded in recovering from his dependence on amphetamines. But later that year he suffered from the effects of a Staph infection he picked up during heart surgery. His poor health had put him a deep depression, according to his son David. On July 21, 1982, Garroway used a shotgun to take his own life at his home in Swarthmore, Pennsylvania. He was sixty-nine years old.

During the thirtieth anniversary edition of *Today*, a photograph was taken of the three decades of on-air talent as they were seated across the set. Said Gumbel, "I had everyone sign the photo not knowing that for some that would be the last time they would be there."

Front Row (l to r): Tom Brokaw, John Chancellor, Hugh Downs, Barbara Walters, Bryant Gumbel, Jane Pauley, Dave Garroway, Jack Lescoulie, Frank Blair and Pat Weaver

Back Row (l to r): Betty Furness, Estelle Parsons, Lee Meriwether, Betsy Palmer, Joe Garagiola, Jim Hartz, Edwin Newman, Gene Shalit, Florence Henderson and Helen O'Connell.

· JOHN ·

PALMER

FIRST
SHOW
1982

LAST
SHOW
1989

IN THE EARLY 1970s, John Palmer was a newscaster for WNBC when he got a late Sunday night telephone call from NBC News asking him to fill in for Frank Blair on *Today*. "I guess as the years went on Frank would sometimes miss Monday mornings," he recalled. Palmer was told to go back to bed and he would get a wake-up call at 4 a.m.

"Go back to bed?" he said. "I was up ironing my shirt, washing my hair and getting ready. I was kind of terrified." He was so nervous on the set that the sweat had to be wiped from his brow during the program. "It was like having a cut man during a boxing match," he said. But Palmer settled down once *Today* regular Joe Garagiola walked over to him and placed his arm on his shoulder. "I'll never forget it," Palmer recalled. "Joe said 'I just talked to my mom in St. Louis and she says they're loving you out there.' It was a nice thing."

Garagiola may have been being kind that day, but eventually he was right. After working at NBC stations in Chicago and New York, Palmer was named White House correspondent and covered the administrations of Jimmy Carter and Ronald Reagan. A trusted figure in Washington, Palmer was the first reporter called on the night of April 24, 1980, and given word that a military rescue effort of the hostages at the U.S. embassy in Tehran had tragically failed, leaving eight servicemen dead. It was the always-steady Palmer standing outside of the White House on March 30, 1981, in the hours after the nation was shocked by the news that President Reagan was seriously wounded in an assassination attempt. The East Tennessee native's flowing baritone voice and economical choice of words was always clear even when there was chaos around him. He was a natural choice to help bring stability to *Today* when NBC News executives decided the triumvirate of Bryant Gumbel, Jane Pauley, and Chris Wallace wasn't working.

Palmer joined *Today* in September 1982 and stayed for seven years. His *Today* newscasts often brought overnight developments in international news during a period rife with Middle East conflicts and geopolitical turmoil in Europe. "We probably had a disproportionate amount of foreign news," he said. "In much of the world the people who were up shooting each other and having coups and things like that were well into their day by the time we came on."

To his mild dismay, Palmer had to remain anchored at the news desk in New York whenever *Today* hit the road for its spectacular overseas trips (as a gag he was once sent on his own trip—to the outer boroughs of New York City). Palmer needed to be ready to broadcast in the event a satellite feed from a remote location was lost, which once happened when *Today* traveled to Rio. "You always had to have somebody back here," he said. "I just didn't like the idea that it was always me."

Lombardo was corny and he lasted longer than Glenn Miller. When my wife died, Bryant wrote a beautiful letter to me. We've since seen each other. I swear to you with all of my heart."

Looking back, Gumbel still felt betrayed that a confidential document in his personal computer was made public. But he did not believe what he wrote was worthy of the front-page treatment it received. "I always said that if anybody ever actually read it, it does not warrant the ruckus it caused," he said. "I would venture to say it's the kind of assessments that your superiors, and

The Today *family in front of the Channel Gardens at Rockefeller Center.*

mine, too, do all the time, when they write job reviews. But I guess in the world of morning television, where everybody wanted to believe that never a word was said, that it was a big deal."

But the memo was a reflection of how Gumbel was a perfectionist who wanted *Today* to be at its best all of the time. He had little tolerance for anyone who did not care about it as much as he did.

● ● ●

By 1989, all three major broadcast networks had been sold by their founding owners. The new corporate parents, including NBC's General Electric, were committed to controlling costs as cable viewing proliferated and began to chip away at the audience share for broad-

cast TV. CNN had also become a force to be reckoned with as a twenty-four-hour news service.

Through the first four decades of television, the news divisions at ABC, CBS, and NBC had long been considered acceptable loss leaders. Operating them at a loss was considered the price of admission for using the public airwaves for highly profitable entertainment programming. But it was a new era, and news no longer escaped fiscal scrutiny. General Electric was looking for a better return on its investment and that included the already highly profitable *Today.*

GE executives looked at untraditional ways to manage the news division and put Dick Ebersol, the newly minted president of NBC Sports, in charge of *Today* (by many accounts with Gumbel's blessing). While *Today* was still number one, it had been losing young women— a viewing audience that was most highly prized by advertisers—to *Good Morning America.* Ebersol believed the program could stem the ratings loss with a newer, younger member to the *Today* cast, who had boosted ratings on the network's early morning news program *NBC News at Sunrise.* In the hard-charging business era of the 1980s, power brokers and chief executives were up earlier than ever and the vision many of them saw giving them their news was Deborah Norville. One of those executives was General Electric chairman Jack Welch, who tuned into *NBC News at Sunrise* while pedaling his exercise bike. Norville had beauty pageant looks, read the news with a silky smooth fluidity, and possessed a rock-solid work ethic that helped her succeed at every local station she passed through, including the gauntlet of WMAQ in Chicago.

Norville frequently filled in for Pauley and, in the summer of 1989, she was tapped to replace John Palmer at the *Today* news desk. Within a couple of months, she was no longer sitting apart from the hosts, as had been the tradition on *Today.* Norville was right next to Gumbel and Pauley at the opening of the program. The positioning was not lost on TV critics. "Watch Out Jane Pauley" read a headline in *USA Today.*

Pauley believed she never was properly briefed by management about Norville's role on *Today.* She considered the changes and how they were handled as she

1988 — *George H.W. Bush is elected as the 41st president of the United States.*

Publicity photo for a 1986 London trip

FIRST
SHOW
1980

· WILLARD ·
SCOTT

Present

B **EFORE WILLARD SCOTT ARRIVED** on *Today* in 1980, he was already a broadcasting legend in Washington.

As the son of an Alexandria, Virginia, insurance salesman, most of Scott's boyhood friends were the children of government or military employees, including one who worked at the White House. "I'd go to the White House and swim every Saturday," Scott recalled. "And Harry Truman would come by—'How you boys doin'—havin' a good time in my pool?' I'm twelve years old and the President of the United States says hello to me. Those were good times." He hosted a radio program while in high school and was still in his teens when he started working at NBC's DC station WRC in 1950 as a staff announcer. Within a few years he was in front of the camera as "Farmer Willard" on a Saturday morning show called *Barn Party*. He worked alongside a young puppeteer named Jim Henson, who brought along an assortment of cloth characters he called Muppets. "I remember saying to him—'Jim these are cute. Don't sign them over to NBC,'" Scott recalled. Scott was later chosen to serve as the station's Bozo the Clown for a children's program. He used his clowning skills to develop a character for the local franchises in the McDonald's hamburger restaurant chain that was eventually used in its national advertising—Ronald McDonald ("Never paid a nickel for it," Scott said). On radio, Scott was one half of the Joy Boys, a comedy team that had an avid following in the city for nearly twenty years. His partner was Ed Walker, a college pal who was blind from birth. "We wrote our own sketches, and we both adlibbed for each other," Scott said. "So all we had to do is get an idea and we'd adlib it. We were a good team. Because I knew what punch line he was going for. And I also knew when to shut up when he was doing his bit. We never talked over each other. Never." The two men had such trust in one another, Scott even let Walker get behind the wheel of his car when they drove along the Whitehurst Expressway. While succeeding on the radio, Scott started doing TV weather forecasts for WRC, where he became known for his unpredictable stunts, such as coming out dressed in a barrel one April 15.

Today had depended on Gene Shalit for humor, but his wordplays and anecdotes were on the urbane side. The gap-toothed Scott had a broad folksiness that played in the heartland, which is where the *Today* audience really lived. "I had watched him in Washington," Tom Brokaw said. "Willard was as natural a performer as I had ever seen on television. He was authentic, funny, and very quick and I knew he would connect in the rest of the country because I've lived out there in those parts of the world where every town had one—a big jolly funny guy who was smarter than hell—and that was Willard. I knew he would be successful."

Scott's act was always built on warmth and a state of wonderment that never changed in a world that became more cynical. In 1983, a *Today* tradition was born when Scott received a card from a viewer that asked if he would mention his uncle's name on television on his 100th birthday. It became a regular feature that has lasted for decades. "How can you not like somebody that's lived 100 years, and listen to one or two little adlibs about what they thought helped them live to be 100?" he said. "Most of them were people that had a little garden, nice families and I'd say that most, if not all of them, were religious." It was a reflection of Scott's relentlessly upbeat outlook that he never apologized for. Over time, Scott's centenarian birthday greetings became a coveted platform for *Today* advertisers who wanted their product names attached to it. Scott himself became one of the most popular product pitchmen of the 1980s. He was so in demand, NBC News had to exempt him from the policy that kept major *Today* talent performing in commercials. Scott was not a journalist. By his own admission, he was barely a weather forecaster. "I never even took it seriously," he said. "I spent years trying to figure out what the hell an occluded front was. I'm still not quite sure. I said, 'It's a girl with an overbite.'"

In August 1983, a *Today* viewer offered to contribute $1,000 to the United Service Organization if Scott was willing to dress up as Carmen Miranda—the 1940s-era South American singing star whose signature look included a headdress made out of tropical fruit. Scott did his Miranda drag act at USO shows when he was in the service. He performed a song and even did the weather in Miranda attire after Bryant Gumbel collected the check.

Willard Scott was such a big star on *Today*, even his hairpiece got special care and handling. "We were doing a feature at Martha Stewart's farm out in Connecticut," he recalled. "We had dinner and a few drinks. And when I got back to New York, I realized I had forgotten my hairpiece. I'd left it in her bathroom. I didn't give a shit about it you know? But when you wear it every day you've got to wear it tomorrow. So they had to call a limo to pick it up and bring it to New York."

assessed the priorities in her life. At age thirty-nine, she had been on *Today* for thirteen years, had three children, and had two years to go on her NBC contract. Her twins were about to start kindergarten and her youngest son had turned three. "Two years is a long time to be somewhere you're not wanted," she wrote in her 2004 autobiography. "I realized I was wanted at home." Rather than contend daily for airtime with an assertive and ambitious newcomer who was given an

expanded role on the program, Pauley decided to leave *Today*. "With three small children at home, I couldn't kick it up another notch," she said. Pauley was willing to settle out her contract, even if it meant giving up millions of dollars. At first, NBC executives did not take Pauley's request seriously. They thought it was a negotiating ploy. But after the situation dragged on, Tom Brokaw reminded them that "Jane is from Indianapolis—she does not 'ploy.'" Pauley ended up extending her

The Exxon Valdez tanker runs aground off the coast of Alaska, ——**1989**
causing the largest oil spill ever in U.S. coastal waters.

deal with NBC News with the promise of a new prime-time news magazine. But her run on *Today* was going to end in December.

After Pauley's new deal was announced, Norville was named as her successor. On October 27, 1989, Pauley announced her planned departure to *Today* viewers. She joined hands with Gumbel and Norville at the anchor desk in a show of solidarity and an attempt to prove that neither was directly responsible for her decision. She handed Norville her alarm clock, which turned out to be broken. ("It was meant as an artifact but the symbolism was unfortunate" Pauley told *TV Guide* years later.)

Jane Pauley was the first baby boomer on *Today*. Her cohorts who watched had embraced her as she grew into her job, became a mother, and balanced her family and career. They were upset by the perception of her being replaced by a younger woman. The notion—reinforced by relentless press coverage—was unshakable and overcoming it became the biggest challenge *Today* would face in its long and storied history.

Meanwhile, historic news events were unfolding on *Today*, and more often it was Norville who delivered the details to viewers. She conducted a live in-

fan letters since the announcement of her departure, including one from longtime *Today* viewer actor Robert De Niro. In the final minutes, clips rolled showing her travels around the world, her laughter on the set and as she described it, "a cavalcade of Jane's hairdos—the best of the worst and the worst of the worst." Helen Fisher, an anthropologist from the Museum of Natural History, even provided analysis of Pauley's enduring appeal. "She's come on very much as a person you can identify with," she said. "We do feel that we know Jane Pauley."

When the taped tribute was over, she turned to Gumbel with tears in her eyes and pulled "a precautionary Kleenex" out of her pocket. Showing the poise that got her there, she read a prepared statement. She thanked NBC for giving her "an incredible front row seat for thirteen years." She thanked her colleagues. She thanked the viewers for watching and for their outpouring of support. She then noted one piece of mail that made her realize what every *Today* cast member eventually learned during their experience on the program. They were part of something larger, something that kept going day

terview with Tom Brokaw when he reported live in front of Brandenburg Gate on November 10, 1989, as German citizens freely crossed the barrier that separated their country for the last three decades. "This is the day that the Cold War ended not with a bang but with a street party throughout East and West Berlin," Brokaw said.

Pauley had her final day as a *Today* co-host on December 29, 1989. She had received four thousand

after day, year after year, providing a link to several generations of Americans. "I'm thinking particularly of one man who wrote me a fine long letter and closed it with a phrase that proved he went back a lot further with the show than even I did," she said. "He quoted the late Frank McGee, who used to sit here. Frank never said goodbye, but at least a thousand times he said 'Don't go far.' And I won't. And don't you either."

Deborah Norville replaced John Palmer as news anchor in 1989.

MATT

ANN CURRY B

CHAPTER FIVE

KATIE

AL ROKER
JO

• FAITH DANIELS •

LAUER

YANT GUMBEL

1990-1999

COURIC

· GENE SHALIT ·

GARAGIOLA

1990 – 1999

THE 1990s STARTED OUT AS A DECADE OF monumental global change that would require a rewrite of history books. Nelson Mandela was released from a South African prison after twenty-seven years and apartheid would be repealed. East and West Germany were reunified. Communist regimes collapsed across Eastern Europe and the Soviet Union was dissolved. Such significant stories often came into America's living rooms with the immediacy that Pat Weaver predicted when he created *Today*.

The American television landscape was being reshaped as well. A fourth broadcast network, Fox, had emerged, and gave Australian media mogul Rupert Murdoch a foothold in the United States. More than half of the country's 95 million television households had a wide array of channels to watch beyond the offerings of broadcasters thanks to cable and satellite services. Sixty-seven percent of those homes owned a videocassette recorder, giving viewers the freedom to watch feature films and tape their favorite shows for later playback whenever they wanted. Affordable video camcorders enabled people to see themselves on television as easily as going through a scrapbook of photographs. The hottest new program on prime-time television at the start of 1990 was ABC's *America's Funniest Home Videos* where viewers provided their own content.

> ## The 1990s started out as a decade of monumental global change that would require a rewrite of history books.

But amid all the tumult, morning television programs were largely doing what *Today* had done since Dave Garroway gently rambled into the camera at the RCA Exhibition Hall nearly forty years earlier. They came on, said hello, reported the news and weather and interviewed guests. The key difference between the programs was the bond viewers had with the people they saw on the screen as they had their morning coffee, and that meant trouble for *Today.* The relationship with its audience was more tenuous then ever following the botched transition from Jane Pauley to Deborah Norville. The program's five-year reign of ratings superiority over *Good Morning America* ended. In the year since Bryant Gumbel's memo had been leaked, the audience for *Today* declined by more than 20 percent and the program was back in second place.

Deborah Norville simply did not have a chance. Critics were tough on her, always playing on the scenario that she was the other woman who broke up the *Today* family. Norville thought the ill feelings would pass once it was announced Pauley was getting her own prime-time news magazine and named the main substitute for Tom

Brokaw on the *NBC Nightly News.* (Pauley's stock at the network had risen to the point that it was rumored she would be made Brokaw's co-anchor.) "She was well taken care of," Norville recalled. "She was going to be fine. And I knew that. And I figured, 'Now the press will leave us alone, and we can just do what we do, which is to do good television.' Unfortunately, I was wrong about that scenario." Even NBC's *Saturday Night Live* satirized the story with a sketch that portrayed Pauley and Norville as the Margo Channing and Eve Harrington characters in *All About Eve.*

The public saw Gumbel as an accomplice in the fiasco and his image suffered as well. The drumbeat of bad publicity had gotten so loud, he agreed to an interview with Barbara Walters on ABC's *20/20* news magazine. At the time, a national confessional with Walters was almost a requirement for celebrities who were vilified by the public and wanted to absolve themselves. Gumbel insisted he played no role in the decision to elevate Norville's presence on *Today,* and he wanted the public to know he was feeling their pain for Jane Pauley.

 **1990** — *The Americans with Disabilities Act is passed by Congress.*

"I miss Jane," Gumbel told Walters. "Which should not be taken as a slam against Deborah, but I miss Jane. I think any time you work with somebody for eight years and you're joined at the hip and suddenly you're separated, you wind up missing them. Yeah, I miss Jane." Walters even got Gumbel to shed his tough exterior and get a little misty-eyed when talking about his father.

But it didn't help. *Today* continued to lose viewers at a rapid pace. In May 1990, Dick Ebersol, the executive whose idea it was to bring in Norville, gave up his responsibilities for *Today* and went back to running NBC Sports full time. In a rare display of network executive accountability, he acknowledged that the transition was his idea, and he had to go. "I felt it was the necessary thing to do," he told the *Los Angeles Times*. "The events of the last eight to nine months have been a soap opera, and viewers are mad at NBC management."

In attempt to smooth over the damage, *Today* stalwart Joe Garagiola was brought in as a co-host along side Gumbel and Norville. At sixty-five years old, he hardly seemed like the answer to the

change was the naming of Katie Couric (then billed as Katherine) as national correspondent for *Today*.

NBC's Washington bureau chief Tim Russert hired Couric as a correspondent in 1988 after seeing her local reporting on WRC. Russert put her at the Pentagon as a back-up to NBC News veteran Fred Francis. "Dick Ebersol is the one, in the midst of all the behind-the-scenes turmoil, who thought that she would be a good addition as national correspondent," said Jeff Zucker.

In a short time, Couric was getting the attention of NBC News with her work as co-anchor on *Sunday Today* and during fill-in stints during the week. "I do remember the day I filled in as the main anchor," she said. "I think Willard had done his weather and, in typical Willard fashion, had mentioned a horny toad convention. And then I saw Gene Shalit in the studio, and I said, on the air, 'Hey, speaking of horny toads, Gene Shalit just walked in . . .' I think maybe people realized that I could be perhaps a little spontaneous, and have fun with the format. But, of course, everyone on the staff knew what I was talking about. And I adore Gene, but you know,

---

> ## *Joe Garagiola was brought in. . . . He was a Gumbel pal who knew how to bring out the host's playful side.*

---

problem *Today* was having holding onto female viewers. But he was a Gumbel pal who knew how to bring out the host's playful side, something that had all but disappeared in recent months. Faith Daniels was poached from CBS to be the *Today* news anchor ("a young mother, a professional woman from a two-worker household . . . the very person who we want to watch the show," was how NBC News president Michael Gartner described her, as the dire situation forced the network to be overly transparent about every move). But the most significant

he was always sort of flirting with the girls. And I think everyone was shocked, but also delighted that I had made that joke. And then I also remember doing the news. There was a story about a skier who had been lost, and lit his dollar bills on fire to attract, I guess, the attention of the search party. And I think I threw back to Bryant and said, 'Gee, with my luck, I would have only had change.'"

The rest of the time viewers saw Couric as a solid correspondent. She was frequently seen on *Today* and other NBC News programs as tensions built in the Mid-

The Couric era begins in 1991. (Clockwise from left): Faith Daniels, Gene Shalit, Joe Garagiola, Willard Scott, Bryant Gumbel, and Katie Couric.

1991 — *Kodak introduces the first digital camera for consumers.*

dle East after Iraqi troops invaded Kuwait. While in Saudi Arabia, she scored an eleven-minute exclusive interview with the commanding officer of U.S. troops Gen. Norman Schwarzkopf. During a visit to Shaw Air Force base she flew in an F-16.

Couric eventually became a ray of hope for the program, and within months the press started touting her as a replacement for Norville. Couric wisely stayed above the fray, defending Norville against the criticism that came her way. But Norville made the decision easy for NBC News by deciding not to return from maternity leave for her first child. "When I got pregnant, people in the press purported this fact that I had deliberately become pregnant so that I could save my job," Norville recalled. "Because of course, Jane's ratings went up when she had her kids. So it was just kind of part of this revolving door spinning more and more rapidly. And I read that and the light bulb went on: *Deb, they don't want you. You can go back and you can try to fight it, but it is clear you will never get any support from the people whose support you must have to be successful at NBC. You will not get their support. And you're a damn fool if you try.*"

Norville settled out her contract. On April 5, 1991, Couric was introduced as the program's co-anchor. "In case you haven't gotten the message, Katie is now a permanent fixture up here, a member of our family and an especially welcome one," said Gumbel.

"I guess this means you're stuck with me," said Couric. "Or maybe I'm stuck with you."

While Norville was unfairly portrayed as the other woman, Couric was embraced as the approachable girl next door, or as one magazine put it "America's Kid Sister." But she represented something more. In the 1960s, Barbara Walters was the trailblazer, working tirelessly and patiently, as she waited for men in the industry to recognize her ability. In the 1970s, Jane Pauley was selected for her youth and her persona developed over time before viewers' eyes. Couric arrived fully equipped as a professional and as a personality. She had the self-assurance of a woman who came of age while the feminist movement had reached critical mass in the 1970s. She grew up believing equality for women was a right. She built on the inroads that the women who came before her had made. She was attrac-

(Left): Katie Couric with Katherine Hepburn in 1991 and (right) as Today *national correspondent with Norville in 1990.*

tive, but her short bob (which she refused to change at the request of NBC executives) was a statement that she was all business and ready to spring into action at anytime. When Couric appeared as a co-anchor on *Today* (the term co-host was no longer used), she was completely comfortable being herself. While bantering at the anchor desk or on the couch, it was typical to see Couric express her displeasure by opening her mouth wide and inserting her index finger as if she were gagging, or even delivering a solid but playful punch to Gumbel's arm. They were not moves you'd expect to see from Barbara Walters or Jane Pauley. But they were in sync with a new generation of women who were freer to express themselves and be irreverent. Couric laughed easily and was fast with a wise crack, but she instinctively knew when to keep it serious and respectful. "My humor just seemed to work well in the morning," she said looking back. "I think I was able to say funny, unexpected things. But then I knew when to pull back. When things were getting too much out of control and the yuks were just too much, and it sort of felt too much like an inside joke, and was leaving the viewers out; then I was always sort of able to pull it back and kind of move on."

Couric was a hit with the audience and created a sense of relief that the worst was over at *Today*.

"I think I benefited from the turmoil, to be honest with you," Couric said. "And I always felt bad about that. Because I think Deborah is a fantastic person. But I think the transition from Jane to Deborah was handled so terribly. People felt that Jane wasn't being treated with the respect she deserved, because she was beloved. It was sort of like this beautiful, younger woman was coming in to steal Jane's TV husband. I think it was just very insensitively handled. They shouldn't have had Deborah sitting with Jane and Bryant, with the feeling that had already been created that somehow she was going to take over Jane's role. I think it was a hard period, and I did feel bad for Deborah, because it's hard to go through that publicly. I remember people saying that when Deborah was on TV in the morning, you felt like you had to be dressed when you watched her; she was so beautiful and put together. And then I came

Couric arrived fully equipped as a professional and as a personality. . . . She was completely comfortable being herself.

along, and I was just much more, I think, approachable, in terms of my appearance and my persona. I think I was more like Jane than Deborah, and I think, as a result, it helped me be more readily accepted."

ON APRIL 5, 1991, THE NEW CO-ANCHOR OF *TODAY* was introduced as Katherine Couric. Everyone called her Katie, but she had been going with Katherine because she wanted to have more gravitas ("Latin for balls," she once said) while covering the State Department for NBC News. Couric was four months pregnant and threw up in her hotel room before she showed up for the program that morning in a red dress from A Pea in the Pod, a maternity clothing store. She still managed to sparkle when Bryant Gumbel instructed the director to play the audio of the program's introduction with her name a second time.

Raised in Arlington, Virginia, Katie was the youngest daughter of John Couric, a journalist turned public relations executive, and his wife, Elinor, a homemaker who volunteered at Planned Parenthood. Couric had an idyllic, happy childhood, filled with friends and games in a neighborhood that she described as being straight out of the wholesome TV sitcom *Leave it to Beaver*. She was so outgoing she used to say she was born on a sunny day. In high school she was a cheerleader and her yearbook cited her for having a fantastic smile. Her parents put a strong emphasis on education. Each day, all four of the Couric children were expected to bring a new word to the dinner table. But there was also time for a lot of TV. Couric came of age in the 1960s when prime-time TV was saturated with sitcoms. She loved the escapist fun of *Bewitched*, *Gilligan's Island,* and *The Andy Griffith Show*. She enjoyed music as well, taking piano lessons and spending hours in the family basement singing along with her father's Frank Sinatra albums.

Encouraged by her father, Couric wrote for her college newspaper at the University of Virginia. She thought about a career as a print journalist, but gravitated to TV because it paid better. Her first job after graduating in 1979 was as a desk assistant for the Washington bureau of ABC News.

Couric's duties included making coffee, distributing newspapers in the newsroom, and picking up ham sandwiches for anchor Frank Reynolds. Early on, she met ABC's always-exuberant White House correspondent Sam Donaldson. After Couric told him her name, Donaldson jumped onto a desk and wildly belted out a ditty from World War I called "K-K-K-Katy" ("K-K-K Katy, beautiful Katy—you're the only g-g-g-girl that I adore . . ."). An extrovert herself, Couric realized at that moment she was in the right business. Donaldson then brought her along to a news briefing at the White House.

In 1980, Ted Turner founded the Cable News Network, the first twenty-four-hour cable news channel. Broadcast network news executives at NBC, CBS, and ABC sneered at the idea. They were still operating in the days when they had no competition and answered to owners more

concerned with prestige than profits from their news divisions. They often said CNN stood for Chicken Noodle News. But Couric, who saw few women in significant jobs at ABC News, believed it could offer more opportunities for her to get hands-on experience in producing and reporting. She left to join the Washington bureau of the startup. She was a gofer no more, as CNN made her an assignment editor. There was a rough patch early on when Couric got her first chance to be on the air. She was getting ready to give a report outside of the White House when the voice of the studio anchors came in her earpiece. She heard them say that Couric looked like she was sixteen years old. After her appearance went poorly, CNN President Reese Schonfeld said he never wanted to see her on the air again.

But Couric didn't give up. She moved to CNN headquarters in Atlanta to work on a two-hour news program hosted by Don Farmer and Chris Curle, an experienced husband-and-wife anchor team. They gave the eager Couric guidance and airtime. It led to an on-air news job at the NBC affiliate in Miami. There she developed a reputation as a scrappy, hard-working street reporter who was glued to the city police scanner at all hours. She covered the drug busts and murders that were the dominant stories in Miami during the 1980s. Couric took a similar job at WRC in

HE DEVELOPED A REPUTATION AS A SCRAPPY, HARD-WORKING STREET REPORTER.

Washington, where she quickly caught the eye of NBC News Washington Bureau Chief Tim Russert. Once Couric was hired to cover the Pentagon, NBC News executives immediately started developing her as an anchor. Couric was surprised. She didn't think she had the glamorous looks—or at just under five-foot-four, the height—to be an anchorwoman. She thought her round face and chubby cheeks made her look like a Campbell's Soup kid. "So it wasn't that all of a sudden I got a call and they said, 'Hey, Katie, we're going to make you a star!'" she recalled. "It was sort of a slow, evolving process." In 1990 she co-anchored *Sunday Today* with Garrick Utley out of Washington. "I remember calling Nelson Mandela's wife Minnie Mandela instead of Winnie," she said. "Not one of my finest moments."

Couric did not have time to fully reflect on her ascent to *Today* as Deborah Norville's replacement. "I think I just sort of went with it," she recalled. "I didn't overthink it. Because if I had, I'm sure I never would have done it because the risks attendant to that situation were probably huge. You know, I think that I was welcomed because I was a reporter. I'd been covering the Pentagon. I'd been working in the business at that point for about twelve years, as a reporter. I had paid my dues. It wasn't as if I had just won the Junior Miss competition and they were trying to give me a shot at television. So I had a lot of support from the rank and file people here at NBC. I think honestly, a lot of it wasn't about me. I think it's very hard to follow in the footsteps of someone like Jane Pauley. And I think that it might have been that I was fortunate to not be the anchor to follow Jane, but the second anchor. And I think maybe it was so awkward and tense, and it was such a tumultuous time for the show; I think that people were just relieved, more than anything else, that they had a fresh face. They probably wouldn't have cared whose face it was at that point."

But before Couric took the job, she made a point of telling NBC News President Michael Gartner that she did not want to limit her *Today* role to the traditional female segments of cooking, fashion, or parenting. She wanted a 50-50 arrangement with Bryant Gumbel with an equal shot at interviewing major newsmakers. Gartner promised her 52-48.

Couric proved she was worthy of every percentage point. The notion that she was perky or cute—as the press often described her—led some politicians to underestimate her tenacity as an interrogator during her early years on the program. In 1992, former Ku Klux Klan member David Duke tried to reposition himself as a legitimate conservative Republican candidate for president. Some TV interviewers treated Duke with deference given to a respectable contender during his bid for governor of Louisiana. Couric did not. She pushed him to try to explain past anti-Semitic and racist statements. "I really let him have it," Couric said. "And I remember my dad called me and said, 'Edward R. Murrow would be really proud of that interview.'" Columnist Frank Rich wrote Couric a letter praising her aggressive approach. "As an American, a journalist and a Jew, I watched in horror as the big guns of television news let David Duke barrel through with his own virtually unchallenged agenda," Rich said. "What you did this morning was not only right, but also smart and courageous."

NO ONE COULD SWING FROM THE HARD TO SO

Couric later stood up to the pugnacious 1992 presidential candidate Ross Perot, challenging him to clarify his populist-pleasing positions on reducing federal spending. Perot, who often snapped back with a rapid-fire "Katie, Katie, Katie" before answering, claimed Couric was trying to "prove her manhood" with her tough queries. Couric said she took it as compliment. In the 1996 presidential campaign, Couric pressed Republican candidate Robert Dole on the contributions he received from the tobacco industry and his claims that there was no proof cigarette smoking was addictive. Dole was on *Today* with his wife Elizabeth to promote the paperback reissue of a book they wrote about their marriage and seemed taken aback by Couric's persistence. "He really thought, *Oh, a morning show. We've put out the paperback of our book and it's going to be about our lives together*," Couric said. "And he was running for president. I thought, *The hell it is. It's going to be about the issues of the day.*"

While Couric developed a reputation for asking probing questions on *Today*, she was also able to be completely uninhabited and freewheeling when it came to performing outside of her role as a journalist. No one could swing from the hard to soft elements on *Today* as well as Couric did. It sent her popularity into the stratosphere.

"I joked often about Katie, although I mean it very seriously—Katie was the best combination of Lucille Ball and Edward R. Murrow," said Matt Lauer. "She had complete ease in front of the camera. I look at Jane Pauley, and Jane was so wonderful. And America fell in love with Jane. Jane wasn't the person who was going to put the lampshade on, and dance around on the show. She held it a little more close to the vest, even though you knew a little bit about her family and her husband, and the birth of her children, which kind of played out in the national spotlight. Katie would walk out there and just say what was on her mind. She wasn't afraid to absolutely ham it up. And then all of a sudden, she'd be standing there with the president and it was as good an interview as you'll ever see. So there was this huge range that Katie has, that I think was something that was really new for the genre. And I think it was what made her mark."

Couric loved to sing on the program, whether it was old TV theme songs of her youth, Broadway show tunes, classic Top 40 hits from the 1960s, or ballads from the Disney movies she watched with her daughters. "If I could do anything in my life, I wish I could sing," she said. "If I had a fantasy career, I would be Kristin Chenoweth."

While she was aware her musical talent was limited, she stepped up to the microphone with the likes of Tony Bennett and other performers. "Katie also loved to dance on the air," said Lauer. "Every time we'd have a dancer on the air, it had to be built into every segment that at some point, the music would strike and Katie would get out there and dance with them. Now, Katie's a good dancer, but she's not a professional dancer. But don't tell Katie that. She loved to get in there and do it. While she was willing to go out there and lay herself on the line, she also took herself pretty seriously in some of these things. But it was fodder. It was great for us. Because we could kind of poke fun at that."

EMENTS ON TODAY AS WELL AS COURIC DID.

Couric was also a force of nature behind the scenes on *Today*. "You just felt that she was always on, always pushing for more, always pushing for better," said Ann Curry. "And she pushed everyone. She pushed all of us. She pushed the cameramen, the producers, everyone, to make the broadcast better. And working with her was like working with a big sister who is always telling you what you should wear. She would say, 'Oh, Ann. Those earrings. You know what? Those are so not *Today*. You need to take those off.' And she would give me her diamond earrings to wear. She actually did that once. So Katie amazed me. I thought, *Wow.* It wasn't always easy. But I did admire her skills, her ability to get good interviews, and make us laugh and encourage us to be our best. I thought she was great. It was like working with an exploding star. You were blinded by her light."

Couric's effect on Gumbel was immediate. His demeanor brightened as the tension that hung over *Today* diminished. Journalistically they were a formidable combination. For newsmakers who agreed to appear on the program, there was no place to hide. Some who worked with Gumbel, already considered the best interviewer in the business, said he became even better when he was paired with Couric.

Soon *Today* was making news again with what was happening in front of the camera. When stories began to circulate about Sen. Edward Kennedy's public boozing

in Palm Beach (including a night out that led to his nephew William Kennedy Smith being tried for rape), Gumbel skillfully shifted from questioning about health-care legislation to whether the senator believed he had an alcohol problem.

"Absolutely not," Kennedy said.

"You see no need to alter or modify your behavior in any way?" Gumbel said with an air of disbelief.

Couric had the same kind of persistence. She refused to let Vice President Dan Quayle brush off a poll that said only 34 percent of the country was comfortable with the notion of him being president. "Doesn't that bother you?" she said. "That's a very small percentage." Rather than explain his role in President

George H. W. Bush's administration, he had his customary deer-in-the-headlights look. On October 9, 1991, Couric landed the first television interview with law professor Anita Hill who went public with charges of sexual harassment against Supreme Court justice nominee Clarence Thomas. Thomas survived a confirmation vote, but it was a landmark in public discourse on the issue. "When they describe him in history books, there will always be a paragraph about this," Couric told Gumbel that morning.

With a more confident and happy team at the anchor desk, the ratings climbed back up and the family atmosphere returned to *Today* in time for its fortieth anniversary celebration on January 14, 1992. The cast—Bryant Gumbel, Katie Couric, Joe Garagiola, Gene Shalit, Willard Scott, and Faith Daniels appeared together the day before on *Donahue*. A viewer called in with a question about whether Gumbel and Scott were getting along after the controversy over the memo. Shalit stood up and started collecting cash from the other cast members as they had taken bets on what time during the program the topic would come up. The scene got a big laugh from Phil Donahue's studio audience. But Scott used the moment to put his seal of approval on the new team—especially Couric—and cast Gumbel's memo as a genuine attempt to improve the program. "Our show has never been better—I wouldn't have always said that," he told Donahue. "I have never seen anybody work harder in trying to change things then Mr. G—I love him."

Around the same time, Gumbel backed the promotion of Jeff Zucker, then supervising producer, to executive producer. NBC News president Michael Gartner told Gumbel the idea was "insane,"—as Zucker was only twenty-six years old with only a few years of TV producing experience. But Gumbel, in the midst of contract negotiations, made it happen. A Harvard graduate, Zucker was hired in 1986 as a researcher for the network's Summer Olympics coverage in Seoul, Korea. After spending two years compiling four thousand pages of background information, he moved up to writer-producer on the morning Olympics broadcast where he had gotten to know Jane Pauley. She recommended him for a job on *Today* when he returned to New York. It took

Zucker a year to get through the door for vacation relief work. He arrived a week before Gumbel's scorching memo became public followed by the Pauley-Norville debacle that sent the program into a tailspin. "I didn't really understand what the hell was going on," he recalled. "I just assumed that this was par for the course. It was an incredibly tumultuous time. And the next two years were obviously as low as it gets. It was difficult to watch and be a part of. It was sad to watch that television institution go through that."

But the discord enabled Zucker to rise quickly through the ranks. He had an innate ability to manage strong-willed talent and developed strong ties with both Gumbel and Couric (he was her producer in Washington and traveled with her to Iraq during Operation Desert Storm). Gumbel believed Zucker had the passion, fortitude, and self-confidence to take some risks with the program. "Bryant basically said to me, 'Look. It's time to reinvent the *Today* show,'" Zucker recalled. "He believed

it needed reinvention. I think that's where, in his heart and in his gut, the memo came from. I think it wasn't meant to be mean-spirited, although it came off that way. That's just the way Bryant writes. And he said to me, 'Look. We should just try new things.' And he said, 'Let's just make mistakes.' And it's why I always believed that it was okay to make a mistake; just don't make the same mistake twice. That came from Bryant, really."

Zucker—whose youthfulness led *Time* to compare him to Miles Silverberg, the baby-faced news producer character on the sitcom *Murphy Brown*—worked hard at bringing an element of unpredictability back to *Today*. He respected the legacy of the program, but was not bound by it. The 1992 presidential campaign became the laboratory where Zucker could truly experiment. President George H. W. Bush looked virtually unbeatable after the success of Operation Desert Storm in 1991. The military action to halt the aggression of Iraqi dictator Saddam Hussein was swift and relatively light on

Katie Couric, Bryant Gumbel, and Gene Shalit celebrating the 40th anniversary of Today *in January 1992.*

casualties. Bush's Democratic opponent, Arkansas Governor Bill Clinton was a charismatic but flawed candidate who outlasted a weak field of opponents in the primaries. The campaign was upended by populist third party candidacy of Texas entrepreneur billionaire Ross Perot, who warned that the federal government's deficit spending was putting a stranglehold on economic growth. Perot, with outsized ears and a twang in his rapid-fire speech, was a compelling and occasionally odd figure. He drove up his standing in the polls by making his case in half-hour infomercials on the networks that he paid for out of his vast personal fortune. At times they drew better ratings than the entertainment shows he pre-empted.

Outside of election nights and debates, presidential politics rarely made exciting television. But Zucker

THE 1992 PRESIDENTIAL CAMPAIGN BECAME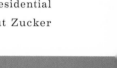

understood the dynamics of the 1992 election were unlike any other, with a breakout renegade character with props (Perot and his budget flip charts), generational and cultural divisions (World War II hero Bush against former pot-smoking Vietnam protestor Clinton), and polarizing feminist politics (Hillary Clinton versus Tammy Wynette). Zucker also knew that the news cycle had become faster. Through its first thirty years on the air, *Today* could set the agenda for the country in its own leisurely fashion. But by 1992 CNN was a serious competitor offering viewers news twenty-four hours a day. The most-watched TV show of the early 1990s was *60 Minutes*, and its success spawned nearly a dozen other news magazine shows across the prime-time schedule. ABC's *Nightline* with Ted Koppel gave viewers the authoritative last word every evening in late night. Outlets such as MTV and daytime talk shows were also giving unconventional platforms to candidates. To stand out, the election coverage on *Today* had to be bold and distinctive. "If I wanted to do a two-

Today viewers spoke to Ross Perot and Bill Clinton during the 1992 presidential race.

1995 — *Senator Bob Packwood of Oregon resigns over charges of sexual harassment.*

hour phone-in, call-in show with Ross Perot, I said, 'We're just going to do it,'" Zucker said. "And people at *Today* would say, 'We don't do that.' And I'd say, 'I don't care.' We had Ross Perot on for two hours—the only guest for two hours. You know, he was originally scheduled to be on for one, and we just decided to keep going." Gumbel loved it. "Jeff Zucker deserves an awful lot of credit for that, " said Gumbel. "He recognized an opportunity early on and was willing to scrap the format in order to do whatever. And so, as a result, we would do an hour with Bill Clinton. I mean, it was unusual and it bought us a degree of attention that got people to look at us."

The campaign provided an unexpected—and defining—moment for Couric. With less than a month left before the election, and President Bush trailing in the

I got work to do," Bush said. But Couric convinced him to stay.

Even though Couric and Zucker had discussed what topics to cover in the event President Bush made an appearance, her head was immersed in the details she needed to do the lengthy segments on the First Lady. "Initially, my career flashed before my eyes," she said, "because I was deeply unprepared to talk with him. I was so focused on Mrs. Bush and all the historical anecdotes and tidbits about life in the White House and, you know, Dolly Madison's tea set, that I really wasn't focused on the possibility that the president might actually stop by. But when I heard Ranger's footsteps on the White House floor, followed by the President of the United States, I thought, *Oh, my God. This is where the rubber hits the road.* I think that's when all my years of reporting really were

BORATORY WHERE ZUCKER COULD TRULY EXPERIMENT.

polls, Couric was scheduled for a live interview with First Lady Barbara Bush and a tour of the White House.

The second hour of the program on October 13, 1992, was set in the Blue Room, where Couric was seated with Barbara Bush while her brown and white springer spaniel, Millie, was sprawled out nearby on the rug, occasionally dozing off. After they wrapped up President Bush unexpectedly entered with the first family's other dog, Ranger. "Look who wandered in—President Bush and Ranger," said Couric. She asked the president if he would stay to answer a few questions. "Listen

helpful. I think Jeff was as surprised as I was. But we always sort of could complete each other's sentences. So I'd run out of questions, he'd say, 'What about this?' And I'd ask a few questions. He'd pop something else in my ear. 'Hey, what about this?' That was one great thing with my relationship with Jeff. I could make an expression, and up in the studio he would know exactly what I was thinking, and what I needed. He was really an incredible safety net for me for those first few years of doing the show, when the nuances and the complexities of doing a live program like this were just something I wasn't familiar with."

The president seemed beguiled by Couric, who smiled as she kept the queries coming like a one-woman press conference.

With Zucker's guidance coming through her earpiece, Couric engaged President Bush—still standing as if he was on his way to a meeting—for more than nineteen minutes. The president seemed beguiled by Couric, who smiled as she kept the queries coming like a one-woman press conference. Looking more relaxed and confident than in any of his debate performances during the campaign, Bush attacked Clinton's character, especially his antiwar activities overseas during the Vietnam era and defended his own position that he was not aware funds were being

good morning on this Thursday but frankly there is nothing good to be said about this last morning of April of 1992," Gumbel said after the program opening that showed a Los Angeles building engulfed in flames. "This one's a tough one."

Gumbel spoke live on the phone with one of the jurors of the mostly white panel that reached the not guilty verdict. "Rodney King was directing the action," the woman said. "He was the one who determined how long it took to put him in handcuffs."

diverted from covert arm sales to Iran to help Contra rebels in Nicaragua. As American politics had moved into the era of packaged candidates and carefully orchestrated campaigns, it was perhaps the last time TV would capture such an unfiltered, impromptu moment in political life, especially with an incumbent president.

"We were on such a high following that interview, because it was completely spontaneous, unexpected, unscripted television," Couric said. "Talk about pulling questions out of your hat. It was intense. But it was great. And it was sort of what live television's all about."

The circus-like atmosphere of the presidential race was almost an entertaining distraction from some of the more disturbing stories *Today* covered in the early 1990s. Perhaps none of them upset Gumbel more than the violence and looting that erupted in the predominantly African-American community of South Central in Los Angeles. It was in response to the acquittal of three of the city's police officers in the beating of Rodney King, despite the notorious videotape that showed him on the ground being pummeled by nightsticks. "We'd like to say

"At what point when he was lying there taking blows do you think he lost control of the action?" Gumbel asked.

Throughout the program, there were the horrific images of the aftermath of the verdict, including motorists being pulled from their vehicles by rioters and beaten senseless on the Los Angeles streets. "It was reminiscent," Gumbel said over the videotape, "of what happened to Rodney King."

Gumbel was even-handed as he reported the story, but it was hard not to see the pain in his eyes that morning. "It took my breath away," he said years later. "It was as close as I came to losing objectivity. None of it came as news to me. Just seeing evidence of how broad the racial divide was, just how intense the passions were. That you could on the one hand see people crying about something, see people beating the hell out of someone else for the same thing. . . . It was just mind-blowing. And I don't think any of us were prepared for the depth of hatred and the expressions of violence."

But later that year Gumbel also saw the realization of a longtime ambition for *Today*. "Africa," he intoned at

"Africa," said Gumbel, "was the only habitable continent we hadn't been to."

1995 — *A budget impasse between Congress and the White House leads to a shutdown of the federal government.*

the start of the program on November 16, 1992. "At once basic and mysterious, it is a continent of contradictions. It is beautiful yet frightening, ancient but modern. It is peaceful yet violent, joyful and pained. It is inviting yet foreboding, barren and bountiful. It is Africa." The program opened each day that week from such visually spectacular locations as Zimbabwe's Hwange National Park and Victoria Falls and presented pieces on preservation of ancient ruins, wildlife, economic development, overpopulation, tourism, and culture in several countries.

only our feelings for what we had done, but also my feelings and hopes for the continent and for the people."

• • •

In January 1994, the future of *Today* settled in behind the news desk when Matt Lauer joined the program, replacing Margaret Larson. He had grown up in the New York suburbs as a viewer of the program, and he set his sights on it as he pursued a degree in broadcast-

The week of *Today* programs in Africa was the result of years of lobbying by Gumbel. "We had been to Asia; we had been to Europe; we had been to North America; we had been to South America; we had been to Australia," he said. "There was only one habitable continent we hadn't been to. And to say, 'Oh, nobody cares' wasn't a good enough answer." Michael Gartner told Gumbel if he could come up with a plan to have it make sense logistically and editorially he would support it. After Gumbel negotiated with diplomats and had the network's finance department crunch the numbers, he was able to get a commitment for the trip.

The profound importance of the week to Gumbel was apparent when he and Couric closed out their Friday broadcast in front of Victoria Falls. Before the credits rolled, Gumbel, his eyes welling up, put up the palm of his right hand in a position familiar to long time *Today* viewers. He used Dave Garroway's sign-off of "Peace."

"It just seemed appropriate," Gumbel recalled. "If I were a smarter man, I would have just shut up, because the picture was so beautiful. But I wasn't that smart. And I was really looking for something just to express not

ing at Ohio University. He almost gave up before he finally arrived.

After Lauer had toiled in a number of local market TV station jobs around the country throughout the 1980s, he landed a spot as a co-host of a sprawling, daily live three-hour talk show called *Nine Broadcast Plaza* for WWOR, named after the location of the station's studios in Secaucus, New Jersey.

"The show was all over the lot," Lauer recalled. "I would have Jesse Jackson for an hour one day, and the next day they would ask me to do an hour on women who fake orgasm. It was very difficult for me, because I was very comfortable with the more serious things, and even some of the celebrity things. I was not at all comfortable, nor cut out for, the tabloidy, in my opinion, trashy side of things. It just didn't fit with me. I was uncomfortable. I think the viewers knew I was uncomfortable. And I do remember one time the producers did come to me and they said that they had this great brainstorm, and they were going to kind of do a throwback to early television, where I, as the host, would be doing live commercials on the air. The way I took it was, they would expect me to

FIRST
SHOW
1994

· MATT ·
LAUER

Present

M **ATT LAUER HAD A MOMENT OF RECKONING** on January 3, 1997, as he sat in Studio 1A during Bryant Gumbel's final *Today* broadcast. The following Monday he would be in the co-anchor chair next to Katie Couric. Even though he had filled in for Gumbel more than 150 times over the previous few years, the prospect was daunting. "I remember watching the retrospective tapes of Bryant's run," he recalled. "I'm thinking, *How am I going to do this? My God, I've done nothing. How am I going to fill these shoes*?"

Lauer had toiled in local TV without much success for a dozen years before he got the call to work at WNBC. Throughout that time he studied Gumbel on screen and later on the *Today* set. "For those fifteen years, when I was trying to be the best I could be at what I was doing, and trying to figure out what it was exactly, or where it was I wanted to go, there was this guy, Bryant Gumbel, just starting on *Today*," Lauer recalled. "And then I watched him as he went through. Bryant was extremely comfortable in his own skin. It was clear that he was wildly prepared. And then, fast-forward, as I started to even work on the fringes of the show, filling in for the news desk and for Bryant, it was that preparation that still kind of connected me to Bryant. I still saw it up close. While a lot of the others were kind of goofing around in between commercial breaks, Bryant was always glancing down at what was coming up next. He always knew where the show was going."

Lauer successfully modeled his own work ethic after Gumbel's. But his pairing with Couric brought a distinctive change in tone to *Today* as well. The assertive personalities of Gumbel and Couric created a compelling sense of tension in their last year together on the program. "I think it was a little more uneasy toward the end, between Bryant and Katie," Lauer said. "I'm not sure how I would describe it, other than maybe it was interesting to the viewers because you were sometimes watching and it was, 'How's this going to go?'"

Lauer's approach with Couric was more laid-back and playful. Even as they volleyed mildly sarcastic barbs at each other, viewers could tell they got along well. "I think you always knew that at the end of the show, we were going to have a good time and kiss and walk away," he said. "It's the reason I got the job, when it comes right down to it."

The Couric-Lauer dynamic could be brother-sister, boyfriend-girlfriend, or husband-wife. There was edginess to their banter, even a bit of naughtiness. But they never crossed the line in a way that would have made some viewers uncomfortable. "It was flirtatious but it wasn't inappropriate," said Couric. "You never felt icky. It was friends who were never going to be

NO ONE WAS PRETENDING TO BE AN ANCHOR ON THE TELEVISIO

more than friends but found each other attractive. At least he found me attractive—I'm kidding. He's really quick and clever—sometimes quicker and more clever than I am, which annoys me because I'm very competitive. He has this great touch. He kind of always knows the right thing to say."

Lauer said the relationship with Couric was the same off the air as it was on. That helped, as viewers had become more sophisticated about television and celebrities. Authenticity mattered more than ever. "I think it's one of the keys to the *Today* show over the last twenty-five years, in a way that the other shows never really figured out," said Jeff Zucker. "Bryant was who he was; Katie was who she was; Matt was who he was. Nobody was pretending to be an anchor on television and I think that that came through, loud and clear. And I think that that was so different than anything you saw on the other shows. I think that was one of the secrets to the success of the last twenty-five years."

Viewers fully embraced the Lauer-Couric team like no other in *Today* history, as the program, already back in first place at the end of Gumbel's tenure, became a dominant leader again. Lauer was named "sexiest anchor" by *People* in 1997. That didn't hurt, but what made viewers like him even more is that he came off as a decent, funny, self-deprecating guy who didn't seem the type to take such an honor seriously. Even after his career took off, he still bought his clothes at the same retail shop in Greenwich, Connecticut, where he once worked.

ND I THINK THAT CAME THROUGH LOUD AND CLEAR.

Lauer never took his stardom for granted. His parents divorced as a child and he grew up as a not-so-rich kid in a rich town. He said he did not possess the discipline to be a great student. Yet he eventually mastered one of the most rigorous daily routines in all of television. Making it to the anchor chair on *Today* was more than reaching a career pinnacle. "This was part of my family tradition," he said. "When I grew up, there were all the greats of the *Today* show before I'd go to school every morning and I watched them all—Hugh Downs, Frank McGee and Barbara Walters, and all these other people at various stages of my life—they were on in my home every morning. So to even consider the fact that I would get to sit in that chair and a different generation of viewer would one day say, 'Oh yeah I remember that guy Matt Lauer in my living room' was mind boggling." Lauer will always remember the moment when he was told he got the job. The news had come in time to tell his father, who was terminally ill with lung cancer. "They had been talking to me for a while," he said. "And it was just a question of it becoming formal. But I remember when I finally got off the phone—I was on vacation, and we kind of settled the deal and dotted the *I*'s and crossed the *T*'s. It was official, and a date was handed to me. I remember hanging up the phone and just waiting long enough to get a dial tone, and calling him. It was one of those great father-son phone calls that is almost difficult to describe."

interview Mario Cuomo for a half an hour, then go to commercial. The first commercial would be whatever tape they rolled. Then we'd come back in the studio and I'd be sitting on a bed; and I'd do a live commercial for Dial-A-Mattress." Lauer did not have a background as a journalist, but he knew he did not want to be pitching products on local TV.

"I just couldn't believe it," he said. "I just said, 'You've got to be kidding me.' I said I would not do that. And, as it turned out, about three months later, my contract was not renewed."

Lauer remained unemployed for the next eighteen months. He had to move out of his Manhattan apartment and rent a small cottage in North Salem, New York, a town in upper Westchester County.

"I lived there with my dog and watched my bank account dwindle, because the phone simply wasn't ringing," he said. "And when it did ring, it was ringing with the types of things that I knew would not bode well for my future: game show offers, infomercials. And although it was hard because I needed the money, I chose not to do them. It came down to a week where I literally had just looked in my checkbook. I had less in the checking account than I needed to pay the rent that was due in about ten days. I was in pretty desperate straits. I took my dog, put him in the car, and I drove to get coffee that morning. And I passed a tree service truck on the side of the road that was parked right in my neighborhood. It had a sign in the back window that said, 'Help wanted,' and a phone number. I jotted it down, and I called from my car phone, right there. I left a message on their machine, and said, 'I'm willing, ready, and able,' and left my number. Later that afternoon, I'm sitting there and the phone rings. It was the first phone call since I had left my number. I figured it was the tree trimming service. I kind of put my best deep, outdoorsy voice on. As it turned out, it was the assistant for the general manager of WNBC in New York.

She said, 'Would you talk to Bill Bolster?' And he got on the phone. He said, 'I saw your tape about a year ago. I've always wanted to call you. I have an opening. Will you meet me at 21 for dinner tonight?' I said I had to check my schedule, which was wide open. I drove in. We had a great meeting and I was hired, basically, that night."

In 1991, Lauer became co-anchor of *Today in New York*, the early morning local news program that preceded *Today*. Part of the job was doing daily "teases" with Gumbel and Couric previewing what was ahead on the network program. "I guess they kind of liked the fact that Bryant and Katie and I had a pretty good on-air buzz," he said. "We seemed to relate well to each other. It was very casual and freewheeling. There was a lot of give and take."

After ten months on the air at WNBC, Lauer received a call about subbing for Gumbel on *Today*. "I immediately thought it was one of my buddies playing a joke on me," he said. "As it turned out, it was Jeff Zucker. And I immediately said yes . . . and then the panic began. I had like four or five days to think about what I said I would do. And I filled in the next week."

He was more than ready as he had done hundreds of hours of live unscripted television. "On *Nine Broadcast Plaza* I was forced to sit there, really just ad-libbing and winging it for thirty, forty minutes at a time, with newsmakers, politicians, and other people, and I always felt very comfortable in that setting," he said. "Filling in for Bryant was certainly a step up into the big leagues. I felt comfortable with the interviewing part. I was a little uncomfortable with being thrust into that bright a spotlight. But Katie, because of the good relationship we had, even back then, made it easy for me. And Jeff Zucker produced it in a way that it was easy for me. It really was not a shock to the system."

The tabloid culture that was a major part of daytime television by the 1990s (and which Lauer was trying to

Tom Brokaw, Katie Couric, Bryant Gumbel, and Matt Lauer unveiled Studio 1A on June 20, 1994.

escape) was seeping into network news. Cameras in the courtroom had turned murder trials—once reported with artist sketches—into ongoing televised sagas. Nothing had ever transfixed American viewers as the trial of O. J. Simpson for the brutal murder of his wife, Nicole, and her friend Ronald Goldman on June 12, 1994. Over the next sixteen months that followed, live continuous coverage on the broadcast networks and cable gave viewers the opportunity to experience the case in real time—from the day of Simpson's arrest at his Brentwood home, through the moment

The future of Today *settled in behind the news desk when Matt Lauer joined the program.*

in the Los Angeles courtroom when he tried on the bloody glove found at the crime scene, to the dramatic not guilty verdict that divided the nation along racial lines.

"Sometimes you'd feel like you'd want to take a shower right afterward," Gumbel said. "But people were so caught up in it." Making the story even more bizarre for Gumbel was his longtime friendship with Simpson, who had been an announcer for NBC Sports. "We played golf together, we had dinner together, we traveled together," he said. "It was a strange time."

Jeff Zucker's rescue effort at *Today* put him on a fast track at NBC. He left the program in 1993 to produce a prime-time news magazine for Katie Couric and Tom Brokaw. The reins were turned over to Steve Friedman, who had been in charge during the program's extraordinary run in the 1980s. The revenues and profits at *Today* had multiplied while Friedman was at the helm (so much so that he asked for a piece of the program, an idea that NBC rejected). Friedman had returned to the NBC News family and back to *Today* with a plan that would be the foundation of the program's success for years to come.

Friedman always admired Pat Weaver's original vision for *Today* as a video newspaper that could take viewers anywhere and to anything that was happening. That happened with the advancements in satellite technology, which *Today* fully embraced in the 1980s. Friedman also believed that the street-level studio of the 1950s—"the window on the world" as Weaver called it—made *Today* accessible to the viewers and was an idea worth trying again.

Since moving out of the Florida Showcase in 1965, *Today* originated in windowless and often sterile looking studios submerged in the RCA Building at Rockefeller Center. There had been talk of returning *Today* to a street-level location over the years, but there was little corporate will by NBC to take on the expense. Plus, any innocence that New York City had during the 1950s and 1960s was long gone by the 1970s. During that decade, bomb-sniffing dogs were routinely led around the *Today* studio before the program in response to threats that were called in. The world seemed a much less stable place for a live program to be exposed to random people on a New York street than it was in the days of Dave Garroway and Hugh Downs.

But when *Today* traveled to cities across America during its many trips during the second half of the 1980s, there was an intensity among the fans of the program that could not be measured by Nielsen ratings. "If we stopped in Jackson, Mississippi, I understood people were going to be out there to see Bryant, Jane, Willard, and Mike Leonard, and whatever," Friedman said. "I got that. But all through the routes, as we're going through these small towns, they would find out when the train was coming through and a hundred people would be at the crossing with signs, just waving at the train. And I said, 'You know what? Here's what we've got to do. We've got to get these people to come to New York to watch the show.'"

NBC brass said no when Friedman raised the idea of a street-level studio in the mid 1980s and when Gumbel mentioned it again in 1989. By 1993, New York was coming back as a tourist destination. Friedman asked that NBC at least strongly consider the studio idea if he returned to the program as executive producer. To his surprise, he received that commitment and the strong backing of the new NBC News president Andrew Lack.

Friedman knew the studio would be a distinctive home for *Today* that the morning competition on ABC and CBS could not easily replicate. "The fact of the matter is the other two shows have copied what *Today* has been doing for the last ten years," he said during the lead up to the studio's launch. "They can copy our interview with Lloyd Bentsen; they can't copy our location." Never afraid to make bold predictions, he added, "As years go by, *Today* will dominate morning television like it did again in the '50s, '60s, and '70s and did in the late '80s." He would eventually be proven right.

The three-story, eighteen-thousand-square-foot studio was built on the corner of East Forty-Ninth Street and Rockefeller Plaza in a structure formerly occupied by a bank. A giant steel girder that ran through the middle of the building had to be removed to open up enough space for sets and equipment. Surrounded by Art Deco buildings, the studio offered views of the nearby skating rink, the Channel Gardens, and the mid-

in 1965. President Clinton was the first guest, interviewed via satellite from the Oval Office. After Gumbel and Couric finished their exchange with the president, several people outside were given an opportunity to step up to video kiosks that were set up on the plaza and ask their own questions. The second one came from a woman who said she had graduated with First Lady Hillary Clinton from Maine South High School in Park Ridge, Illinois, in 1965. How about a thirtieth high school reunion at the White House? President Clinton replied he was planning on holding his reunion there and would pass the suggestion along to Mrs. Clinton.

"I knew right then and there that this thing was really going to take off," Friedman said.

The *Today* talent had to adjust to the plaza over time. "I was slightly trepidatious, honestly, only because it was such a new concept—an old concept, but such a concept that was new to me," said Couric. "And I remember thinking, *Oh, God. What if people misbehave and are rowdy, or do things that are not appropriate?* So I was nervous, initially. And my husband, at the time, I think, was

"THE WINDOW ON THE WORLD" AS WEAVER CALLE

town Manhattan skyline. The city-block-long plaza provided ample room for pedestrians, devoted fans, and tourists to gather and connect with the program in person while friends and family watched back home.

Studio 1A, as it was christened, went live on the morning of June 20, 1994. The crowd that showed up was subdued and the *Today* team looked tentative as they were still getting a sense of the new surroundings. "It was like flying to the moon for the first time," said Friedman. "Nobody knew how to react or how to get in and out of things, or how free the technical people were going to be." But overall the program went smoothly with visits from former New York Mayor Ed Koch, who brought bagels, Tom Brokaw, and even Barbara Walters, who reminisced about becoming a *Today* panelist when the program originated from the last windowed studio

nervous, too. But I quickly realized that it's a wonderful opportunity for people to show up and be in the action, and have a good time. It was a brilliant idea."

Gumbel had his own reservations. When he finished his work on *Today*, he often left the studio wearing a hat and attempted to walk the streets of Manhattan unrecognized. Heading into a throng of sign-holding fans every morning was simply not in his nature. "The spontaneity of it was less of a problem for me than the fact that—and people think I'm lying when I say it, but people who know me will tell you—I may be as shy as any person who has ever been on television," said Gumbel. "And that shyness is accentuated when people want to make a big deal about who I am or what I do. I'm not comfortable with it. I never, ever, ever have been. I don't like being noticed. I don't like being singled out. I don't

— MADE *TODAY* ACCESSIBLE TO THE VIEWERS.

like being made a big deal of. I'm just not good at it. So it wasn't the spontaneity that was the problem. Coming out and going, 'Hey, everybody!' That's not me. I mean, I'm the guy at the party who is always in the corner; and I'm the guy in the restaurant who has always got his back to the crowd."

But Gumbel was a pro as he welcomed the people who turned out every day with signs that said hi to the folks back home—just as they did in the program's early days. "Like everything else, once he saw it was good for him, he was great at it," said Friedman. "They got more and more comfortable as they did it. And as they got more successful, they got more comfortable."

● ● ●

After more than a dozen years on *Today*, Gumbel maintained his meticulous approach to the program. Steve Capus was a supervising producer on *Today* (and on his way to becoming president of NBC News) during the mid 1990s. He remembered how Gumbel arrived at the studio with scripts that he had either rewritten the night before or filled with notes and questions. "I would write the cold open for *Today* and then hold my breath and wait to see what Bryant thought of it," Capus recalled. "One morning he said to me 'I'd like to think you're still drunk after last night.' Or it was 'What in the world was this?' He could be tough. But I loved working with Bryant. He was an amazing talent to watch. We always used to sit there and watch the body language. If he was engaged he'd be leaning on

"I think the plaza was a stroke of genius," said Couric.

I **F THE PLAZA OUTSIDE OF** *TODAY* were a city, Al Roker would be its mayor. It's a role that Al Roker was elected to by default. In the early years of Studio 1A, the simplest way to put the plaza to use was to go outside and talk to the crowd. "It just kind of became my thing," Roker said. "It's not unlike what I would do when I was doing local news. They'd send me out on remotes all the time, to local fairs and things like that. You always talk to the crowd. So this was no different. The difference is, people weren't from Lodi, New Jersey, or from Levittown, doing a local fair there. They were coming here, and they were from all over the country."

Roker remembered how the plaza was greeted with skepticism at first. "The critics were saying, 'Nobody's going to stand outside a window. People are too sophisticated—they have home video cameras, they don't need this,'" Roker said. "Yet everyday, people stand and they want to wave and they want to be seen back home. It's the original interactive TV. In the very beginning, if the weather was just a little bit inclement, nobody showed up. But now, sometimes we have to tell people to go home because they're standing out in either a dangerous lightning storm, or it's brutally cold. The plaza gives us an immediacy that allows us to really show it firsthand—not just point a camera out the window, but to actually be out in it." When major winter storms paralyzed the Northeast in the 1990s, there was no better way for Roker to report the story than walk up a mountain of snow piled high outside of the studio.

Roker possessed a lightning quick wit (he once described himself as being "a black Don Rickles" during his high school years) that was ideally suited for any unexpected situation in the days when the plaza was uncharted territory. "There was a guy who had a sign that he was in love with this girl—her name was Jill. Would she marry him? And so I went up to him," Roker recalled. "And Jeff Zucker said in my ear, 'Don't do it.' But I didn't listen to him. I said 'So, you want to marry Jill?' And this is live. And the guy says, 'Well, I love Jill, but I love Jeff more' and turns to the guy next to him and just gives him a big, open-mouthed kiss. I just kind of let it finish, and I said, 'See? They won't even show that on *Will & Grace*.'" (The sitcom later based an episode on the incident, with Al Roker playing himself.)

Performing on camera was not part of Al Roker's original plan when he was a radio and TV major at the State University of New York at Oswego in the early 1970s. His goal was to produce or direct in television—until the school's department chairman told him that a Syracuse station was paying ten dollars a newscast for part-time on-air work. "I got a weekend

weather job at the end of my sophomore year in college, and never looked back," he said. After graduating in 1976, he headed to Washington where he did weather forecasts for WTTG. Not long after he started, he received a phone call from Willard Scott, then a local market legend working at WRC.

"Is this Al Roker?" asked Scott.

"Yeah," said Roker.

"Come on. I'm outside. Let's go to dinner."

Roker got into Scott's Cadillac and they drove to a restaurant. "I watched everybody and their brother come up and say hello to Willard," he said. Scott immediately became a mentor to Roker.

"The two best bits of advice Willard gave me were, 'Always be yourself. Because that, at the end of the day, is all you got. They can do whatever they want to you but as long as you are yourself, you've always got that.' The other was, 'Never give up your day job.' Willard was one of the original multitaskers. While he was doing weather at WRC, he also did radio. He had a farm in Belle Plaine, Virginia. On weekends, he threw birthday parties for people. You know, he did it all. And I've always remembered that. And I can honestly say I would not be here doing what I'm doing if it wasn't for Willard. He is like my second father. I love him."

HE INSTANTLY BECAME A FAVORITE FOR HIS RELAXED AMIABILITY.

Scott went to *Today* in 1980 and Roker followed him to New York (his hometown where his father drove a city bus) to work at WNBC. He instantly became a favorite for his relaxed amiability. The "What Is Cool?" issue of *Entertainment Weekly* named Roker its "Cool Ordinary Guy."

Roker became Scott's regular fill-in on *Today* and took over as the full-time weather forecaster in January 1996. "I would have to say, to a certain extent, I patterned myself after Willard," said Roker. "And then to work with him, and to eventually fill in for him, was just a dream come true. I couldn't believe it." Roker also followed Scott's advice about diversification. Once daily exposure on *Today* raised his profile, he wrote books and formed his own TV production company.

As one of six children growing up in Queens, Roker spent many mornings in front of the television watching cartoons. Animation became a lifelong obsession. "My wife says I would probably give up everything I own to find a portal to Toontown," he said. In one of his early report pieces for *Today*, Roker went out to Los Angeles to chronicle the making of an animated *Superman* episode that featured him in a cameo. Not long after that passion was recognized, Roker received a call from the wife of *Peanuts* comic strip creator Charles Schulz. He was dying of cancer and she wanted his final interview to be with Roker.

the edge of his seat and not sitting back. If he was sitting back, you'd know Bryant wasn't liking the answers he was getting."

"He was unpredictable," Matt Lauer recalled. "You never knew when Bryant was going to absolutely kill someone with kindness or get caught off guard in a kind of goofy, funny moment, and he almost looked uncomfortable. Then there were the moments where Bryant just went after someone like a pit bull. And it was riveting. You'd stop and you'd go, 'Did he just say that?'"

While Gumbel was still at the top of his game, he decided to

and I had been close, almost since the day he started," Gumbel said. "And he and I would have dinner together. He'd always have Christmas dinner and Thanksgiving dinner at my house. We'd go on golf vacations together. We were just very, very close; we always have been. I was always confident that Matt would do well, because he's a bright guy, and he's easy and relaxed, and he's willing to work."

Gumbel did his final program on January, 3, 1997. His departure signaled a new era for the program—one that belonged to Couric. It was recognized as Couric and Lauer had equal billing as co-anchors—only Barbara

"I THINK OF MATT AS THE **JAMES BOND** OF OU

make 1996 his final year on *Today*. "I never wanted to stay on longer than was healthy for either the show or the audience or me," he said. "And when I signed the last contract, I remember thinking, 'You know what? Fifteen years has a nice ring to it. All these other times, you've talked about walking away; maybe it's time to force yourself to do it.' And so when we signed the contract, we said, 'This is the last one. It's over. This will be the last year. And that will be it.' And I'd be lying if I said during that year I didn't start having some regrets, on certain days, about having said that. But having said it, I still felt confident that it was the right decision. For the sake of the audience, and for the sake of the show, it should be changed every now and then. It should be changed, no matter how facile, or how effective, or how good anyone might be. It's good that it changes. I just think that's necessary."

Gumbel said no one at NBC ever asked him who his successor should be. But it was easier for him to walk away from *Today* knowing that it was Matt Lauer. "Matt

Walters and Jim Hartz had a similar arrangement during their two-year tenure together in the mid-1970s. Gumbel had opened the program every day. Under the new team, Couric opened it three times a week, with Lauer handling the other two.

It meant a lot to Couric. "One of the most important accomplishments for me was to make women seen as equal partners," she said. "There are a lot of subtleties about the show. I was very pleased when people at NBC decided to make sure that the woman co-anchor was an equal partner with the man. And I think that was really ushered in when Matt came."

"These were symbolic things, but they were important," added Zucker, who returned to produce *Today* in 1994. "And I think this was the evolution of society. I think it was the evolution of the show. And it was the evolution of the relationship from Bryant and Katie to Katie and Matt."

By 1996, Al Roker had regularly relieved Willard Scott, and took over his role as resident funnyman and

"This had always been my dream job," said Matt Lauer.

OADCAST. HE IS SO GOOD AT EVERYTHING." — *Ann Curry*

weather forecaster, but was more contemporary and not quite as folksy. (Scott still appeared regularly with his centenarian birthday greetings.) Roker was another familiar face to the audience. As NBC News had learned, the transitions on *Today* needed to be handled with care. "Bryant to Matt: they were incredibly good friends. Willard to Al: Willard was Al's hero and mentor," said Zucker. "And so it was a very warm relationship. Al, who looked very different at the time when he came on (Roker weighed 320 pounds before having gastric bypass surgery), was the jolly weatherman, and had a great sense of humor, and was so quick. When you see Matt and Katie and Al, in particular: how quick they were, with their minds—they were all great live broadcasters." Rounding out the new team in 1997 was Ann Curry, the anchor on the early morning program *NBC News Sunrise* who had frequently filled in at the news desk for Lauer. "The audience liked her," Zucker said. "She had a very warm sensibility. She had a very engaging personality. She was beautiful. And so she worked as well."

It was a reinvention of the morning program family formula—four cohorts close in age (all in their early forties), with shared experiences in pop culture (they grew up with the same TV shows and hit songs that had been served up by the networks and Top 40 radio when they were at the peak of their influence) and family life (they all had young children). They were all serious about delivering news and information but felt free to show their personal side and a sense of fun. "Al and Ann had big personalities, and I wanted to make it an ensemble show that really played off all of their personalities," Zucker said. "Katie and Matt were the stars of the show, but we worked hard to make it a family, and to make them all integral parts of the show. And I think that that ended up paying off. They were youthful. They all had a sense of humor. They all could play. And they all got along."

The other element was the studio on the plaza. Zucker called it the Fifth Beatle. "I wanted to take advantage of it and use it as a real differentiator," he said. With the proliferation of channels and choices, TV

C *ARPE DIEM.* **THE WORDS WERE** on the last letter that Ann Curry received from her brother, Gordon. Curry first noticed it after learning the horrible news that he was gone. A twenty-three- year-old medical technician in the Air Force, he died in a vehicle accident during a transport mission to Wiesbaden Medical Center in Germany. He had hoped one day to become a doctor. "Seize the day is what carpe diem means," Curry said. "That sort of set the tone for the rest of my life. Don't regret. This is not a dress rehearsal, as they say. And don't be afraid of things that, in the end, really are not going to get you. Fear is what gets you; it's not living boldly."

It was 1983 and Curry was twenty-seven years old at the time, working as a TV reporter in Portland, Oregon, near her family home. Soon afterward, an offer for a reporting job came from KCBS in Los Angeles. Her father, a retired military officer, and mother, a Japanese immigrant, didn't want her to go.

"They were so upset, and so afraid," she recalled. "They were afraid of losing another child. Finally, I told my father, 'Dad, look. If I stay, a part of me is going to die. And so you have to decide what you think. But I think I need to run toward life, arms open—watching that I don't fall, but arms open.' And I remember he paused, and he stifled a tear, and he said, 'I think you're right.' And I haven't stopped running since."

From that point forward, Curry was drawn to stories of service and sacrifice. After she took a job at WMAQ in Chicago, she covered the first Iraq war from the home front. "I remember seeing a farmer who was a National Guardsman get up one morning and leave his crops that were now ripening on the vine, kiss his wife and his children good-bye, and drive away—knowing that his entire year's salary was going to go down the drain because he could not harvest his crop," she said. "And then to hear the sound of all of these huge turbines come toward his farm. Americans came—his neighbors—to harvest his crop, so his family would eat. That was a great story, I thought. That was a great moment for me."

Her work in Chicago earned a promotion to the anchor chair at *NBC News at Sunrise* in 1994. "My first real anchoring job, ever in my life," she said. "And I pretty much sucked at it. But for some reason the numbers went up. So, there you go. People liked it at that hour, to watch somebody suffer."

But the role put her in the early morning proximity of *Today*, where she handled the news-reading duties when Matt Lauer substituted for Bryant Gumbel at the anchor desk. She was

embraced again. "When I first came to fill in, I decided to stay back and just do my job, and not sort of intrude on the space of those who were actually on the broadcast," she said. "I was just the fill-in chick, as I thought of it. And Matt looked at me and said, 'Why are you standing back over there?' I said, 'Well, I'm just filling in.' He goes, 'No you're not. You're one of us.' And he put his arm around me and had me come stand up with the rest of everyone else."

Curry smoothly moved into Lauer's role after he was named co-anchor in 1997. "I never imagined there would be a place for me," Curry said. "I remember saying, 'God somebody pinch me.'" Growing up in a military family that moved around the country, watching *Today* was a comforting constant in her life. She read Barbara Walters's book about interviewing, *How to Talk with Practically Anybody about Practically Anything*. She studied Bryant Gumbel and Jane Pauley. "I learned a lot watching Bryant," she said. "His questions were studied and smart and curious and on target."

After her first two years on the program, Curry developed a deep interest in the reports on ethnic cleansing happening in Bosnia and Kosovo. "I remember being upset by what had happened—women being raped; men being killed because of their ethnicity—to move them off of the land," she recalled. "I went into Jeff Zucker's office and told him that we, as a news program, had to cover this story in a big way. And within a few days I was on a plane—me. I didn't expect to be sent myself. I was on a plane, and I was heading into Kosovo."

CURRY PURSUED ASSIGNMENTS THAT REQUIRED COURAGE AND HEART.

Curry, her cameraman, and her producer entered a refugee camp on the border of Macedonia, sneaking past rifle-wielding police and soldiers who were keeping journalists out.

"This program put on more than a week of stories about this ethnic cleansing going on in Kosovo, every single morning," she said. "And do you know what? The next week, one of our competitors did the same thing. And the following week the other competitor did the same thing. And I love being a part of that. Because, you know, *Today* does a lot of lightweight stuff—cooking and fashion and how to raise your kids stuff—which is all important for many different reasons. But it felt good to see what this program can do on a serious story—to have this program step up and start a wave of coverage that occurred all across the airwaves in America, and caused people to talk about it and care about it in a deeper way. . . . This program helped do that."

From that point forward, Curry pursued assignments that required courage and heart. She made global humanitarian issues her specialty—traveling around the world to bring attention to the suffering caused by war, genocide, or natural disasters. Her approach has always been intense, caring, and earnest. She developed the ability to present the difficult stories with honesty but not a hint of cynicism, no matter how hopeless the scene around her appears. "She wears her heart on her sleeve," said Lauer. "She reaches out to so many people. And I think the warmth she exudes has been one of the great things in the history of this show."

programs needed to be more distinctive to break into the public's consciousness. Zucker used the plaza outside Studio 1A to make *Today* an event every day with various stunts in front of the crowds, which got larger and louder over the years. He initiated live music concerts every Friday during the summer. Viewers voted on engaged couples seeking to have their weddings on the program. The winners were joined together in matrimony in front of family and friends on the plaza with Couric and Lauer delivering a fact-filled commentary worthy

of a royal couple. Halloween became an annual giant party with a costume contest. The *Today* cast members tried to top themselves year after year with often hilarious costumes and spectacular entrances—the greatest being Couric flying into the plaza on a guy wire as Peter Pan (as a child she had loved the musical NBC production of *Peter Pan* that starred Mary Martin). A laughing Lauer (dressed as swinging sixties secret agent Austin Powers) went limp and fell to the ground when he saw her.

"We had really talented people putting those costumes together," Couric recalled. "They were

I was very pleased when people at NBC decided to make sure that the woman co-anchor was an equal partner with the man.

all beautifully done. One of my favorite years was when I was Dorothy, and I was surrounded by Richard Simmons lookalikes. And that was sort of just so, so strange, but hilarious."

Zucker believed in integrating the personal lives of the cast into the program. "It was a big change from the way the show had been done previously," he said. "And I think that's the way society evolved at the time. It was the advent of all these magazines on newsstands that told us about your favorite TV star and celebrities. We were in an era where people wanted to know more about the people they were spending time with. I thought those were the people who were really watching the show, and they wanted to know that you were going through the same issues that we were going through."

All of the cast members suffered personal losses in the years that ensued, but the one that was most public was the death of Jay Monahan—Couric's husband since 1989 and the father of her two daughters. An attorney from Virginia, Monahan was working as an on-air legal analyst covering the O. J. Simpson civil trial for cable network MSNBC in 1996 when he started to feel fatigued. It lasted for months into the following year until a bout with severe abdominal pain sent him to a doctor. He learned he had advanced colon cancer that had spread to his liver. He was forty-two years old when he died on January 24, 1998.

Couric was off the air for more than a month. When she returned to the program, she wore her husband's wedding band on a gold necklace. She addressed viewers directly at the start of her first day back, thanking them for their outpouring of support and contributions to the National Cancer Institute in her husband's memory. "Jeff Zucker, who was such a close friend of mine was very sensitive, because he had gone through colon cancer and, thank goodness, survived," she said. "He understood, I think, better than most people, what I was going through. And he had me tape the beginning of the show that day because it was so questionable how I was going to be able to handle it. And it was really hard."

The support of the viewers helped sustain Couric. "It was a surreal bonding experience with people who were watching," she recalled. "When Jay died, I had

Katie Couric with husband Jay Monahan in 1995.

boxes upon boxes of letters. The condolences came from celebrities such as John F. Kennedy Jr. and grandmothers from Peducah. And I really did feel the collective embrace of people who were at home, watching. Something that I had learned from the experience is that dealing with an illness, terminal or otherwise, is a very isolating feeling. You really do feel like the rest of the world is going on, and they're laughing and having lunch and pushing baby strollers without a care in the world. You feel like you're *here* and the rest of the world is in such a better place. And I wanted to really reach out to other people who were feeling the same way I had been feeling since Jay was diagnosed, to say that I learned how much suffering does go on, with so many people, 24/7. But I wanted them to know that I knew they were out there and that I understood."

MATT LAUER

INTERVIEW WITH HILLARY CLINTON

JANUARY 27, 1998

THIS VAST RIGHT-WING CONSPIRACY has been conspiring against my husband since the day he announced he was running for president," Hillary Clinton told Matt Lauer on January 27, 1998.

It was a headline-making powerful defense by the first lady to counter charges that had rocked the nation six days before. Kenneth Starr, the independent counsel, was investigating allegations that President Clinton pressured Monica Lewinsky, a twenty-four-year-old White House intern, to lie about whether she had an affair with the president.

It was remarkable that Hillary Clinton showed up on *Today* at all that day. The interview, intended to be a discussion about childcare, had long been scheduled with Katie Couric. But Couric was off dealing with her ailing husband that month and Lauer returned from his vacation to find he would be handling the interview. Once the scandal that linked the president to Lewinsky hit the front pages, it was assumed that Mrs. Clinton would cancel. "To her great credit, she did not," Lauer recalled. "And it was one of those things that, as

the interview came closer, and we realized she was going to show up, we realized it was going to be somewhat monumental."

Before the appearance, Lauer spent an entire day prepping with Executive Producer Jeff Zucker, which was highly unusual. "Even if it's the president, it wouldn't be like that," he said. The next morning, as the car taking him to the studio came down to West Forty-Ninth Street, Lauer's driver asked, "What's going on here?" Lauer looked up and saw TV satellite trucks all around Studio 1A. "As I got out of the car, there was a little bit of a hum," he said. "And people pointing and saying things. I got upstairs and I turned my television on. And the news came on at 5:00 a.m. And the lead story was, 'Today is the day we hear from Hillary Clinton. She's scheduled to appear live in two hours with Matt Lauer on the *Today* show.' I flipped the channel, and the other station was doing the same thing."

Lauer said he believed the success or failure of the interview would be judged on whether he could strike the right tone. "There was no way we were going to shy away from certain questions," he said. "But there was also no way that we were going to beat her over the head with certain questions."

Lauer talked to Hillary Clinton for twenty minutes. He asked what the exact nature of the relationship between Lewinsky and her husband was. She refused to comment on any specific allegations. Lauer was persistent, but Mrs. Clinton remained calm and steady, keeping her indignation focused on her husband's political enemies.

"It was extraordinary to me that she sat through it," Lauer said. "Extraordinary. Some of her answers became so poignant and were played so many times over the course of the next many years. It was also a difficult interview because of the delicacy of the subject. We had the first lady of the United States, who commands a certain amount of respect, naturally. But we also had, if the stories were true, a woman who was the victim of adultery. And so you have to treat that with kid gloves. It was a difficult tightrope to walk."

COLUMBINE MASSACRE

APRIL 20, 1999

G **UN VIOLENCE IN AMERICA** was a story that led *Today* often during the 1990s. At the end of the decade, Matt Lauer told a journalist it was the one story he wished he could offer an opinion on. "People at cocktail parties now talk about their personal safety," he said. "There's something really wrong here." The pain from the loss that resulted from senseless killing rarely came through with more intensity than on April 22, 1999, when *Today* reported on the aftermath of the shooting massacre at Columbine High School in Littleton, Colorado. Two teenagers

 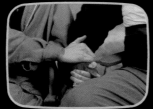   

had taken the lives of a dozen students and one teacher in the suburban Denver school. Katie Couric went to the scene and sat with the father of Isaiah Shoels, an African-American student who was killed. Michael Shoels's son was targeted by the killers for the color of his skin. Sitting at his right during the interview was Columbine High School student Craig Scott who witnessed the killing of Isaiah in the school library. He escaped injury, but lost his sister, who was shot and killed in another part of the building. Scott described what happened as Shoels wept. Couric took Shoels's left hand while Scott reached out and clasped his right one. Executive Producer Jeff Zucker kept the camera on the sorrowful tableau and just let them talk. He ignored the commercial break for local stations. ("We're staying here, and I don't care," he said in the control room.) "Jeff instinctively understood how powerful that moment was," Couric recalled. "From the scene of the falling snow to this white, blond kid who had lost his sister, Rachel, to this kind of burly African-American father. I think visu-ally it was very powerful. Jeff knew that, 'wow, this is more than television we're watching.' This is a profound moment in time, where the pain of these two people was just so, so raw, and so exposed. And Jeff had the good sense, and that sort of intangible knowingness to let it run." Said Lauer, "It was one of those interviews where within the studio, the world stopped."

WHERE IN THE WORLD IS MATT LAUER?

IN THE 1990S, IT WAS NEARLY IMPOSSIBLE for parents to escape the infectious theme song of the PBS series *Where in the World Is Carmen Sandiego?* Based on a series of computer games, video games, and books, the children's game show was a popular tool for teaching children geography and history.

Executive Producer Jeff Zucker, who had a knack for appropriating whatever was hot in pop culture for *Today*, and his second-in-command Michael Bass, were inspired by *Carmen Sandiego* to attempt a new travel stunt for the program in 1998. "I liked the theme song," Zucker recalled. "So I said, 'Well, why don't we just do *Where in the World is Matt Lauer?* and use the theme song?'"

The co-anchor would go to five secret locations—five countries on four continents—in five days. It took a staggering amount of planning and preparation. On the first trip in May 1998, Lauer delivered the first-ever live American broadcasts from the great Pyramids in Cairo, the Acropolis in Athens, and the Taj Mahal in Agra. The Taj Mahal telecast required three months of negotiations with Indian government officials, as live TV signals out of India were prohibited. Cranes were needed to get camera equipment up to the Acropolis.

Lauer rode camels in Egypt, sampled baby octopus in Venice with chef Marcella Hazan, listened to a didgeridoo in front of the Opera House in Sydney, Australia, and endured 110-plus degree temperatures in Agra. Lauer, well-prepared by the team, delivered a pithy information-packed travelogue at each stop, remaining astonishingly lucid for someone who spent forty-two hours in a plane and slept for ten hours over the course of a week.

The concept was a sensation with viewers. Over the next ten years, Lauer did the stunt eight more times, logging nearly two hundred thousand miles in air travel as he treated viewers to tours of Angkor Wat, the Great Wall of China, Easter Island, and the slopes of the Swiss Alps. A crew of twenty producers and technical people—many from NBC News bureaus throughout the world—were at work in advance at each location to make the process a smooth one for Lauer when he arrived.

One thing the advance work could not control was the weather. But the uncertainty only added to the dramatic effect when the camera pulled back to reveal Lauer's location. During a trip in 2001, Lauer's first stop was Machu Picchu near the Andes Mountains of Peru. "We spent the weekend shooting around the place, and then comes Monday morning," he recalled. "We're staying in this town along the river below, and we take our trip up early, five in the morning,

whatever, to get there, so at seven o'clock we're ready. The best part of *Where in the World* is the reveal. We had this place where we were set up where all of Machu Picchu on the hillside was behind us. All weekend long we had looked and said, 'This is going to be breathtaking.' We get up there at 6:30 a.m. It is so foggy that I could barely see the cameraman ten feet in front of me. He could not see a foot behind me. None of what we were hoping the viewers would see was visible. It was socked in. At ten of seven, they're in the control room, going, 'Maybe we should hold off. Maybe we'll reveal you at eight. Maybe we'll come back and do this tomorrow; stay there an extra day.' There was nothing to see. At two minutes of seven, I'm standing there with the camera guys and the producers, and someone said, 'You know, it looks like it's starting to lift a little bit.' At thirty seconds till seven o'clock, the fog swiped away. And there, with the sun, was Machu Picchu. And I remember turning around and thinking, *You've got to be kidding me*. And we came up, and boom, they went into it. And there it was, like no fog had ever been there. It was magical, absolutely magical."

ANN CURRY

· MATT

SAVANNAH GUTHRIE

CHAPTER SIX

MEREDITH

AL ROKER

WILLARD SCOTT

LAUER •

NATALIE MORALES

2000–2011

VIEIRA   HODA
         KOTB

KATHIE LEE GIFFORD

Katie Couric

2000 — First Lady Hillary Clinton is elected to the U.S. Senate.

2000–2011

AMERICA HEADED TOWARD a new millennium with uncertainty and fear. On December 31, 1999, NBC News correspondent Robert Hager was stationed at the Y2K Command Center in Washington for the rollover to 2000. Would our ATM cards work? Would water and sewer systems continue to function? Would terrorists use the event to make a statement with an attack? The anxiety went beyond the calendar. Everyday life was chang-

ing rapidly with the emergence of new technology in the digital age. (Just six years earlier, Bryan Gumbel asked on *Today*: "What is the Internet anyway?") Ann Curry recalled how it was all a lot to absorb. "We were very much shifting into a new gear," she said. "And we could feel it. We were going faster. And we were trying to figure out how that felt. We were just starting to figure out how to work a mouse. We were just starting to understand what the Internet meant to our lives. And we didn't know what the future was going to bring. We were worried about terrorism. In the '90s, we had a lot of terrorism. We had the bombing of the USS *Cole*. We had two U.S. embassies bombed in Africa. We had the Oklahoma City bombing, which was homegrown terrorism. We recognized that we were maybe vulnerable."

"We were very much shifting into a new gear. And we could feel it. We were going faster. And we were trying to figure out how that felt." —Ann Curry

If America and the world were in for a cataclysmic event on Y2K, *Today* was going to be there even if it occurred at night. "We were all on the scene of the dropping of the ball in Times Square, because we were worried something was going to happen," Curry recalled. "There was a lot of tension leading up to it. There was a tremendous amount of security. The police were checking under manhole covers. They had lots of barriers. It was very loud and very crazy, but also very exciting. A little nerve-racking, too." As the clock reached midnight in New York, a sense of relief came with the jubilant celebration. "The entire world connected," said Curry. "By the time it came to New York, I mean, half the world was already going to bed and was hungover. It was wild. It felt as though the world had become one. And that's a rarity."

Today came into the new millennium on a roll. Since ABC's *Good Morning America* had become a solid competitor in the late 1970s, the ratings leadership in the morning seesawed back and forth in five-year spans. But *Today* was into its sixth consecutive year on top. The program had become a finely tuned hybrid of news and entertainment that was at its peak influence. NBC's *Friends* was the top-rated program in prime time in

2001. Viewers who watched the team of Katie Couric, Matt Lauer, Ann Curry, and Al Roker were seeing *Friends* without a script. They depended on them for reliable information but became emotionally invested in them as well.

Today *came into the new millennium on a roll. It was into its sixth consecutive year on top.*

Couric's relationship with the audience was particularly deep. She called the support she received after her husband's death from colon cancer in 1998 "a virtual embrace." *Today* provided an escape for her during her

Foundation, she formed the National Colorectal Cancer Research Alliance to promote screening for colon cancer. The organization distributed informational brochures in drugstores and created public service announcements for television. It also supported the opening of the Jay Monahan Center for Gastrointestinal Health at New-York-Presbyterian Hospital.

But the boldest action Couric took on behalf of the cause came in March 2000 when the cover of *Time* described her efforts as "Katie's Crusade." Testifying before a congressional committee about colon cancer, she noted that embarrassment and discomfort in the screening process was an obstacle to diagnosis and prevention of the disease. "A lot of people don't want to talk about it," Couric said. "Colons. Rectums. Bowels. Not exactly the stuff of cocktail party conversation." She believed the best way to get past the reluctance was to undergo a colonoscopy herself on *Today*. "I think that

"THEY SEE YOU DOING SAD STORIES....THEY SEE YOU CELEBRATING....TH

    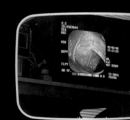

personal crisis. "I needed to keep working. I had two children. I loved my job. It was a sanctuary for me. Even though it invaded my mind all the time, for two hours I could think about something else. Or at least try."

In return, Couric used her powerful platform to raise awareness for the disease that took her husband's life. She had done a five-part series on *Today* called "Confronting Colon Cancer," explaining diagnosis and treatment. With the support of the Entertainment Industry

that was effective because it came from the purest of all places," she said. "The desire to educate people and spare them the pain that my family had endured."

Couric's report began in her Manhattan apartment, where she was shown drinking from the large plastic container filled with a polyethylene glycol-electrolyte solution used to cleanse the bowel the night before the examination. She went to work on *Today* the following day and after the program headed to New York-Presbyterian Hospital for the procedure. She remained conscious while under sedation, still able to banter with her doctor and deliver wisecracks as she watched an image of her internal organ on a monitor. "I have a pretty little colon," she said. When Couric showed the report on *Today*, she assured viewers that there was minimal discomfort. "I'm a big baby," she told them. "So for me to say that, that's a lot." There was a 20 percent increase in colonoscopies during the years that followed Couric's on-air demonstration.

"Maybe a life was saved," she said. "Maybe many lives were saved because I talked about what happened to Jay. I felt an obligation to educate the public. I had this incredible platform—a bully pulpit and I thought I've learned the hard way. If I don't share what I've learned with people, it's a terrible reflection on me."

It was certainly a positive reflection on *Today*. Couric believed the intimacy of morning television made her

EALLY DO GET TO KNOW EVERY FACET OF YOUR PERSONALITY." — *Katie Couric*

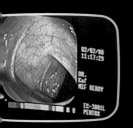
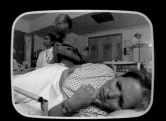

a more compelling advocate. "I always laugh when people say 'I know you,'" she said. "And I say, 'Well you really do.' They see you in all sorts of situations. They see you doing sad stories talking to people who experienced loss. They see you celebrating. They see you trying to get to the bottom of complicated issues. They see you trying to pin a politician down. I think they really do get to know every facet of your personality. I think they see you going

through life experiences. I had two children while I was on *Today*. My husband was diagnosed with cancer. My sister was diagnosed with cancer. That combined with the early morning hour, going about their daily business getting ready to face the day—all those things make it a very familial experience for people."

● ● ●

Top: Couric duets with Bette Midler on the plaza.

LIVE
EDT

WORLD TRADE CENTER
NEW YORK CITY

WORLD TRADE CENTER
NEW YORK CITY

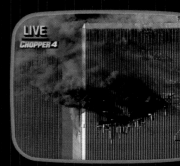

LIVE
CHOPPER 4

"A PLANE JUST HIT THE WORL

LIVE
EDT

THE PENTAGON
WASHINGTON, DC

—*Lauer heard in his earpiece.*

RON INSANA
CNBC'S "BUSINESS CENTER"

2003 — *The U.S. begins its military occupation of Iraq.*

TODAY HAD TO HELP GUIDE THE COUNTRY THROUGH ITS SHOCK AND THE GRIEF OV

Two days before the nation went to the polls on November 7, 2000, to choose between Vice President Al Gore and Texas Governor George W. Bush, Washington Bureau Chief Tim Russert gave *Today* viewers a tutorial in Electoral College math. "Florida, Florida, Florida," he told Matt Lauer. "Matt as goes Florida will go the nation. If I'm mistaken, I'll be the first to admit it. But I think that is the critical state."

On some NBC News programs, Russert had been using a telestrator—a device made popular by football analyst John Madden—to explain the complex paths to victory in the tight race. But on election night, Executive Producer Jeff Zucker went for a more low-tech approach. "I asked someone to go out to get a board for him to write on," he said. Russert used a white dry-erase board and a marker through the nail-biting night as the results came in. The all-night marathon continued into *Today*, which used an on-screen graphic that said "Indecision 2000." "Good morning," said Katie Couric, who napped briefly in her office after co-anchoring the night before. "We do not have a winner."

The results for Florida and its twenty-five electoral votes were too close to call (after faulty exit polling data had given the state to Gore early on). Russert was on the set with his white dry-erase board that read "Florida, Florida, Florida." Gore was ahead in the national popular vote tally—his lead over Bush was larger than the one John F. Kennedy had over Richard Nixon in 1960—but without Florida, he did not have the 270 electoral votes needed to win.

America would not have a winner until December 12 when the Supreme Court ended the state's recounts. Bush went to the White House and Russert's board ended up in the Smithsonian Institution.

Once the country got past the acrimony of the disputed election, television news slipped into an era of tabloid story-

Lauer and Couric were reporting live when a second hijacked airliner struck the south tower of the World Trade Center on the morning of the September 11 terrorist attacks.

telling. There were now three twenty-four-hour cable news channels—CNN, Fox News Channel, and MSNBC—which could turn shark attacks at the beach or a missing congressional intern named Chandra Levy into ongoing sagas. *Today* was getting drawn into following those stories as well—until September 11, 2001.

"I remember it being the most gorgeous New York City day," said Jonathan Wald, the executive producer for *Today* at the time. "And I remember spending extra time outside, opening both the 8:00 a.m. and the 8:30 a.m. half-hours outside." Wald recalled, eerily, how Al Roker greeted a group of nurses from Youngstown, Ohio, that morning on the plaza. They came with a sign that said "Hug A Nurse Today."

"We all thought it was an accident," said Lauer. "It had been described to us as a small plane. So I'm thinking Cessna. In my mind's eye, that's what I'm thinking. Except I was seeing a lot of damage, and I was thinking, *Wow, that must have really hit.*"

Couric joined Lauer back on the couch. "We come up on the shot of the smoke coming out of the World Trade Center, and had to figure out the story as we were seeing it happen," Lauer said. "So that is when everything hopefully you've learned in your years of being a broadcaster kicks in, and you describe what you're seeing. You try to add color to it by giving viewers who aren't from New York a little more about the location:

ASTONISHING CASUALTIES CAUSED BY THE WORST ATTACKS EVER ON AMERICAN SOIL.

Near the end of the second hour, Matt Lauer interviewed Richard Hack, the author of a new biography about Howard Hughes. At 8:51 a.m. he heard Wald in his earpiece. "It's very rare they speak in your ear," Lauer explained. "If they talk in your ear, something needs to be changed. They came in my ear and they basically said, 'We've got to get to commercial, quick. Get to commercial.' So the guy finished his sentence. I said, 'You know what? I'm going to take a break right now.' As soon as we dipped to black, in my ear they said, 'A plane just hit the World Trade Center. A small plane.'"

Couric was off camera in the news production area. "I looked up, and I saw on CNN one of the Twin Towers was on fire," she said. "And I think I thought, *Oh, God, what happened? A small plane must have flown in there.* Because you couldn't really see how big it was at that point. And I thought a guy had a heart attack and a plane flew in there. I guess it just shows how I try to see the glass as half full. And I thought, *Thank God, it's before nine o'clock. Hopefully a lot of people aren't at work yet.*"

What is the World Trade Center? What is the area? What time of day is it? Either way, that's the two largest buildings that we have, and thousands of people work there. And at this time of day, a lot of people would be in there."

Wald looked to get correspondents into place to cover the story, but depended on any firsthand information he could get. "A bunch of producers started to call in," Wald said. "Friends of mine who were down there called and we put them on the air. Anybody who was in the area who had seen it and who called in—we put them on the air."

One of them was *Today* producer Elliott Walker. "She's on the phone with us," Lauer said. "She lives right down there, and witnessed the first impact. She's describing what she saw as she's looking up at that first tower on fire. And we're saying, 'Did you see what kind of a plane it was, Elliott?' And all of a sudden, she goes, 'Oh, my God. Here's another.' And as she's saying it we're looking and into the frame comes a second plane from behind. And then we saw that iconic image of the flames. We are live and she screams, 'Oh, my God, there's been another collision . . . *Oh, my God!*' A chill went through my body as that fireball came out of the front of the building and I looked at Katie, and Katie looked at me. And I mouthed to her, 'Terrorism.' And we looked at each other. The next hour was surreal. Everyone in America realized it at the very same time that this was not an accident. We had camera people, stage managers, who've been there, seen and done everything, sitting in the studio, crying. So you're looking at a camera and there's someone standing there, with tears in their eyes. You're thinking, again, this is as bad a thing as we've ever witnessed."

The situation only got worse when Lauer and Couric connected with Washington to get a live report from Pentagon correspondent Jim Miklaszewski. "As he's on the air with us, and we're watching the World Trade Center burn, he goes, 'Oh, my God. Something has just hit the Pentagon!' He's in the building. And it's like this can't be happening again. God Almighty, it was world changing." A fourth hijacked passenger jet went down south of Pittsburgh. It had been heading toward Washington, D.C.

Lauer and Couric had to remain steady on the air while wondering how the unfolding disaster was affecting the people important to them. "I'm a New Yorker," said Lauer. "My family is somewhere in the city, and I'm wondering, *Are they watching this? Are they?* You know, my wife used to live downtown. Is she downtown? She lived blocks from there. She had friends down there. By any chance, is she down there? I can't get to a phone. Normally that happens. The first thing you do: you call your loved ones. I can't do that. Throughout the next hour or so, we all managed to get notes to floor managers and producers: 'Please call my wife.' So we got those calls out and found out that our families were okay."

Couric knew her two daughters were in school. "I thought it was as safe as anyplace else," she recalled. But she was concerned for her parents who lived in Arlington,

Virginia. During a commercial break, she called them and instructed them to stay in the basement of their house. "I was also dating somebody at the time who was on a flight from Boston to Los Angeles," she said. "So I was worried about him. It was just really terrifying, the whole thing."

Tom Brokaw joined Lauer and Couric as they described the towers crumbling down into a white cloud. "The profile of Manhattan has been changed," Brokaw said. "There's been a declaration of war by terrorists on the United States." By 1:00 p.m., the *Today* anchor team had been on the air for six hours as they reported on how a beautiful day had transformed into a surreal, catastrophic horror show. Once they were done, they were allowed to feel what the rest of America was going through. "We finally got up, and we just kind of hugged each other," said Lauer. "We both cried."

They headed across the street into Rockefeller Center to do a special hour report from the *NBC Nightly News* studio later that afternoon. "A good buddy of mine named Harry Crosby came on as one of our guests in the studio," said Lauer. "He had been downtown and he told this story of seeing people jumping out of the windows. He was there. He was witness to this. And that made my hands shake, to listen to him. It's five o'clock in the afternoon, and we got done with the special. I looked over in the corner of the studio and saw my wife holding our two-month-old son, and I just lost it. I went over to them, and I just lost it."

"I've had more hard days than I'd like to say in my life," said Katie Couric, "but that was one of the hardest and most challenging days for me professionally. I was as scared, I was as afraid as the rest of the country was when they were watching me."

Lauer knew the following morning's broadcast was going to be a brutal experience. "We need to go out to dinner," he said to his wife, Annette. As they sat in a restaurant with large windows that looked out onto First Avenue on Manhattan's East Side, they could see a steady stream

"That was one of the hardest and most challenging days for me professionally." —Katie Couric

of pedestrians headed north up the street. "It was a sea of people because all the mass transit was shut down," he said. "But, the restaurant was lively. There was a life to it. Except, every time an ambulance would go by, the place would get cemetery quiet. And they'd wait for the firetruck to go by, and then the conversation would slowly start again. I think we all needed a release. We all needed to get out, and get to a place and be with people, and know that life, in some small way, was going to be the same."

The days that followed were bleak, with reports from the site of the unthinkable tragedy, now called Ground Zero. "The *Today* staff is a very close-knit group of people," said Wald. "It was difficult for outsiders to crack. But an event like that sort of lowers some of the walls. All of the security guys, or most of the security guys at NBC News, but specifically the ones that work on the *Today* show—and there's extra security because of the crowd and the street-level studio—many of them are former New York City policemen, and they were instrumental in getting us down there to Ground Zero in the early hours and days after the attack, to broadcast from there, and to do reporting there. And I remember one of the

guys took me down. In the weeks after, stuff was still smoldering. And he said, 'You know what you're standing on? That's the antenna from the building.'"

Today had to help guide the country through its shock and the grief over the astonishing casualties caused by the worst attacks ever on American soil. "Homeland security," "jihad," "war on terror," "Osama bin Laden," "Taliban," and "anthrax" became household names and phrases in the everyday lives of viewers. It became a tricky balancing act for *Today*. The program slowly made its way back out onto the plaza after two weeks of staying inside with the frosted windows up in Studio 1A. "If you watch those shows, I think you'll know we're kind of off our game," Al Roker recalled. "Because even though we were going outside, it was, 'When do we start to have fun again?' It was a really difficult time. And our discomfort was the least of anybody's concerns or issues. But you didn't want to appear callous, or cavalier. So there was a lot of back and forth about—when do we resume normal? Or do we ever? Are we ever normal again? Is this the new normal?"

● ● ●

(left): CNBC's Ron Insana was covered with ash when he arrived at the Today *studio from lower Manhattan. "It was like a scene from* Independence Day," *he said.*

TODAY DOES HALLOWEEN

THE HALLOWEEN COSTUME CONTEST on the plaza started quietly on *Today* in 1994. But like many *Today* events outside of Studio 1A, it grew into an epic extravaganza that offered up a fun house mirror of pop culture past and present. Viewers who might have found Willard Scott's turn as Carmen Miranda on *Today* bizarre back in 1983 could never have imagined Matt Lauer's 2000 entrance as mega-pop-sensation-of-the-moment Jennifer Lopez. Al Roker as Sean "Puffy" Combs decked out in a white suit accompanied Lauer. "It was perfect for the time," Lauer recalled. "It was a little risky for me as the kind of new guy trying to create news chops walking out in this plunging neckline and mini dress. But it was fun." Both Lauer and Roker went drag in the plaza again in 2004—Lauer as a blonde, lapdog-holding Paris Hilton and Roker as talk show legend Oprah Winfrey. "I looked like Isabel Sanford who was Weezy on *The Jeffersons*," Roker said. "I didn't look like Oprah. It's amazing that whenever she sees me she says hello." The duo also parodied classic TV—Ed Norton and Ralph Kramden from *The Honeymooners*, and Gilligan and the Skipper from *Gilligan's Island*. They came down the side of a wall as Batman and Robin. They warbled "Cecilia" as Simon and Garfunkel in front of a giant reproduction of their *Bridge Over Troubled Waters* album cover and recreated the gaudy getups of Vegas entertainers Siegfried and Roy.

In the early years, *Today* cast members did not reveal their costumes to each other ahead of time. But the highly competitive Katie Couric was maniacal about getting intelligence on what her colleagues were wearing so she could make sure hers was the best. She was an unstoppable force on Halloween mornings.

Couric took cues from her young daughters when choosing her getups. When they were obsessed with *The Wizard of Oz*, she became Dorothy. When *SpongeBob SquarePants* was their favorite TV show, Couric dressed up as the character and bounded around the plaza with enough energy to power a Nickelodeon theme park. Once *The Apprentice* became NBC's hottest show, Couric put on a red wig and tapped her inner mogul to become Donald Trump. She was a scene-stealing Mary Poppins, surrounded by a troupe of dancing chimney sweeps ("Katie Couric on Broadway!" Roker said.), a saucy Mae West, and a bejeweled Marilyn Monroe singing "Diamonds Are a Girl's Best Friend."

Ann Curry has been a regal Lady Liberty, a shimmying Tina Turner, and a convincingly elegant Audrey Hepburn. She arrived on the plaza by horse as Joan of Arc and a rifle-toting Annie Oakley. But not every costume has been a hit with the *Today* team, especially the diva-

themed year in which Curry had to take the plaza stage as Cher, alongside Meredith Vieira as Bette Midler and Natalie Morales as Madonna. "I had the cone boobs," said Morales. "I didn't regret it. But it was an interesting choice."

Curry was less sanguine about it. "It was like wearing your underwear on national television," Curry recalled of the Cher getup. "It was so form-fitting, number one. And number two, just before I went on, the costume ripped right in the bum, a hole the size of a grapefruit. I was so mortified. Every Catholic schoolgirl part of me took over. And when I got out there, I couldn't even move. I just felt naked."

Vieira's outfit was also a misfire. She played Midler in her mermaid period. But the clamshell she entered failed to turn on cue, and spectators thought she was Ariel from the Disney movie *The Little Mermaid*. "A very old Ariel," she said. "Kind of pathetic."

But Curry acknowledged that Halloween on *Today* is about giving the people what they want. "You have to be willing at some point to let yourself be mortified, for the good of the viewer," she said. "Ultimately what gives you peace about it is that it's not really about you; it's about them. And if they're having fun; if you're bringing them into their morning in a way that makes them smile a bit more, then it's all worth it. That's how we roll around here."

Halloween on Today through the years (clockwise from top left): The cast of Star Wars, Lady Gaga (Vieira), Batman and Robin (Roker and Lauer), Marilyn Monroe (Couric), Superman (Roker), Tina Turner (Curry), Paris Hilton (Lauer), Oprah Winfrey (Roker),

Donald Trump (Couric), Gingerbread Man (Roker), Yoda (Kotb), Jennifer Lopez (Lauer), "Puff" Daddy (Roker), Cinderella (Curry), Little Red Riding Hood (Kotb), Pinocchio (Vieira), Lucy Ricardo (Couric), Humpty Dumpty (Lauer), and Amelia Earhart (Curry).

THE SUMMER CONCERT SERIES

I N THE 1950S, *TODAY WAS* often radio with pictures. Host Dave Garroway played several records a day on the program, mostly by the jazz vocalists and big band performers he favored. In the 1960s and early '70s, the various themes used for the program were performed by guitarist Django Reinhardt, pianist Erroll Garner, and the Modern Jazz Quartet—all reflecting the rarified tastes of the producers at the time. While jazz greats such as Duke Ellington and Louis Armstrong and classical artists appeared on the program, many of the pop performers who played were crooners or lounge acts—middle-of-the-road music that was favored by the parents of the predominantly young record-buying audience of the times. But as baby boomers grew up they wanted to hear the music they loved on *Today*, and the Summer Concert Series that began in 1994 on the plaza served that audience. Earth, Wind & Fire, Neil Diamond, Smokey Robinson, the Monkees, Santana, Chicago, and Tom Jones— proven acts with longtime followings—served up their hits. "I believed that the audience that was watching *Today* wasn't actually as familiar with the current stars as they were with the music that we grew up with," said Jeff Zucker, who launched the concert series.

Gradually, the acts became hipper through the 1990s (Prince, Sheryl Crow, R.E.M., Will Smith) and the crowds were so large they began to resemble urban versions of the Woodstock festival. As radio became more fragmented, *Today* became an ideal way to reach a broad audience in one shot and music sales saw a boost after an appearance on the program. By the time 2000 rolled in, the booking of a hot act could have fans camping out on West Forty-Eighth Street on a Wednesday night as they waited for a Friday morning performance. "I like the ones where you're catching someone at their apex," said Matt Lauer. "We had Ricky Martin on the show when all anyone could talk about was Ricky Martin. Sometimes the gods are smiling on you and a song explodes, and . . . oh, by the way, at the end of the week, we have that person on the plaza. We had a crowd I had not seen before. It was just enormous. And he put on this extravaganza, with these wild dancers. And he came out, and I thought this must have been what it was like to be in that theater when Ed Sullivan said, 'The Beatles!' Because the place went crazy." It was a scene that would be repeated over the years.

"The number of people who come is amazing," said Meredith Vieira. "They will stretch for blocks, literally. And people sleep here the night before, because they want to be first in line. There's no way some of them are even going to see the performer, but they want to be part of the scene. I'll be out there, and I'll look up at the windows, and very often, in the office buildings, the

windows will be open a little bit, and people will be looking out. I just think, *I have the coolest job*."

The Summer Concert Series was such a fixture in the popular culture, it became a plotline in the 2010 comedy *Get Him to the Greek*, starring Russell Brand as debauched British rock icon Aldous Snow. An appearance on *Today* (where he performed his hit "The Clap") was the first stop on Snow's treacherous comeback trail.

But there could not have been a better script written for the most memorable concert moment yet. In August 2010, Lady Gaga appeared on the plaza just as she became the most talked about pop diva since Madonna. "It was a spectacle," said Executive Producer Jim Bell. "The crowd, her white-hot luminescence, and her just breathtaking talent as a live performer. But there was a great moment when, between songs two and three, it started to rain. And we were in a commercial. It was one of those summer spot showers that just kind of popped up out of nowhere, and really started dumping a lot of water on the plaza. There were any number of frantic members of her entourage, and *Today* staff and producers going, 'What are we going to do? Can she do it? She's going to get hurt because she's such a performer and dancer. And she's wearing nine-inch heels or whatever she's wearing.' And I was out there, speaking to her folks. They spoke to her, and she just said, basically, 'Get out of my way.' And she went out and just knocked it out of the park with a performance in the rain. It looked really like as if we had planned it. It was so beautiful, with the water coming down. And she didn't miss a beat."

Gaga, Sting, Kenny Chesney, and Neil Diamond. Today *headed to Atlantic City to host a concert with Bruce Springsteen.*

After twelve years at *Today*, Katie Couric was the biggest star in all of television news. She was a vibrant personality who could be entertaining while never putting her journalistic credibility at risk. As part of a *Today* stunt in May 2003, she traded places with Jay Leno for a day and hosted *The Tonight Show*. "I have to be honest with you. I have not been this nervous since I was at the NBC Christmas party, and I was French kissed by Willard Scott," she said in her opening monologue. Her sexy black dress would never be worn on *Today*. Her guest host spot lifted the ratings for *Tonight* by more than 40 percent. It was evidence as to why whenever her contract with NBC came up, she was courted with offers from other networks and TV syndication companies. She was by far the highest-paid person in network news and based on the ratings and profit performance of *Today*, well worth it. Behind the scenes, Couric was known for being demanding, always pushing producers to come up with new ideas. She made her feelings known when she believed the program did

not meet her standards. Her issues became the subject of industry gossip and, for the first time in her career, bad press in 2005. It didn't help that ABC's *Good Morning America* was closing the ratings gap with *Today*, as the network's new prime-time hits *Desperate Housewives* and *Lost* helped deliver more viewers to the morning team of Diane Sawyer and Charles Gibson.

> *By the end of 2005*, Today *had a commanding lead in the ratings. . . . The program had won every single week.*

Jim Bell, a veteran of NBC's Olympics coverage, was brought in to replace Tom Touchet as executive producer in April 2005. He believed *Today* turned around that year when he allowed longer interviews of serious newsmakers and made the program less tightly formatted so that Couric, Lauer, Roker, and Curry could interact more naturally with each other. But what *Today*—and Couric—did best was breaking news coverage. The program was given a chance to prove it again when Hurricane Katrina, the most severe storm to ever hit the United States, struck the Gulf of Mexico region in late August 2005. "We went through April and May, basically trying to pull the program out from a nosedive, and it kind of lasted through the whole summer," Bell recalled. "But the way *Today* covered Hurricane Katrina live that morning—we had Brian Williams, Lester Holt, and Campbell Brown down there when the storm hit, and our competitors were definitely just completely flat-footed. Shortly thereafter, Katie was down in New Orleans. And she went to Houston, and she went to Mississippi. And you saw her out there, covering the sucker. Matt did a big, live, twenty-minute interview from New Orleans with President George W. Bush. We had already kind of established the framework, in terms of our priorities in hard news, of

Katie Couric showed some leg and raised ratings as guest host of Tonight *in 2005.*

being willing to get them back to working without a net a little bit more. It changed the tone. It changed the conversation. It was a huge difference maker. And that really kind of resonated for weeks afterwards."

Today did not leave the disaster in the Gulf behind when it returned to New York. For a week, the program turned Rockefeller Plaza into a job site where *Today* staff members and volunteers built more than sixty houses for Habitat for Humanity that were shipped to the stricken region.

By the end of 2005, *Today* had a commanding lead in the ratings race again and celebrated ten years as the number one rated morning program. The streak was not an average measured annually or quarterly. The program had won every single week. By that time, Katie Couric was coming up on fifteen years as co-anchor. "I thought that was a big chunk of time," she said. "I always thought you want to leave before they want you to leave. I had such a great run. I was so proud of a lot of the work I did over those years." As her contract expiration approached in 2006, she was wooed by CBS with an offer to become the first solo woman anchor of a network evening news-

cast. While Couric loved *Today*, she also valued her status as a role model for women. Unlike morning television, the audience for network evening newscasts was eroding every year as more viewers got their news during the day from cable and the Internet. But the perception of the programs as the traditional flagships for their news divisions remained. Barbara Walters felt the lure of making history when she left *Today* in 1976 to become co-anchor with Harry Reasoner on the *ABC Evening News*. Couric knew that being the first to do such a program alone was an even bigger step. "There are very few things I would leave the *Today* show for," Couric said. "I care deeply about women having opportunities and equality. The history was important."

Couric announced on April 5, 2006, that she was leaving *Today* to take over on the *CBS Evening News*. Lauer had known for months that the historic run the co-anchors had together was coming to a close. "Once those ratings got back up and we were securely in first place again, I think that takes a lot out of you," he said. "Being number one sounds great. It's hard. You have that target on your back every single day. It took a lot out of all of

TODAY AT THE OLYMPICS

SINCE 1996, *TODAY* HAS BEEN the gateway to NBC's coverage of the Olympic Games, still among the most dependable events on television for attracting massive audiences. NBC Sports had handled the morning programming during the two and a half weeks the games aired, but that changed under Jeff Zucker's reign as *Today* executive producer. "I had come into the company working on the Olympics," Zucker said. "So I understood the power of them." Zucker had *Today* broadcast from the Olympics' location and opened each morning with the games' signature rings and fanfare theme. The program's proximity allowed it to capture the fresh emotions that came from the competition. *Today* delivered its coverage live no matter what the time zone—even when it meant going on the air at 4:00 a.m. in Vancouver during the Winter Games in 2010.

"We met some people who were experiencing the greatest moments of their lives on live television and had a chance to embrace them as they were competing for their country," said Matt Lauer.

"The American team did so well, and the athletes were willing to join us on the side of Grouse Mountain, in the middle of the night," said Jim Bell. "For many of them . . . it was a continuation of the celebration. It was the most fun you could ever have at that time of day."

The games also enabled the *Today* cast members to serve as surrogate Olympics fans who could try some of the events viewers only experienced through television. Perhaps the most unforgettable stunt was the two-man luge demonstration by Matt Lauer and Al Roker during the XX Olympic Winter Games in Torino, Italy, in 2006. "The sight of us in Spandex was revealing in many different ways," said Roker. "But the best moment was when Matt found out he was going to be on the bottom, and I was going to be on top. It just went against all logic. It was one of those moments that you look at and you go, 'That's just ridiculous.' And people just seemed to love it."

M EREDITH VIEIRA'S DAILY ROUTINE FOR *TODAY* began at 2:30 a.m. After her alarm went off, she got out of bed, trying not to wake her husband, Richard Cohen, and laid down on the floor ("I have no idea why," she said) in a space just off from the bathroom in her Westchester home. She put her feet up on a chair and rested her head on her backpack while she read the e-mail messages that came in on her BlackBerry, most of them having to do with that morning's program. She headed down to the kitchen where her dog and two cats were waiting to be fed (they had adjusted to her schedule). Right before Vieira left the house to enter a car that took her into Manhattan, she often prepared Cohen's coffee cup or plugged in his mobile phone. "I always put my stamp on the kitchen in a way that said 'I've been here,'" she said.

Throughout her career, Vieira has always been there for her family. Her commitment to home life was a rarity for someone with such a high level of success in a business filled with massive egos. Vieira's devotion to her husband, who she met when they both worked at CBS News, was worthy of a romance novel. Cohen told her on their second date that he had multiple sclerosis. Other women headed for the exit when he mentioned his condition. Vieira was already in love and knew she was going to marry him.

Vieira was raised in Providence, Rhode Island, the daughter of a Harvard-educated doctor. Her mother was homemaker who encouraged her daughter to pursue a career. After graduating from Tufts University, Vieira's husky voice, natural beauty, and strong writing ability led to jobs in local radio and television and eventually *60 Minutes*, the gold standard of TV news magazines. When Vieira chose to walk away from the program after three years to spend more time caring for her family, it led to sniping from inside CBS News, where some producers and correspondents resented her desire for a more accommodating schedule. The situation played out in the press and newspaper opinion pages as it struck a nerve with millions of career women who were struggling to find success in the workplace while raising families.

Vieira's skill at delivering compassionate, award-winning news pieces kept her in demand. In 1993, she headed to ABC to work on the news magazine *Turning Point*. But it was canceled several years later during a period of cost cutting at the news division. Vieira was ready to leave ABC until Barbara Walters came to her with an offer to be the moderator of her new topical daytime talk show, *The View*. She believed Vieira was empathetic, smart, and unpretentious, and by 1997 filled with life experiences she could share with the daytime audience.

Walters understood what Vieira had been up against in her effort to have children and a TV news career. She once said if she brought a child to work during her era on *Today* in the 1960s and '70s "it would be like bringing in a puppy that was going to pee on the desk." Vieira had put in nine years on *The View* when Jeff Zucker approached her in 2006 about taking over for Katie Couric at *Today*. Before she accepted the offer, she made sure she had the full support of her husband and children. They showed it to her with a bracelet she wore on her first day on the air. It had a charm with the inscription "We are with you—Love, Richard, Ben, Gabe, and Lily." Vieira never went to work without it. After it fell off her wrist and was lost in Minneapolis while she covered the 2008 Republican National Convention, her husband had it remade with a second charm that said "x2."

VIEIRA'S SKILL AT DELIVERING COMPASSIONA

ARD-WINNING NEWS PIECES KEPT HER IN DEMAND.

the probability that she was going to leave," he recalled.

Meredith Vieira topped Zucker's wish list for a replacement. In the 1980s, Vieira was a beautiful, fresh-faced, and highly capable broadcast journalist who rode the fast track to stardom from local TV to become the youngest correspondent ever on the prestigious CBS news magazine *60 Minutes* when she was hired to replace Diane Sawyer. She became a hero for working moms when she decided to walk away from perhaps the most coveted—and demanding—job in television journalism after becoming pregnant with her second child. "She's a great broadcaster," *60 Minutes* creator Don Hewitt once said. "As she put it, her baby was more important than my baby." Vieira's messy split with *60 Minutes* sparked a national debate about how women balance motherhood with their careers. "I certainly wasn't the only one who made those choices," Vieira said in 2006. "I was just kind of out there and very visible. When you're on television you become public whether you want to or not."

In 1997, Barbara Walters hired Vieira to be a part of her new ABC daytime talk show, *The View*. Vieira was by far the most accomplished and intelligent member of the original panel Walters put together. But what surprised viewers and network executives was her range and her ability to be spontaneous and a bit zany on the program. She led the show's daily discussion of "Hot Topics" and spoke honestly about her family. Viewers knew about Vieira's husband Richard Cohen, and his battles with multiple sclerosis and cancer. They heard her express self-doubt over her skills as a mother of three

us, getting that cushion back up. So I knew she was looking to do something else. She and I talked about it a lot. So for a year, I knew it was cooking."

THE HISTORIC RUN THE COANCHORS HAD TOGETHER WAS COMING TO A CLOS

Jeff Zucker, who by that time was president and CEO of NBC, attempted to keep Couric. He even offered her the chance to develop her own late night program that would have followed *The Tonight Show*. But Zucker knew Couric well and understood her fixation on the groundbreaking opportunity at CBS. "While she was considering it, I was also behind the scenes, preparing for

children. But she also tap-danced while dressed up to look like a giant hot dog. "If there was anybody ever built to do *Today*, it was Meredith," said Zucker. "She had news credentials. And she had a bawdy sense of humor, and a fun side. I'm not sure, given what Katie Couric had just come off of, after some fifteen years on the *Today* show, it was going to be near impossible to find somebody to

"It was sad for me," Couric said of her departure from Today. *"And I still miss it."*

step into those shoes. And Meredith was probably the only one with the stature to be able to do that."

Zucker was not the first to approach Vieira about doing the morning shift. She once turned down an offer to co-anchor *Good Morning America*. CBS nearly nabbed her for *The Early Show*, but ABC sweetened her deal for *The View* by also making her host of the syndicated version of the game show *Who Wants to Be A Millionaire*. Vieira was generally reluctant to take a job in the early morning hours. "In a nutshell, that was the reason," Vieira said. "I'm a night person. It's very hard for me to get up."

Zucker was aware of Vieira's misgivings, and believed getting her to come to NBC was a long shot. But it was worth a try. "I knew that she'd turn them all down," he said. "But I was coming with the *Today* show. And I thought that was different. I'd been talking to her agent and eventually, she agreed to allow me to see her for about ten minutes."

When Zucker first called Vieira to set up a meeting in late 2005, she would only give him a short window of time she had between the morning broadcast of *The View* and her afternoon taping of *Millionaire*. "We didn't want anybody to see us," he said. "So I would pick her up and drive her from one show to the other."

Zucker showed up at ABC's studio on the West Side of Manhattan in his chauffeured SUV with tinted windows. They drove together for the short distance to the studio for *Millionaire*. Vieira recalled, "He's sitting in the back and, literally, in the five minutes it took he said to me, 'Katie's leaving the show and you are my choice to replace her. I'm not talking to anybody else. We'd love to have you on board.' The first thing I said to him is 'I think you're skewing pretty old.'"

Vieira was fifty-two at the time.

"And he said, 'We want experience.' Because I was thinking, Why? Why wouldn't you get someone who has less miles?"

"I told her it didn't scare me at all," Zucker said. "In fact, I wanted to embrace it and I wanted to make a virtue out of it. And the fact is that she was young at heart and filled with experience. And that was exactly what we needed at the time."

Soon afterward, Vieira met with Lauer and they quickly developed an easy rapport. "I had dinner with her at my apartment and it was one of those meetings where the conversation never lagged," Lauer recalled. "It was Meredith being real and Meredith sharing parts of her life with me."

"In a business of big egos, Meredith is almost egoless," said Matt Lauer.

· NATALIE ·
MORALES

FIRST
SHOW
2006

Present

N **ATALIE MORALES'S FIRST JOB IN TELEVISION** was with Cabelvision News 12, a local cable channel that aired in the Bronx, New York. The bare bones operation required her to report, shoot, and edit her own stories. "I even lugged my gear around," she said. "I was a one-man band." But the 1990s was an era of TV news expansion, and Morales rode the wave. She joined NBC News in 2002 via its cable news channel MSNBC. Her route to *Today*, where she succeeded Ann Curry at the news desk in June 2011, began in what is known as "the third hour."

Today had become such a strong franchise for NBC, the network decided in 1999 to make more of it. A brand extension called *Later Today* was tried at 9:00 a.m. It attempted to tap into the program's history by featuring former "*Today* Girl" Florence Henderson (known to a whole new generation who grew up watching her on *The Brady Bunch*) as a co-host with Asha Blake and Jodi Applegate. *Later Today* was a misfire, as its separate set and a studio gave it little connection to the juggernaut that took over Rockefeller Plaza every morning. A year later, the hour was absorbed into the *Today* flagship and evolved into a platform to develop new talent. Morales, who joined *Today* as a national correspondent and a co-anchor of the third hour in 2006, is the first to ascend to a role as one of "the Fab Four," as she calls it, joining Matt Lauer, Ann Curry, and Al Roker.

Going out onto the plaza to greet people in front of Studio 1A takes her back a bit to her days as a community reporter. "It's actually my favorite part of the job," she said. "In those little glimpses of the people that we shake hands with and embrace. You really get a sense of how much of an impact you can make sometimes. I'll hear 'Oh, my gosh, I just ran my first marathon!' And they connect with me because I've run marathons. Or, 'Oh, we had our babies around the same time.'

Morales, an air force brat who grew up in Panama, Brazil, and Spain speaks Spanish and Portuguese (her mother is from Brazil and her father is Puerto Rican). Her multilingual skills helped during her award-winning coverage of the rescue of the thirty-three Chilean miners who were trapped underground for sixty-nine days in fall 2010. "It was an incredible moment," she said.

Since 2010, Morales has also anchored *Today In Two Minutes*—an online streaming video that condenses the day's events, weather, and content from the program. It's the very same name of a feature that Dave Garroway did in the earliest editions of *Today* in the early 1950s—except he used a bulletin board and still photographs.

2010 — *Director James Cameron's Avatar becomes the top-grossing film of all time.*

The full court press was working. "I started to think about it," Vieira said. "My contract was up with *The View*. And I always contemplate change every time my contract is up—or take a look at the landscape, and my own landscape. And I thought, *You know what? It's the* Today *show. If I don't take this now, I'm never going to get this opportunity again, probably.* And I realized that I would be a part of that history."

On September 13, 2006, Meredith Vieira joined *Today* as a co-anchor. "I feel like it's the first day of school and I'm sitting next to the cutest guy in the class," she said to Lauer. The ratings held up and she was a runaway hit with her colleagues who discovered that the warmth, sense of humor, empathy, and compassion she always showed on camera, was completely genuine. "Meredith is exactly as people see her," said Ann Curry. "She is just as generous behind the scenes."

"She just came here and relaxed," Lauer observed. "And it made us all relax. She has the ability to just present the real side of her. It was if she had been with us for ten years."

Curry wanted the co-anchor job when Couric left in 2006. Yet she never complained when Vieira was

encourage her. Because that's ultimately what's going to help everybody.'"

It was not just the ratings that told Vieira she was reaching viewers. In April 2007, she was sent to Blacksburg, Virginia, to cover the massacre of thirty-two students at Virginia Polytechnic Institute and State University. The gunman was a mentally ill student who committed suicide after his murderous rampage.

"I'll never forget Jim Bell calling me up in the afternoon," she recalled. "I guess it was breaking at that point. I didn't have a television on. And he said, 'Meredith, we're all getting on a plane,' and told me what was happening. And then the story was unfolding as I'm getting ready to go. It's sort of a numbing feeling. Because you know something awful has happened, and you're going to go there."

On her second night on the Virginia Tech campus, she was with a camera crew taping interviews during the candlelight vigil being held for the victims. "A kid came up to me," Vieira recalled. "And he said, 'Can I hug you?' And I said, 'Sure.' And then a few others came. And they were crying. And one of the kids said, 'You

CURRY WAS HEADED TO THE SOUTH POLE WHERE ONLY SEVEN THOUSAN

brought in, especially after she saw how well she blended into the team. "Initially I was sad," she said. "But then I also realized early on—and I really kind of sort of yelled at myself a little—and I said, 'Ann, come on. No one is deserving. It's about, what is good for the broadcast. And, more importantly, what is good for the American people. And Meredith seems to be great for the American people. So let's just jump on this train and let it ride. And just let it go as fast as it can go and

know, we miss our parents so much and we feel like you're our parent.' They saw me, in many ways, as their mom. They couldn't get to their moms. The college was on lockdown, and so much had gone on there. I was very touched by that. Not only were we telling the country this story—and obviously, it's extremely upsetting—it was the biggest thing like that since Columbine, really—but also we were providing comfort for those kids who had experienced it, who were feeling it so intensely. And

"The shooting at Virginia Tech was one of the first major stories that I covered here," said Vieira. "And one of the most upsetting."

that's when the power of this show hit me—that we had that kind of effect on people, that these kids felt a real connection to me because of what I did. And that was really humbling, and one of those moments where you go, 'I'm really proud of what we do.'"

Providing a seamless transition from Couric, a figure whose legacy at *Today* rivaled that of Barbara Walters and Dave Garroway—was a powerful testament to Vieira's ability and appeal. "Ultimately there are a finite number of people who can do these jobs, and have the range that they require," said Jim Bell. "But there's an even smaller number of people who can fit the position when you're actually talking about having them join an existing team from a cold start, completely unknown. And the fact that, even though she was obviously a known quantity because of her work on *The View* and at *60 Minutes*—Matt, Ann, and Al, and me and the crew, we didn't know her from a hole in the wall. What's she going to be like? And at the end of the day, it was probably because of who she is off the air that it went so well on the air. Because you just can't fake what Tom Brokaw used to call the strain of having to basically prepare to take exams in front of the country every morning and know what you were talking about, on any number of possible subjects. Going from politics to talking to Dr. Nancy Snyderman about this new breast cancer study. That's difficult enough, as it is. And then you factor in

the volume of programming, and the early hours with all these people you don't really know. And I'll be honest—as well as it went, it was not easy. There was no guarantee that it was going to go well, despite the wonderful person she is and the immense talent that she is. It still was very hard, and there were some tough days and weeks in there. I don't think we ever quite got enough credit, and she never got quite enough credit, for essentially replacing Katie, arguably the most important personality in the history of morning television. I mean, those were some serious Jimmy Choos to fill."

Bell also had the challenge of bringing more innovation to *Today*. If the program became stale in the new media age in which choices seemed to continuously proliferate more all the time—by 2007 you could add satellite radio, smartphones, and iPods to the list—there was no place to hide. In the fall of that year, Bell sent Lauer, Roker, and Curry "To the Ends of the Earth" to report on climate change and its effect on the environment. It was a morning program travel stunt on steroids. "Matt was inside the Arctic Circle, and Ann was in Antarctica, and Al was on the equator, and Meredith was home in Studio 1A, connecting the dots," he said.

It was Curry's part of the journey that provided a layer of drama.

"We were able, miraculously, to get a live shot out of Antarctica through the Internet," Bell recalled. "It was

:OPLE HAD GONE BEFORE AND WHERE NO ONE HAD EVER BROADCAST LIVE.

"Today Goes to the Ends of the Earth" has taken the program to Australia, Kilimanjaro, and Iceland.

KATHIE LEE
AND
· HODA ·

FIRST
SHOW
2008

Present

THIS IS A LOVELY ACCIDENT," is how Kathie Lee Gifford described the rollicking fourth hour of *Today* that she has co-hosted with Hoda Kotb since 2008. "If you think about it, on paper, a post-menopausal has-been and an award-winning Egyptian journalist: 'Hey, that's going to be a riot of a show.'"

Gifford is one of those television personalities who viewers identified by her first name. She held forth for fifteen years every morning on *Live with Regis and Kathie Lee*. The syndicated hit was built on the first twenty minutes of the program where Gifford and co-host Regis Philbin riffed on their social lives, their families, the day's headlines, or whatever else that came into their heads in a spontaneous daily coffee klatch. "Perky and pesky, popular and polarizing but seldom, if ever, dull," is how the *New York Times* once described Gifford's freewheeling zaniness.

In the later years of her run on *Live*, Gifford's image took some knocks over marital problems that played out in the tabloids and charges that she used child labor for her clothing lines. After leaving *Live* in 2000, she focused on her children and on writing books and stage musicals. She was rarely seen on television until she made an appearance to plug one of her projects on the fourth hour of *Today*.

Jim Bell saw that she had not lost the ability to pull viewers toward the screen to wonder, *What will she say next?* NBC executives were looking to make the fourth hour of *Today* more distinctive and Gifford could certainly do that. After she filled in a few times, it seemed like a natural fit and she was convinced to join the program full-time and make a TV comeback at age fifty-four.

Kotb, an accomplished NBC News correspondent who had been co-anchor of the fourth hour with Ann Curry and Natalie Morales, had some misgivings about being paired with Gifford. "I had done serious news. I'd been in Iraq during the war. I'd been in Afghanistan. I'd been in Pakistan. And then suddenly, I was going to be laughing and scratching with Kathie Lee. I was thinking, *Oh, my God; what am I doing?* And I tried to keep my newsy-ness going, which doesn't work. You can't put your big toe in the pool and say, 'Well, hey, I still have this.' You just sort of have to dive in. And I just felt like I kind of ripped off my news corset one day and said, 'The hell with it,' and tried it. And then I really started enjoying myself."

The program found its personality when comedian and author Chelsea Handler was on the show during Gifford's first month. "She had a book that came out, *Are You There, Vodka? It's Me, Chelsea*," she said. "We were out on the plaza, and the producers, they prepared cocktails for her. Well, it went over so well, they just kept bringing cocktails on the show."

Call it *Today* on the rocks. An instant kitsch classic was born.

"We create the environment of a party. We create the illusion of one. And people are buying into it. They just are. And I'm stunned. I remember when we started getting away with all this stuff and I went, 'Aren't there any standards and practices anymore on the networks?'"

"WE CREATE THE ENVIRONMENT OF A PARTY." — *Kathy Lee Gifford*

KATIE COURIC LEFT A DEEP IMPRESSION on a generation of young women who saw her debut on *Today* in 1991. One of them was a University of Arizona journalism student named Savannah Guthrie. She was struck by how the co-anchor was completely comfortable being herself. "Everyone does it now, but it was very novel then—she was very real," Guthrie recalled. "That's what appealed to me about her and that's what hooked me on the show. I think seeing her made me realize it didn't require artifice or faux personality to be in that job."

Twenty years later, Guthrie went from being an avid viewer to a member of the *Today* family when she was named co-anchor of the program's third hour. But her route there was circuitous. Guthrie started out as a local news correspondent in her hometown of Tucson in the mid-1990s around the time when more television cameras were making their way into courtrooms. She enjoyed covering trials and also became hooked on watching the legal system play out on real time on Court TV, where she eventually worked. But first, at the age of twenty-seven, she decided to become a lawyer. "There was a part of me that wondered what it was like to stand up in court and make an argument," she recalled. "I was also starting to think about what to do next in television. I took the LSATs thinking I would have that in my back pocket. Then I got a letter from Georgetown Law School inviting me to apply. I felt it was a sign from above."

She fully expected to have a career in law. She practiced for a year as a white-collar criminal defense attorney in the Enron case and was even selected to serve as a clerk for a federal judge. She turned down the position, as she still felt drawn to television news and a desire to cover national stories. "I still had that hunger for it," she said. "The only reason I wasn't doing it was because I thought I wasn't good enough and that no one would give me a chance. But there was no excuse not to at least try."

Guthrie hired an agent and soon became one of the many lawyers who made their on-air bona fides as legal analysts on Court TV. The cable channel encouraged its talent to appear on other outlets and Guthrie, who covered pop star Michael Jackson's 2005 trial on charges of child molestation, showed up as an expert on numerous programs including *Today*. "Katie Couric interviewed me," she said. "When I first heard her say my name, I thought, 'OK, keep it together, Savannah.'" The exposure led NBC to eventually hire her as a Washington correspondent in 2007.

Guthrie spent time at the White House, the 2008 presidential campaign trail, and on MSNBC before landing on *Today*. Standing at nearly five foot ten before slipping into towering high heels, she is hard to miss on the plaza out in front of Studio 1A. "To be a part of something you've admired for so long—it's almost too much to comprehend."

2011 — *Osama bid Laden is killed by U.S. forces in Pakistan.*

from McMurdo Science Station. But that place was like a seven-hour flight from the actual geographic South Pole. So Ann and her team became obsessed with actually getting to the South Pole. There was no easy way to get a camera shot out of there. But she had a satellite phone. There was a crazy plane ride that you have to take to get there. For two and three days, the plane wouldn't take off because of the weather. At one point, we lost track of her for almost twelve hours. I mean, it was hairy." During that period, Curry's husband called Bell to ask where his wife was. Bell had to say he didn't know.

But Curry ended up calling into NBC News overnight and indicated that the U.S. Air Force plane making the flight was ready to go. She was headed to the South Pole where only seven thousand people had gone before and where no one had ever broadcast live. It was another *Today* first.

When Bell came in that morning at 5:30 a.m., he asked where Curry was and the control room had not heard. But this time it likely meant she was on the plane.

"She calls into the control room at, like, 6:50 in the morning and says, 'I'm here,'" said Bell. "I mean, we almost fell out of our chairs. We said, 'Hold on a second. Hold on a second.'

And so we come out at seven o'clock and we say, 'She made it!'" There was Curry in her red parka, standing in fifty-three-below-zero-degree temperatures, reporting live from the South Pole. "And everybody in the studio starts standing up. Tim Russert happened to be in the studio that day. Everybody was celebrating," said Bell.

Such acts of derring-do had become Curry's signature on *Today*. Viewers saw her go skydiving to honor the 250th birthday of the U.S. Army and bungee jump off the Middlesbrough Transporter Bridge to raise money for Save the Children. "I don't have a lot of fear of physical danger," said Curry. "Being a family women, I try not to take risks without some sort of purpose. You should be careful and measure the risks of things. But it is, I think, a greater mistake to regret that you have not done enough." In 2006, Curry headed out on the first of many dangerous trips to Sudan to deliver dogged and unflinching reports on the violent genocide taking place in the Darfur province. Twice she traveled there with *New York Times* columnist Nicholas Kristof who wrote how they stayed in a "$4 a night hotel, several people in a ramshackle room, with a pit toilet that was a home for a bat that zoomed in and out at the worst possible moments. . . . Ann put up with the bats, the scorpions and all kinds of militia with guns."

●　●　●

Meredith Vieira never expected to be a long-timer on *Today*. She added a year to her original four-year contract. But again, she put her family first instead of continuing beyond 2011. "Richard is in good health, and that's part of the reason I want to leave right now," she said when she announced her departure from *Today* in April of that year. "I want to be there with him, and I want to have fun, and I want to appreciate our time together and not have to punch a clock so much."

Ann Curry on the slopes in Vermont, in the kitchen with Matt Lauer and Martha Stewart, and zip-lining in Vancouver.

As much as NBC News wanted Vieira to stay, *Today* had bench strength to call upon. Ann Curry had put in fourteen years on the program at the news desk and filled in at the anchor desk hundreds of times. The viewers also recognized and respected her willingness to report from hot spots (and a few extreme cold ones) around the globe. "They've actually shaken their fingers at me and said, 'You know, I've worried about you. You shouldn't go to those places,'" she said. "And I'll look at them and say, 'If I don't do it, who does?' And they kind of melt and they say, 'Yeah, you're right.'"

"She's a genuinely good soul who cares deeply about what she's doing, about the segments she's doing about the people's she's interviewing," said NBC News President Steve Capus who first worked with Curry on *NBC News at Sunrise* in the mid-1990s. "She's always had that as long as I've known her. When I first started working with her she had a newborn baby and a young daughter. I watched her raise her family while she had this incredibly demanding job while staying true to who she is." Curry was a

broadcaster, but she understood the immediacy of the new media age in which Americans—and the world—no longer relied solely on the TV screen for news and information. While covering the major earthquake that hit Haiti in January 2010, Curry delivered a message on the social media network Twitter urging the U.S. military, which had taken control of the country's airfield, to clear the landing of a plane carrying medical supplies (It read: "@ usairforce find a way to let Doctors without Borders planes land in Haiti: THE most effective at this."). The message convinced the Pentagon to give the plane clearance to land. Twitter declared it "The Most Powerful Tweet of the Year."

The day after Vieira's tearful final program on June 8, 2011, Curry switched over to the anchor desk alongside Matt Lauer.

"It's a little bit like a member of the family moving to a new seat of the table," said Lauer, as the crew in Studio 1A applauded.

Said Curry, "If you're willing to put up for me that long and you're clapping—that's a good sign."

THIRTY YEARS AFTER *TODAY* **BROUGHT THE** Royal Wedding of Prince Charles and Lady Diana to American households, the program returned to London for to see their son Prince William wed Catherine Middleton. Nearly 10 million viewers turned to *Today* — the program's largest audience in eleven years — to watch live coverage of the sumptuously dressed guests making their entrances and a historic Westminster Abbey ceremony for a young couple that exuded glamour and warmth. "It was the perfect combination of tradition and the modern monarchy," said Matt Lauer. "And the spin in the Astin Martin sealed it for me."

TODAY GOES VIRAL

BY THE END OF THE FIRST DECADE of the twenty-first century, the TV technology used by the behemoth cameras that broadcast the first *Today* program in 1952 could sit in the palm of your hand. Not only could consumers create their own video images, they had the power to distribute them immediately online through YouTube or other social media sites. A homemade video shared with friends who watched them on their computers at work or home could "go viral" and be seen by millions in matter of hours. The staff at *Today* was no different. "We all are getting sent the links to these viral videos," said Jennifer Long, a producer. "It was Don Nash, the senior broadcast producer, who decided: 'Why don't we make imitations of these?' Just because we thought it would be fun. I don't think we thought it was anything groundbreaking."

A video showing 172 students at the University of Quebec at Montreal dancing while mouthing the words of the Black Eyed Peas's party anthem "I Gotta Feeling" as a camera followed them in one long continuous take with no edits had become an online sensation. It inspired similar "lip dub" routines on campuses around the world, and Long found herself charged with creating a *Today* version. Long went to Montreal and talked with students to learn the process of rehearsing and organizing such an elaborate undertaking. "It has to be in sync perfectly," she said. "And every single movement has to be choreographed. If one person says the wrong word, doesn't sing the right word, or the cameraman moves to the left or the right of where he's supposed to be going, then you have to start the whole thing over. And all I kept thinking was, given our crew schedule and our staff schedule and the few rehearsals that we would have to do this, there was no way that we were going to be able to do this in less than dozens of takes. I knew that we didn't have that. I can't ask five hundred people who work at *Today* to spend the entire day lip-syncing over and over again. Because of everyone's different schedules, I broke it down into five different groups, depending on if you worked overnight, or during the day, or during the early evening. And I started choreographing people in groups. I made people listen to the song over and over and over till they wanted to vomit. We played it in the control room. We played it in the studio."

After the *Today* staff and crew members learned the words and their dance moves, the producers assembled them along a route around Rockefeller Plaza starting in Studio 1A, winding through its stairways and corridors, moving out onto the concourse into the Channel Gardens and the skating rink, and back onto the plaza. A camera operator using a Stedicam strapped in a harness and a technician who kept the shot in focus moved in tandem while Long was by their side shouting cues for the next location.

"They needed to know that they had ten seconds to get to the control room; twelve seconds to get to Kathie Lee Gifford; forty more seconds till they get to Al Roker," she said. "I was counting. I had these little time blocks where I would have a stopwatch and would count down, screaming at the top of my lungs, 'Nineteen, eighteen . . .' So they would have a sense of how fast they needed to go. Because we wanted to make sure we weren't getting behind. I basically had to arrange a dance between two camera operators and myself so we wouldn't be seen on camera."

The easy part was getting every member of the *Today* on-air family involved (along with special guest star, *NBC Nightly News* anchor Brian Williams and *Weekend Today* anchors Lester Holt, Amy Robach and Jenna Wolfe). "It was almost never a question of *if* they would do it," said Long "It was '*when* do you want to do this?' And it always has been. They are up for anything. If they think that the audience is going to enjoy it, they're willing to do it."

The finished product that aired on November 19, 2010, went on to win a prestigious Edward R. Murrow Award for best use of video. It may not have been a piece of TV journalism in the traditional sense. But it was a vibrant visual slice of the culture that will be as representative of its time just as an old kinescope of Dave Garroway in the RCA Exhibition Hall reflects the pace and feel of American life in the 1950s. "What we're putting on the air is essentially a time capsule," said Long. "And we want to make sure that we are getting it right. We are portraying what it's like to live today."

WE HOPE WE CAN GIVE YOU ENOUGH TO STA

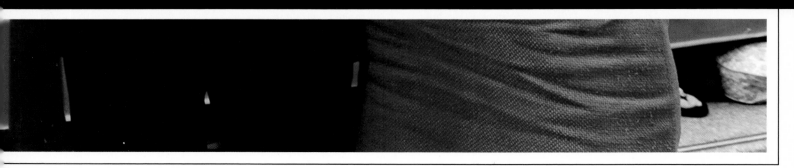

EPILOGUE

TOM BROKAW DID NOT SEE TELEVISION UNTIL he was fifteen years old. "We lived in such a remote part of South Dakota, we couldn't get a signal," he said. "And we finally moved in 1955 to a town where we could. The entire family was immediately transfixed by the *Today* show in the morning. My mother became a huge student of it. She was a working woman. She worked in retail shops and other places downtown. But before I'd go to school in the morning, she would be saying something to me about what she'd just seen on the *Today* show. And I remember the morning of the Bay of Pigs invasion. She said, 'I don't believe these stories we're hearing.' She knew immediately that the United States was probably involved. I remember thinking how great Dave Garroway was, this intellectual but user-friendly guy. And the cast members—you felt like you knew them."

Even nearly thirty years after he served as host and went on to a distinguished run as anchor of the *NBC Nightly News*, Brokaw still meets strangers across the country who say they remember having their breakfast while watching him and Jane Pauley. The men and women who had significant roles on *Today* over its first sixty years are part of a small exclusive club that has touched the lives of several generations of Americans. "I think that there has been a long-form continuity, as I describe it," he said. "It works very hard at getting all the pieces right." Maintaining the program's vitality and its stature in broadcasting history has been part of the job. "I always said that I thought *Today* was the kind of program that you leave in better shape than you found it," said Bryant Gumbel. "I cared about that. I took it seriously. When it seemed to be sinking, it was kind of like 'I'll do anything, I'll do whatever to save it.'"

Consistency has been critical to the success of *Today*. But the program also had the ability to change and adapt to the pace of American life. Jane Pauley remembered how Rockefeller Center was "a pretty sleepy place" at the time of her arrival on *Today* in the 1970s. When she first met Executive Producer Stuart Schulberg, he insisted to her that *Today* was not a "show" but a program. "I think it should be spelled in the British way—*programme*—to capture his meaning," she said. The current version of *Today*, she said, is "still an important news program—but unabashedly a show. In my era, the audience was an abstraction. Today, it's literally rocking and rolling and the hosts work a lot harder. The average segment runs under four minutes. The show moves at a breathtaking pace these days. It feels supercharged. In my day it took a lot of coffee just to keep the staff awake."

"I always said that I thought Today *was the kind of program that you leave in better shape than you found it,"* said Bryant Gumbel.

In the twenty-first century, *Today* is bigger (four hours) and faster than ever. While it has been decades since a chimpanzee romped on the set, the producers and the NBC News executives still have to consider the proper mix of substantive news coverage with soft features and occasionally outrageous stunts that humanize the on-air talent and keep people talking about the program. Working in their favor is the relationship *Today* has with viewers that has extended from one generation to the next. There is a level of trust that has built up, thanks to the program's longevity. "You can go from a government official in one segment, to a segment on postpartum depression, to Martha Stewart's cooking something great in the kitchen—all in the span of ten minutes—and it all works," said NBC News President Steve Capus. "It's really unique in that regard, that the audience gives us a tremendous amount of range in which to operate."

But with that trust is a feeling of ownership. Jennifer Long said when she attends a party and the other guests learn that she is a producer at *Today*, the room practically tips in her direction. "Everybody wants to talk to you," she said. "Everybody has an opinion about the show for better or for worse. And these people are your customers. You can't blow them off. The reason why you get to do what you do is because they're watching. But people do not hesitate to tell you exactly what they think about what they saw on your show that day—everything from the content of the show, to what Matt Lauer was wearing, to why did Ann Curry laugh at that joke. Everyone is very opinionated. It's almost like that we've been elected and they're our constituents, and they have a right to tell you what they think. And we like that. That's how they should feel. We're doing this job for them. And they don't hold back. Every day is like a town hall meeting, no matter where you go, if they find out you work at the *Today* show. They want to tell you what you're doing right, and what you're doing wrong, and how they want you to get it right."

Matt Lauer also knows attention must be paid every day to the fans who gather on Rockefeller Plaza outside of Studio 1A. "There are some days it's rushed and we don't have that much time," he said. "But when you're out there, it just can't be a high five down the row. You have to stop and look them in the eye, and go, 'Where are you from?' And, 'Thank you for coming.' I say, 'Thank you for coming' a million times every morning. They make an effort to come to New York, get up early in the morning, and stand in that position. What's five seconds extra to me to recognize that? So I think that's really what it's all about. You're remembering that while you think what you're saying at that moment, teasing whatever story is coming up, is important, those people also have precious few opportunities to be seen by their friends back home. And if you can take two seconds to turn and recognize someone as you're talking, make a joke about someone, bring someone into the game a little bit, I think that goes a long way."

Over the past sixty years, the delivery system for *Today* evolved from grainy black-and-white images to color televisions to high-definition screens to home computers and mobile devices held in the palm of a user's hand. The talent on *Today* will continue to change and the technology and increased number of choices will only make competition more intense. But the advantage that *Today* has held onto is its almost mystical legacy respected by the women and men who create it every day and the people who watch it. However the media landscape changes in the years ahead, it will never alter the fact that it was Pat Weaver who recognized that people would want an electronic source of authoritative information and companionship at a time of day when they were most vulnerable, preparing to head out into the world to go to work, study at school, pursue their dreams, or maybe even find some peace.

The quotations in this book are derived from interviews with the author in 2002 and 2011, interviews with NBC News producers in 2006, 2007, 2010, and 2011, past *Today* programs from the NBC News Archives and published accounts listed in the bibliography.

BOOKS

Allen, Fred, and Stuart E. Hample. *All the Sincerity in Hollywood: Selections from the Writings of Radio's Legendary Comedian Fred Allen*. Golden, CO: Fulcrum Pub, 2001.

Auletta, Ken. *Three Blind Mice: How the TV Networks Lost Their Way*. New York: Random House, 1991.

Battaglio, Stephen. *David Susskind: A Televised Life*. New York: St. Martin's Press, 2010.

Blair, Frank, and Jack Smith. *Let's Be Frank About It*. Garden City, NY: Doubleday, 1979.

Brooks, Tim, and Earle Marsh. *The Complete Directory to Prime Time Network and Cable TV Shows: 1946–Present*. New York: Ballantine Books, 2007.

Cornog, Evan, and Richard Whelan. *Hats in the Ring: An Illustrated History of American Presidential Campaigns*. New York: Random House, 2000.

Davis, Gerry. *The Today Show: An Anecdotal History*. New York: Morrow, 1987.

Downs, Hugh. *On Camera: My 10,000 Hours on Television*. New York: Putnam, 1986.

Frank, Reuven. *Out of Thin Air: The Brief Wonderful Life of Network News*. New York: Simon & Schuster, 1991.

Gordon, Lois G, and Alan Gordon. *American Chronicle: Six Decades in American Life, 1920–1980*. New York: Atheneum, 1987.

Kurtz, Howard. *Reality Show: Inside the Last Great Television News War*. New York: Free Press, 2007.

Matusow, Barbara. *The Evening Stars: The Making of the Network News Anchor*. Boston: Houghton Mifflin, 1983.

Metz, Robert. *The Today Show*. New York: New American Library, 1978.

Mink, Eric, Laurie Dolphin, and Christian Brown. *This Is Today: A Window on Our Times*. Kansas City, MO: Andrews McMeel Pub, 2003.

NBC. *Today: The First Fifteen Years*. New York: National Broadcasting Co, 1967.

Norville, Deborah. *Back on Track: How to Straighten Out Your Life When It Throws You a Curve*. New York, NY: Simon & Schuster, 1997.

Pauley, Jane. *Skywriting: A Life Out of the Blue*. New York: Random House, 2004.

Probst, Leonard. *Off Camera: Leveling About Themselves*. New York: Stein and Day, 1978.

Walsh, Elsa. *Divided Lives: The Public and Private Struggles of Three American Women*. New York: Anchor Books, 1996.

Walters, Barbara. *How to Talk with Practically Anybody About Practically Anything*. Garden City, NY: Doubleday, 1970.

Walters, Barbara. *Audition: A Memoir*. New York: A.A. Knopf, 2008.

Weaver, Pat. *The Best Seat in the House: The Golden Years in Radio and Television*. New York: Knopf, 1993.

Whitburn, Joel. *Joel Whitburn's Pop Memories, 1890–1954: The History of American Popular Music: Compiled from America's Popular Music Charts 1890–1954*. Menomonee Falls, WI: Record Research, 1986.

ARTICLES

"Ann Curry: News Anchor." *People*. 11 May 1998.

"CBS News Gaining On 'Today.'" *Variety*. 18 May 1983.

"Five Years in a Goldfish Bowl." *TV Guide*. 19 January 1957.

"Garroway Today." *TV Guide*. 10 July 1953.

"Garroway No Longer Will Work by the Dawn's Early Light." *TV Guide*. 1 August 1959.

"Gay Raider Invades NBC-TV Newscast To Protest 'Bigotry.'" *Variety*. 29 October 1973.

"Matt Lauer: Sexiest Anchor." *People*. 17 November 1997.

"NBC-TV's 10-Year Blow-By-Blow." *Variety*. 10 September 1958.

"Now Silent Quiz Star. Charles Lincoln Van Doren." *New York Times*. 10 October 1959.

"Playboy Interview: Bryant Gumbel." *Playboy*. December 1986.

"'Real jerks?' Bryant Gumbel is happy to share his list." *Chicago Sun-Times*. 19 August 1988.

"Tele Follow-Up Comment." *Variety*. 8 February 1967.

"The Press: Pauley Signs On." *Time*. 11 October 1976.

"'Today' May Go-For-Brokaw." *Variety*. 26 June 1974.

"TV Followup: Today." *Variety*. 10 February 1982.

"TV Newspaper." *Time*. 15 September 1952.

"TV Update." *TV Guide*. 26 May 1979.

Andrews, Peter. "With A Folksy Flavor...." *TV Guide*. 26 February 1977.

Angell, Elizabeth. "The Katie Factor." *Newsweek*. 6 July 1998.

Ballad, Richard. "Hugh Downs to Frank McGee: The Big Switch on the *Today* Show." *Look*. 5 October 1971.

Barron, James. "John Chancellor, Professorial Anchor and Commentator at NBC Is Dead at 68." *New York Times*. 13 July 1996.

Battaglio, Stephen. "*GMA* Catches *Today* Snoozing." *TV Guide*. 15 May 2005.

_____. "What Katie Couric Really Thinks About *Today*, Tomorrow and Diane." *TV Guide*. 22 May 2005.

_____. "Katie's Jump to CBS: The Real Story." *TV Guide*. 17 April 2006.

_____. "Living for Today." *TV Guide*. 1 May 2006.

_____. "*Today* Changes Meredith's View." *TV Guide*. 17 April 2006.

_____. "Hit the Road, Matt." *TV Guide. com* 26 April 2007.

Bedell, Sally. "Dave Garroway, 69, Found Dead; First Host of 'Today' on NBC-TV." *New York Times*. 22 July 1982.

Benchley, Peter. "He Never Carried A Pencil." *TV Guide*. 25 June 1966.

Berman, Susan. "TV's behind-the-scenes battle to be No. 1 in the morning." *Us*. 15 November 1977.

Birmingham, Frederic A. "Everything Happens on the 'Today' Show." *The Saturday Evening Post*. September/October 1973.

Black, Stu, Don Kowet. "'How could you take drugs before the fight when it's against your religion?' Whether he's questioning Muhammad Ali or hitting a golf ball, sportscaster Bryant Gumbel plays hard and tough." *TV Guide*. 24 October 1981.

Brady, James. "In Step With: Gene Shalit." *Parade*. 20 December 1987.

Carter, Bill. "New Co-Anchor for 'Today' Is Expected. *New York Times*. 27 October 1989.

_____. "Bryant Gumbel, Forecast for 'Today': Cloudy." *New York Times*. 10 June 1990.

_____. "NBC Names Executive Producer of 'Today.'" *New York Times*. 3 December 1991.

_____. "On the Set with: Bryant Gumbel; Steady in Storm or Calm." *New York Times*. 11 November 1992.

Clarke, Gerald, Mary Cronin, Janice Simpson. "Battle for the Morning." *Time*. 1 December 1980.

Conaway, James. "How to Talk with Barbara Walters About Practically Anything." *New York Times*. 10 September 1972.

Corry, John. "NBC News – Live From Moscow." *New York Times*. 13 September 1984.

Dempsey, John. "Affils Say NBC News Not Up To Muster." *Variety*. 18 May 1983.

Drake, Ross. "Mr. Nice Guy Meets the New Barbara Walters. " *People*. 12 August 1974.

Efron, Edith. "Hugh Downs, Egghead." *TV Guide*. 26 August 1961.

Efron, Edith. "'I'm a Lord-Knows-What.'" *TV Guide*. 5 August 1967.

Feder, Robert. "Joe Garagiola returns as 'Today' boss leaves." *Chicago Sun-Times*. 16 May 1990.

Fisher, Marc. "'60s Radio Days: A Sillier, Simpler Time." *Washington Post*. 13 September 1999.

Frank, Stanley. "The Sweat-shirt Guy Who'd Become a Breakfast Egghead." *TV Guide.* 15 March 1969.

Friedman, Arthur. "Katie Couric: fashion present." *Women's Wear Daily.* 6 March 1997.

Friedman, Steve. "When Jane Pauley Kissed My Ring, I Knew We Were on Our Way." *TV Guide.* 16 January 1988.

Funt, Peter. "How Jim Hartz Won the Great TV Host Hunt." *New York Times.* 22 September 1974.

Gehman, Richard. "Portrait of a Tormented Man." *TV Guide.* 22 July 1961.

Gold, Matea. "When Katie met Jeff." *Los Angeles Times.* 20 June 2005.

Goldman, Kevin. "Gumbel's Memo to Boss Gives NBC 'Today' Staff Poor Ratings." *Newsday.* 2 February 1989.

Goodman, Walter. "TV View; 'Today,' After That Infamous Memo. *New York Times.* 2 April 1989.

Gorman, Christine. "Katie's Crusade." *Time.* 13 March 2000.

Gould, Jack. "Tape Causes Controversy." *New York Times.* 6 December 1959.

_____. "TV: Garroway Departs." *New York Times.* 18 July 1961.

Greeley, Bill. "Tap Hartz To Scale Alpo." *Variety.* 31, July 1974.

Hall, Jane. "Meet 'Today's' new Wake-Up Call. 26-year-old Jeff Zucker's job is to take Couric, Gumbel & Co. back to the top and keep them there." *Los Angeles Times.* 5 April 1992.

Hickey, Neil. "He Starts His Day with Homework." *TV Guide.* 1 August 1964.

_____. "The Man with the $175,000 Smile." *TV Guide.* 30 January 1965.

_____. "The Not-So-Hard Times of a Newscaster." *TV Guide.* 26 February 1972.

_____. "Peace, It's Wonderful!" *TV Guide.* 25 January 1975.

_____. "Too big too soon?" *TV Guide.* 27 August 1977.

Hill, Michael E. "Bryant Gumbel; 'Today's' Outspoken Anchor Leads NBC to Seoul." *Washington Post.* 18 September 1988.

Johnson, Marilyn. "Meredith's View." *More.* May 2006.

Judge, Frank. "Women in Spotlight on Today." *Journal American.* 18 July 1965.

Kleinfield, N.R. "Star Weatherman: Willard Scott A Huckster For All Seasons." *New York Times.* 5 April 1987.

Klemesrud, Judy. "Oh, How She Loves to Get Up in the Morning..." *New York Times.* 2 July 1967.

_____. "What to Wear is Special Problem for Women on Television." *New York Times.* 9 February 1970.

Kristof, Nicholas D. "A Village Waiting for Rape and Murder." *New York Times.* 12 March 2006.

Latham, Aaron. "Waking Up with Sally." *New York.* 16 July 1973.

Lee, Felicia R. "New Morning Platform, Same Perky Candor." *New York Times.* 17 April 2008.

Levy, Jonathan, Marcelino Ford Livene, Anne Levine. "Broadcast Television: Survivor in a Sea of Competition." *OPP Working Paper Series, FCC Office of Plans and Policy.* September 2002.

Lippmann, John. "NBC Makes a Major Overhaul of 'Today' Show; Television Executive Dick Ebersol is sidelined and Joe Garagiola is rehired in an attempt to shore up ratings. 16 May 1990.

Lukas, J. Anthony. "What Does Tomorrow Hold for 'Today'?" *New York Times.* 22 August 1976.

Miller, Merle. "Old Buttoned-Up." *TV Guide.* 25 December 1971.

Millstein, Gilbert. "Meet the Man Who Succeeded Garroway." *TV Guide.* 20 January 1962.

Mink, Eric. "Network Duel Over No. 2 Spot In Morning." *St. Louis Post-Dispatch.* 23 July 1990.

Nieves, Evelyn. "At Lunch With: Al Roker; bright and Warm and Hold the Thunder." *New York Times.* 2 September 1992.

Norville, Deborah. "How Deborah Norville picked herself up, brushed herself off – and became a star again." *Redbook.* 1 October 1997.

O'Connor, John J. "TV: The Folksy Style Comes to NBC's 'Today.'" *New York Times.* 10 September 1980.

Park, Jeannie, Alan Carter, Gavin Moses, Sue Carswell, Michael Mason, Marilyn Balamaci. "Two Was Company, Three a Crowd." *People.* 13 November 1989.

Powell, Joanna. "Mad About Matt." *Good Housekeeping.* 1 May 1998.

Quinn, Sally. "A Day in the Life of Barbara Walters." *Washington Post.* 20 April 1972.

Richards, David. "Handsome Is. Will Handsome Do? Matt Lauer, Reluctant Pretty Boy, Steps Into Gumbel's Large Loafers on 'Today.'" *Washington Post.* 4 March 1997.

Richman, Alan. "Willard Scott Is Blowing His Top." *People.* 20 March 1989.

Rosenthal, Andrew. "The 1992 Campaign: The Republicans; Bush Renews His Attacks About Vietnam and Draft." *New York Times.* 14 October 1992.

Schneider, Karen. "Live Wire." *People.* 9 August 1993.

Scott, Sophfronia. "Here We Go Again." *Time.* 15 April 1991.

Shanley, John F. "Interesting Work. Mary Kelly's Job for 'Today' Program Takes Her to Far Corners of World." *New York Times.* 6 July 1958.

Shepard, Richard F. "Chancellor is Set as Host of 'Today'." *New York Times.* 5 July 1961.

_____. "The New Newsman on 'Today'." *New York Times.* 13 August 1961.

_____. "Early-Morning TV Race Heats Up." *New York Times.* 26 April 1978.

Stein, Lisa. "*Today's* big question: Will Katie Couric be Deborah Norville's substitute – or successor?" *TV Guide* 29 December 1990.

Steinberg, Jacques. "Ann Curry's Ambition: To Witness the Suffering." *New York Times.* 22 March 2007.

Steinem, Gloria. "Nylons in the Newsroom." *New York Times.* 7 November 1965.

Sullivan, Elizabeth. "Early Bird Satellite." *Boston Globe.* 2 May 1965.

Swertlow, Frank Sean. "Barbara Walters and ABC: Is the Marriage Working?" *TV Guide.* 5 February 1977.

_____. "Which Is She – Journalist or Cher?" *TV Guide.* 12 February 1977.

Tauber, Michelle. "100 & Counting." *People.* 18 November 2002.

Van Doren, Charles. "All the Answers." *The New Yorker.* 28 July 2008.

Whiteside, Thomas. "Profiles." *The New Yorker.* 5 September 1959.

Zoglin, Richard. "Jane Pauley: Surviving Nicely, Thanks." *Time.* 20 August 1990.

_____. "Miles in The Morning." *Time.* 23 March 1992.

TRANSCRIPTS

Barbara Walters' Interview with Bryant Gumbel. *ABC News 20/20.* 16 March 1990.

"An Interview With Weatherman Al Roker." *NPR Weekend Edition,* 5 May 1996.

Interview with Willard Scott. *CNN Larry King Live.* 21, May 2003.

ONLINE

Charlie Andrews Interview, Archive of American Television, interviewed by Henry Colman on October 20, 1998. www.emmylegends.org.

Katie Couric Interview, Archive of American Television, interviewed by Karen Herman on June 18, 2010. www.emmylegends.org.

ACKNOWLEDGMENTS

AS A JOURNALIST WHO HAS COVERED THE MEDIA INDUSTRY SINCE 1989, I've developed a deep understanding and appreciation of how *Today* has remained a vital and resilient institution in American television. So to have the opportunity to write a history of the program on the occasion of its sixtieth anniversary can only be described as a great honor.

I am extremely grateful to Cheryl Gould and her office for initiating the project and being such a driving force, and to Lauren Kapp of NBC News for suggesting that I should be the one to tell this story. I felt very fortunate to have Geoffrey Stone of Running Press as my editor. He was open to my every suggestion while keeping the project on track under a tight deadline. Paul Kepple and Ralph Geroni of Headcase Design were instrumental in creating a wonderful design, and Susan Van Horn was vital to keeping the project moving. Ernie Angstadt, a senior researcher for *Today*, was invaluable in providing access to the program's archives. His passion for *Today* and its legacy was infectious. Megan Kopf was, as always, a great help in setting up interviews with talent and producers. Jennifer Hozer and Julie Gollins were an incredible help in pulling together images for the book and providing technical support.

The generous encouragement of Don Nash, Jaclyn Levin, and Michael Fabiano of NBC and Christopher Navratil and Rick Joyce of Perseus Books meant a lot during the writing process. The unwavering support of Debra Birnbaum, the editor-in-chief of *TV Guide Magazine*, was also greatly appreciated.

Special thanks also goes to Jim Bell, Steve Capus, Katie Couric, Steve Friedman, Andrea Gallo, Lisa Goins, Allison Gollust, Matthew Hiltzig, Matt Lauer, Jenny Matz, Mark Segal, Julie Townsend, Millie Verastegui, Jonathan Wald, Jamie Zozzaro, and Jeff Zucker for their assistance.

Finally, an enormous thank you to my wife, Candice Agree, for offering her time, feedback, and most importantly, the endless spousal patience this endeavor required.